CHICANAS/CHICANOS

AT

THE CROSSROADS

CHICANAS/CHICANOS

AT

THE CROSSROADS

Social, Economic, and Political Change

Edited by David R. Maciel and Isidro D. Ortiz

THE UNIVERSITY OF ARIZONA PRESS   *Tucson*

The University of Arizona Press
Copyright © 1996
Arizona Board of Regents
All rights reserved

♾ This book is printed on acid-free,
archival-quality paper.
Manufactured in the United States of America

01 00 99 98 97 96 6 5 4 3 2 1

Library of Congress Cataloging-in-Publication Data

Chicanas/Chicanos at the crossroads : social, economic, and political
change / edited by David Maciel and Isidro D. Ortiz.
p.   cm.
Includes bibliographical references and index.
ISBN 0-8165-1343-0 (cloth : acid-free paper). — ISBN
0-8165-1634-0 (paper : acid-free paper)
1. Mexican Americans—Politics and government.   2. Mexican
Americans—Economic conditions.   3. Mexican Americans—Social
conditions.   I. Maciel, David.   II. Ortiz, Isidro D., 1949–   .
E184.M5C425   1996
973'.046872—dc20   95-41767

British Library Cataloguing-in-Publication Data
A catalogue record for this book is available from
the British Library.

CONTENTS

ACKNOWLEDGMENTS

The completion of any book, in particular an edited work such as this, owes much to many. The various contributors deserve our sincere appreciation. They not only wrote their respective chapters with creativity and professionalism, but offered constructive suggestions that ultimately improved the final draft. Two respected colleagues served as intellectual mentors on this project since its early stages to the present: Juan Gómez-Quiñones and Richard Griswold del Castillo. Besides providing valuable insights and sharing their vast knowledge of the field of Chicano Studies, they gave us constant encouragement.

None, though, merit our deepest gratitude more than the entire administrative staff of the Department of Mexican American Studies at San Diego State University. Laurel Dyke, Paula J. Timmerman, and Evelyn D. Cruz labored tirelessly and with great devotion on every phase of the book. This collective project would not have been completed without their substantial assistance.

Joanne O'Hare, senior editor for the University of Arizona Press, deserves special mention. Joanne consistently offered solid support and demonstrated great patience with our project; she was always there in times of need.

INTRODUCTION

As Chicanas/os approach a new millennium, they find themselves at a critical juncture.[1] After three decades of intense social struggle (from the onset of the Chicano Movement in the 1960s to the present), it is evident that much has been accomplished, yet challenges still remain.

The "Movimiento" (movement) initially brought about a period of dramatic activism, idealism, artistic creativity, and renewed optimism toward significant change.[2] It bore fruit in labor organizing, political participation, community issues, education, and even in self-awareness and culture.[3] It is clear that the Movimiento changed the Chicano community like no other past struggle. Chicanas/os began to overcome their historic invisibility in American society, receiving national and even international media coverage of their plight, grievances, and public-policy concerns. One clear result of the Chicano Movement and its aftermath was the emphasis on the vital need for alternative scholarship that would not only address the serious limitations of previous studies of the Chicano community, but would also contribute more sensitive, better-informed, and more adequately researched interpretative analyses of Chicana/o issues. Initially the first generation of Chicana/o scholars, which emerged concurrently with the Chicano Movement, contributed important early overviews and initial monographic studies. Soon thereafter a new academic trend in Chicano/a scholarship was initiated, becoming known as Chicano Studies. Over time the original conceptual methods and fields of study evolved and diversified to eventually incorporate regional and gender studies as well.[4]

In spite of the impressive gains, setbacks and shortcomings in the struggle were nevertheless apparent. The advancement of the community was uneven at best: while many Chicanas/os were able to achieve a certain social mobility, a greater number remained static. To make matters worse, with the demise of liberalism and radicalism in the late 1970s and 1980s came a conservative backlash. The advent of a Republican presidential administration in 1980 signified a retreat and the initiation of a dismantling by the federal government of many of the triumphs of the Chicano Movement and other progressive movements. Civil rights, affirmative action, bilingual education, labor organizing, Chicano Studies, feminism, political empowerment, job-training programs, financial aid, and immigration came under constant attack during the 1980s, years ironically characterized by the print media and political establishment as the "Decade of the Hispanic."[5] As the decade evolved, it became apparent that it would be many things, but certainly not of the "Decade of the Hispanic." Instead of being years when a consolidation of earlier achievements and successes occurred, the 1980s threatened to become a period of retrenchment and regression in conditions that had taken decades to change for the better.

As the 1990s unfold, certain patterns become visible, particularly a substantial increase in activism. A case in point would be that of Chicano university students. Dissatisfied with the lack of progress for Chicano Studies, faculty, and student recruitment, Chicano students across the United States have resorted to confrontation and direct action reminiscent of the activism of the late 1960s.[6] A second example involves the area of international relations. Chicanas/os in the 1990s have become visible players in U.S.-Mexican relations, on questions of free trade, immigration, and cultural interaction.[7]

The early 1990s, moreover, have been witness to many disappointments, first with the passing away of the heroic figure César Chávez and the near retirement of other activist legends such as Corky González and Reies López Tijerina. In addition, demographic growth continues at an accelerated rate for the Chicano community, thus intensifying the needs of the community. Also, although the Clinton administration has raised new expectations for progress, suggesting new priorities that would aid Chicanos and other Latinos, to date appointments of Hispanics to federal posts have not been as extensive as promised or expected.[8]

Recent investigations by advocacy organizations, governmental agencies, and private non-profit groups reveal that Chicanos and other Latinos continue to be plagued by many of the problems and issues of the pre-1980 years: for example, they continue to experience discrimination in housing and schooling.[9] The institutions have also noted that a disproportionate number of Chicanos and other Latinos remain in poverty or near poverty levels. In addition, Chicanos and other Latinos continue to be victimized by crime and violence and double standards of justice.[10] Politically, the groups, according to these institutions, remain underrepresented in the ranks of elected and appointed officials and in numerous professions;[11] moreover, many Chicanos and other Latinos continue to lack access to health care and insurance.[12] Although highly useful, the analyses offered by these organizations often do not specifically illuminate the conditions and experiences of Chicanas/os; the institutions almost invariably utilize Latinos or "Hispanics" in general, as their unit of analysis rather than Chicanos.[13] Because Chicanos are the largest segment of the Latino population, it is not unreasonable to assume that the conclusions reached in the investigations apply to them. However, it is difficult to assume that with much confidence, especially in light of the historical reality of variation among Latino national-origin groups in terms of dimensions such as histories and opportunity structures.

The condition, fortunes, and experiences of Chicanas/os since 1980 have not received much scholarly attention. Although the scholarly literature on Chicanas/os has been growing steadily since 1970, most has focused on the period prior to 1980, emphasized limited aspects of Chicano activism during the 1980s, or offered cursory overviews of developments among Chicanas/os since 1980. One possible reason for the lack of attention may be the view that the recentness of the years makes it difficult for serious reflection. In any case, in the absence of scholarly attention, a diverse array of significant questions have remained unanswered, and a large gap in knowledge about the conditions, fortunes, and experiences of Chicanas/os persists. This anthology seeks to provide tentative answers and advance understanding and knowledge of these issues through scholarly examinations of developments in Chicana/o socioeconomic, cultural and political life since 1980. To the extent possible, Chicanas/os are the principal foci of the studies.

The anthology strives to be distinctive in several respects. First, it offers an assessment of the Chicana/o experience since the late 1970s with special emphasis on the 1980s and beyond. Second, it offers multidisciplinary perspectives on the conditions, fortunes, and experiences of Chicanas/os in the contemporary era. The authors of the chapters represent a broad array of disciplines, ranging from economics to women's studies. They offer their insights drawing upon their particular training and/or experiences and expertise. In their discussions the authors strive to present fresh data and incorporate the most up-to-date methods and frameworks. By incorporating multidisciplinary perspectives, the anthology extends the multidisciplinary thrust of Chicano Studies.

Lastly, the anthology reflects a conscious attempt to incorporate gender, regional, and disciplinary diversity in authors and topics addressed. As the table of contents and authors' biographical profiles reveal, the authors include Chicanas/os residing in different regions of the United States and with divergent backgrounds. The authors also include scholars and practitioners in specific fields. An attempt was made to include both established as well as promising younger scholars. The chapters attend to traditional foci as well as incorporating treatments of issues that have not received extensive attention in the scholarly literature on Chicanas/os.

Rarely does a single scholarly work offer definitive answers about the conditions, experiences, and fortunes of a group as diverse and complex as the Chicana/o population. This anthology is not an exception. Rather, it is offered with the intent of providing timely and useful insights and stimulating additional reflection and scholarship as this century draws to a close. If the anthology fulfills these tasks, the investment of resources needed to bring the work to fruition will prove to have been sound.

NOTES

1. Historically the entire Mexican-origin community was recognized by the term "Chicano." In this book, "Chicanas/os" and "Chicanos" are used interchangeably to refer to Mexican Americans as a reflection of current trends in scholarship that acknowledge the contributions of women. This usage is consistent with name changes of academic departments and of the most important professional academic organization, the National Association of Chicana and Chicano Studies. Also, "Latinos" and "Latinas" are used here instead of the term "Hispanic" and "Hispanics," unless otherwise noted.

2. Armando Rendón, *Chicano Manifesto* (New York: MacMillan, 1971); and Stan Steiner, *La Raza* (New York, 1970).

3. Phillip Ortego, "The Chicano Renaissance," in *Introduction to Chicano Studies,* eds. Livie Isauro Durán and H. Russel Bernard (New York: Harper & Row, 1973) offers an insightful overview of Chicano cultural trends in this period.

4. See the various published proceedings of the National Association of Chicano Studies for an overview of trends in Chicana/o scholarship in the last two decades.

5. See the last chapter in Rodolfo Acuña, *Occupied America: A History of Chicanos* (New York: Harper and Row, 1989) on this subject.

6. Ralph Frammolino, "A New Generation of Rebels," *Los Angeles Times,* 20 November 1993.

7. María Rosa García-Acevedo, "Aztlán and Contemporary Mexico: An Assessment of Chicano-Mexicano Political Relations," unpublished manuscript.

8. Christian R. González, "Clinton Criticized on Appointments," *Hispanic Link Weekly Report,* 18 October 1993; and Frank Cota-Robles Newton, "Presidential Appointments and Disappointments," *Hispanic Link Weekly Report,* 18 October 1993.

9. Massachusetts Advocacy Center, *Locked In/Locked Out: Tracking and Placement Practices in Boston Public Schools* (Boston: Massachusetts Advocacy Center, 1990); and "HUD Housing Study Finds Discrimination Is Widespread," *Hispanic Link Weekly Report,* 9 September 1991.

10. American Friends Service Committee Immigration Law Enforcement Project, *Human Rights and the Mexico-U.S. Border* (Philadelphia: American Friends Service Committee U.S.-Mexico Border Project, 1990); and Lisa D. Bastain, "Hispanic Victims: Bureau of Justice Statistics Special Report" (Washington D.C.: U.S. Department of Justice, 1990).

11. See, for example, Terese Puente, "Big-City Dailies Show Modest Hiring Gains," *Hispanic Link Weekly Report,* 8 April 1991; and Félix Pérez, "Lawyers' Group Takes Aim at Judicial Underrepresentation," *Hispanic Link Weekly Report,* 25 May 1992.

12. National Council of la Raza, "Lack of Insurance and Underinsurance: Biggest Barriers to Hispanic Health Care," *Agenda* 11 (1992): 1–2.

13. See, for example, Scoban Nicolau and Rafael Valdivieso, *A More Perfect Union: Achieving Hispanic Parity by Year 2000* (New York: Hispanic Policy Development Project, 1990).

ABBREVIATIONS

AB	Assembly Bill
AFDC	Aid to Families with Dependent Children
AFL-CIO	American Federation of Labor and Congress of Industrial Organizations
AGIF	American GI Forum
BANOMEXT	Banco de Comercio Exterior
CAC	Corporate Advisory Council
CANACINTRA	Cámara Nacional de la Industria de la Transformación
CASAS	Comprehensive Adult Student Assessment System
CBS	Columbia Broadcasting System
CONAPO	Consejo Nacional de Población
D/HEW	Department of Health, Education, and Welfare
EEOA	Equal Educational Opportunities Act
ELA	Eligible Legalized Alien
EMR	Educationally Mentally Retarded
GAO	General Accounting Office
GM	General Motors
HEO	Hispanic Elected Officials
HPDP	Hispanic Policy Development Project
IDR	Income derived from interest, dividends, and rents
IMSS	Instituto Mexicano de Seguro Social
INS	Immigration and Naturalization Service
IRCA	Immigration Reform and Control Act
LEP	Limited English-Proficiency
LULAC	League of United Latin American Citizens

MALCS	Mujeres Activas en Letras y Cambio Social
MALDEF	Mexican American Legal Defense and Education Fund
MAPA	Mexican American Political Association
MECHA	Movimiento Estudiantil Chicano de Aztlán
MSA	Metropolitan Statistical Area
NABE	National Association for Bilingual Education
NACS	National Association of Chicano Studies
NAFIN	Nacional Financiera
NAFTA	North American Free Trade Agreement
NALEO	National Association of Latino Elected Officials
NALGA	National Association of Lesbian and Gay Activists
NCLR	National Council of La Raza
NNHW	National Network of Hispanic Women
NOW	National Organization of Women
OCR	Office for Civil Rights
PCM	Politically Correct Movement
PRI	Partido Revolucionario Institucional
PUSH	People United to Save Humanity
SAVE	Systematic Alien Verification for Entitlement Program
SAW	Seasonal Agricultural Workers
SEP	Secretaría de Educación Pública
SLIAG	State Legalization Assistance Funds
SRE	Secretaría de Relaciones Exteriores
SWVREP	Southwest Voter Registration and Education Project
UFW	United Farm Workers
UNAM	Universidad Nacional Autónoma de México
VRA	Voting Rights Act

CHICANAS/CHICANOS

AT

THE CROSSROADS

PART ONE. DEMOGRAPHIC

AND ECONOMIC TRENDS

AMONG CHICANAS/OS

The Chicano population has grown rapidly since 1980, and early on this growth was acknowledged as an important trend by demographers, scholars, journalists, and policymakers. The increase was not the only trend occurring within the population however. It was accompanied by other trends that will have consequences for Chicanas/os and others. Demographer Susan González Baker identifies the important features of and changes in the Chicano population and the specification of the policy implications due to these trends. Echoing other scholars who have identified the existence of a critical linkage between Chicanas/os and the future of the United States and have called for increased investment in the Chicano population, González Baker calls on policymakers to think ahead and accommodate rather than resist the demographic changes occurring within the Chicano population. In her view, such actions are vital to the future interests of Chicanas/os and the nation.

Immigration, particularly from Mexico, is one of the most controversial issues in contemporary American politics. Leo R. Chávez and Rebecca Martínez illuminate the concern over Mexican immigration and the consequences for Chicanos and other Latinos resulting from the debate and reactions toward immigration. According to Chávez and Martínez, during the 1980s immigration fueled the growth of the Chicano and Latino populations. As the number of immigrants increased over the decade, pressure to control immigration, especially illegal immigration, intensified across the United States. In the wake of mounting pressure, governmental authorities resorted to a variety of strategies and policies that during the 1980s had detrimental implications for Chicanos. As a result, Chicano organizations contested the policies and strategies and defended the rights of immigrants. However, the debate and pressure to control immigration continued largely unabated. In the absence of a change in the nature of the debate, Chicanos and other Latinos will continue to experience negative consequences in the 1990s and beyond.

At the onset of the decade the Adolph Coors Brewing Company declared that the 1980s would be the "Decade of the Hispanics." Implicit in its declaration was the notion that during the 1980s Chicanos and other Latinos would experience unprecedented socioeconomic gains. In the aftermath of the declaration, some Chicanos proclaimed their belief that the 1980s would witness the achievement of "Hisparity," i.e., the development of socioeconomic equality between Latinos and Whites. These claims were succeeded by the founding of the magazine, *Hispanic,* whose purpose was to celebrate the Hispanic success story in the United States.

Economists Refugio Rochín and Adela de la Torre provide insight into the actual, as opposed to the declared or anticipated, status of Chicanas/os during those years. In contrast to most of the other authors, they adopt a broader time frame: the year 1970, the year of publication of the landmark study, *The Mexican American People,* is their point of departure. The findings of this study serve as the benchmark for their analysis. Their examination of an array of socioeconomic indicators reveals that the 1980s failed to become a period of significant and unprecedented gains for Chicanas/os. Although the years since 1970 have witnessed some changes in the socioeconomic conditions of Chicanas/os, Rochín and de la Torre conclude that overall the general status of Chicanas/os appears to be no better than before 1970. They argue, moreover, that in the absence of major policy interventions, significant improvement in the socioeconomic conditions of Chicanas/os is unlikely even during the 1990s. Their analysis serves as a useful corrective to misconceptions regarding the conditions of Chicanos. It also reveals the gap between the rhetoric and the reality of the 1980s, touted as a decade of growth, which, as some candidates for higher office described it, was "a tide that would lift all boats."

DEMOGRAPHIC TRENDS IN THE CHICANA/O

POPULATION : POLICY IMPLICATIONS

FOR THE TWENTY-FIRST CENTURY

Susan González Baker

Chicano policymakers, social scientists, and political activists/advocates share a profound commitment to broadening knowledge about the Chicano population in order to advance Chicano social and economic well-being. However, too often information gathered by researchers fails to find its way into the political debate, leaving policymakers and advocates to make claims based on incomplete, outdated, or patently incorrect information. This volume and this chapter seek to promote the sharing of information across disciplines within the academic community and across institutions—from the pedagogical to the political—in an effort to enhance the understanding of the Chicano experience and, in the case of this chapter, the effectiveness of public policies affecting Chicanos.

Demographic evidence about U.S. populations is one of the cornerstones in building effective public policy. One must know who "belongs" in a group before specifying group conditions or suggesting policy reforms aimed toward a group. Identifying populations accurately, however, is a constant challenge to demographers. For example, the core definition of membership in the "Chicano" population has changed dramatically since the 1960s in the data collection protocols of the U.S. Census Bureau. The trend has moved away from counting Chicanos based solely on objective demographic features—parental birthplace, Spanish surname, use of the Spanish language, for example—to relying on objective indicators in combination with self-identification by census respondents. With the trend toward self-identification has come a commensurate growth in the size and demographic diversity of the Chicano population. The analyses in this chapter draw from contemporary census data and thus identify as Chicanos those persons self-reporting "Spanish/Hispanic origin or descent" and identifying the source of that affiliation as "Mexican, Mexican American, or Chicano."[1] Given this definition base, our task is to identify the important features of and changes in the Chicano population over time and to specify the policy implications of those demographic trends. Some of the trends bode well for Chicanos; others are quite ominous. Together, the trends offer an empirical base for some concrete policy suggestions intended to enhance Chicano life chances in the United States of the twenty-first century.

DEMOGRAPHIC TRENDS

Population Size and Population Growth

Mexican-origin population growth since 1980 has been dramatic. From a 1980 base of 8.7 million persons, the Mexican-origin population grew by 4.7 million to a 1990 total of 13.4 million—a 54 percent intercensal increase, outstripped only by the Asian-origin population, which doubled in the same time period, and outstripping African American population growth by a factor of four and non-Hispanic white growth by a factor of nine. This Mexican-origin growth tracks closely to overall Latino population growth, as Mexican-origin persons constitute nearly two-thirds of the Latino population. The Latino population grew by 53 percent from 1980 to 1990 and now constitutes over 8 percent of the U.S. population. By the turn of the twenty-first century, Latinos—owing primarily to growth in the Mexican-origin subgroup—will exceed 10 percent of the U.S. population.[2]

Sources of Population Growth

Half the Mexican-origin population growth since 1980 is due to childbirth, the other half to international migration. In this way, the Mexican-origin population is distinct from ethnic/racial groups like African Americans, whose growth emerges primarily from natural increase, and Asian Americans, whose extraordinary growth as a community was fueled overwhelmingly by international migration.

A population profile greatly affected by immigration patterns is, by definition, heavily influenced by U.S. immigration policy—a policy area examined in more detail in chapter 2. Under prevailing policy guidelines, Mexican-origin population growth can be expected to continue on its steep upward trajectory. The Immigration Reform and Control Act of

1986, for example, adjusted the status of nearly 3 million undocumented immigrants, over 70 percent of whom were from Mexico, to that of legal permanent residents, offering the opportunity to petition for visas on behalf of their immediate family members. In addition, the Immigration Act of 1990, while imposing an overall ceiling on annual worldwide immigration for the first time, also designated a short-term increase in visa allocations for countries like Mexico where certain preference categories are heavily backlogged for adjudication. Together, these policy reforms select for continued Mexican migration to the United States, even as other policy reforms seek to impose new limits on Mexican immigrant settlement in the United States (see chapter 2).

Together with natural increase and migration, mortality patterns complete the demographic equation for a population group. Chicanos offer a sometimes-perplexing mix of positive and negative health indicators, which, taken together, offer a portrait of a population suffering from inadequate access to health care and, not surprisingly, higher-than-average death rates due to preventable disease.

First, the good news. Although only about two-thirds of Latinas reportedly receive prenatal care in the first trimester of their pregnancies—a figure well below that of non-Hispanic white women (79 percent of whom receive such care)—low birth-weight babies are not significantly more common among Latinas than non-Hispanic whites. Additionally, members of the Latino population appear less likely than their white counterparts to die of such chronic diseases as heart disease (among men) and cancer or heart disease (among women).[3]

Next, the bad news. Although some forms of life-threatening disease are less common among Chicanos, others are more prevalent. Death due to diabetes is significantly more common among Mexican American women than among white women, as is death due to infectious disease. Latino males are at greater risk for death due to homicide and AIDS than are white males (homicide ranked fourth among the most common causes of death among Latino males in 1989). Death caused by violent means and death due to communicable disease have long been correlated with poverty in the public health literature. Latinos do not appear to be immune to such patterns.[4]

Along with a higher risk for violent death and death due to preventable disease, Latinos possess one of the most discouraging profiles in terms of access to the health care system. Latinos are much less likely to report having health insurance than non-Hispanic whites, Asians, or African Americans. Fully one-third of U.S. Latinos report having had no health insurance during 1991.[5] Furthermore, while barriers to care, such as language incompatibility and culturally inappropriate treatment are implicated in the low subscription rate, particularly in U.S./Mexico border regions, the most significant barrier cited by Latinos continues to be sheer cost.[6]

In sum, the Chicano population grew dramatically throughout the 1980s, and all indications appear to be that the growth will continue into the twenty-first century, when the Latino population will represent over 10 percent of the U.S. population. Before examining the policy implications of this growth, we should delve more deeply into the composition of the Chicano population, in both demographic and socioeconomic terms. The next sections examine these features.

Demographic Composition

AGE. One of the most common demographic observations about Chicanos is a youthful age structure of the population. Since 1960 the median age of Chicanos has been consistently lower than that of non-Hispanic whites. Even among Latino-origin groups, Chicanos stand out, along with Puerto Ricans, as having the youngest age composition. In 1988, the median Chicano age was 24.1 years, versus 33.4 years for non-Hispanic whites and 39.1 years for the Cuban-origin population. Although this age structure represents a younger population than that of non-Hispanic whites, the Chicano population as a whole is aging over time. The median Chicano age has risen consistently since 1960, exceeding 20 years for the first time in the 1970s.[7]

Age composition patterns emerge, in large measure, from childbearing patterns in a demographic group. The simple image of Chicanos as having larger families than non-Hispanic whites, however, obscures interesting patterns across Chicano subgroups. While it is true that Chicanas give birth to more children, on average, than their non-Hispanic white counterparts, these patterns do not hold equally across all generational cohorts and class categories. In 1980, non-Hispanic white women of childbearing age had borne 1.83 children, on average. Mexican-origin women born in Mexico (first-generation) had borne 2.74 children, on average, while those born in the United States (second or later generations) had borne 2.34 children.

Fertility differentials among Chicanas and non-Hispanic white women diminish further when we control for educational status. Chicanas born in the United States, with increasing educational levels, demonstrate declining fertility levels from an average of 3.56 children born to Chicanas with less than an eighth-grade education to an average of 1.21 children born to Chicana college graduates—a number smaller than the comparable figure (1.3) for non-Hispanic white women with college degrees.[8] Of course, the heavy concentration of Chicanas in the lower educational categories mitigates the fertility-reducing effects of education on overall age patterns in the Chicano population.

The demographic implications of Chicano age structure are twofold: first, Chicanos represent a larger share of the young U.S. population than they do of the overall population. Although Chicanos are not yet 10 percent of the U.S. population, they are already more than 10 percent of the U.S. population under age 15. Indeed in the states featuring large Chicano populations—New Mexico, California, and Texas, for example—their numbers approach one-third of the school age population.[9] Second, this youthful age structure includes a "built-in" demographic momentum for further population growth, with a significant share of the Chicano population at or approaching childbearing age.[10]

NATIVITY. No treatment of Chicano population composition is complete without an assessment of the immigrant/U.S.-born distinction in the Mexican-origin community. The Mexican-origin population in the United States is comprised in the majority of first-generation immigrants from Mexico. In 1980 one in four Mexican-origin persons in the United States had been born in Mexico. Since 1980 Latino population growth through immigration has outpaced population growth through natural increase, so that the foreign-born share now approaches one-third.

Nativity patterns are particularly important for policy in that they determine citizenship status, which in turn determines access to the political process. U.S.-born Chicanos possess formal political rights no different from U.S. citizens of any other ethnic origin. However, immigrants (or legal permanent residents, in immigration policy parlance) are not eligible to vote, with the exception of a few local jurisdictions, and have more limited access to some forms of public benefits than do citizens. To date, significant shares of the Mexican-origin community refrain from adjusting their resident status to that of U.S. citizen, as witnessed by the fact that naturalization rates for Mexican-born immigrants fall far below those of other Latino groups and non-Latino groups. For example, of the 44,400 Mexicans who immigrated in 1970, only 3 percent had naturalized by 1979, versus nearly half of the 16,000-member Cuban-origin cohort and half of the 93,000 Asian-origin immigrants. Roughly 600,000 Mexicans immigrated to the United States between 1970 and 1979. Of those, only 10 percent had naturalized by 1987. Factors contributing to such low naturalization rates include geographical proximity to the country of origin (Canadian immigrants to the United States show similarly low naturalization rates, for example), comparatively low educational levels, and the economic basis for the migration behavior, versus the political refugee status through which most Cubans and many Asian-origin immigrants arrived in the United States.[11]

FAMILY STRUCTURE. Chicano families are larger, on average, than non-Hispanic white families and somewhat more likely to be headed by women. Data from the 1991 March Current Population Survey show an average family size of 4.06 persons in the Mexican-origin community and 3.13 persons, on average, in non-Hispanic white families. One-third of Mexican-origin families have five or more members, versus 13 percent of non-Hispanic white families—a dramatic difference that will be particularly relevant in the upcoming discussion of child and family policy.[12]

Over time, Chicano families have also included increasing numbers of female-headed families. Furthermore, the source of that headship status differs among Chicanas and non-Hispanic white women. From 1980 to 1991, female household headship grew from 18 to 19.1 percent of all Chicana families. The comparable growth rate was higher in non-Hispanic white families, from 13.6 to 16.4 percent, implying higher rates of marital instability among non-Hispanic whites than among Chicanos. However, nearly half the female-headed households in the non-Hispanic white population are the result of widowhood, versus one-fourth in Chicana households. Chicanas are more likely than white women to be household heads as the result of divorce (30 percent) or separation (7 percent).[13] Thus, Chicano family patterns reflect a significant incidence of marital instability— patterns that seem to be gaining ascendance with the passage of time.

GEOGRAPHIC DISTRIBUTION. Although not the most geographically concentrated of Latino-origin groups (a distinction held by the Cuban-origin population), Chicanos are highly concentrated in a single region of the United States. Chicanos reside overwhelmingly in the five Southwestern states—California, Arizona, New Mexico, Colorado, and Texas. Indeed, nearly 75 percent of all Mexican-origin persons in the United States live in Texas and California, both of which now have populations in excess of 25 percent Mexican origin. Latinos, overwhelmingly of Mexican origin, constitute over 18 percent of the Arizona population, over one-third of the New Mexico population, and over 10 percent of the Colorado population. The Latino population also includes significant numbers in Illinois, where 7 percent of the population is Latino, concentrated primarily in the Chicago area.

The persistent regional concentration of Latinos in the Southwest has both historical roots and contemporary influences. Aside from the historical basis for Mexican residence in what is now the U.S. Southwest, a general contemporary shift in population toward the Sunbelt since the 1970s fueled by economic development and expansion has meant a return migration by Chicanos living in other parts of the United States. The combination of established Latino communities and comparatively attractive economic opportunities has attracted both Mexican immigrants and Chicanos to the same areas of the Southwestern United States, producing both new opportunities for community building and new tensions.[14]

Social and Economic Characteristics

EDUCATION. Plotting the educational trajectory of Chicanos over a period of time yields a dramatic mix of advancement and retrenchment. For every positive indicator—increases in the median years of completed schooling, for example—dismal indicators emerge simultaneously; i.e., low levels of college graduation, even lower levels of postgraduate education, and increasingly embattled public school systems fighting for funding in program areas that serve Chicano children.

In most aggregate indicators of educational achievement, Mexican-origin persons stand at the low end of the continuum, in comparison to other Latino-origin groups and non-Latinos. In 1991 fewer than half (44 percent) of all Mexican-origin persons aged 25 years and over had completed four years of high school or more, versus 80 percent of non-Hispanic whites, 61 percent of Cubans, and 58 percent of Puerto Ricans. Nearly 16 percent in this age bracket had completed no more than five years total of formal schooling, compared to 1.6 percent of the non-Hispanic white population and less than 10 percent of other Latino-origin groups. Mexican-origin persons could be distinguished as late as 1988 by a median schooling level falling short of twelve years, below that of non-Hispanic whites, Asians, or African Americans.[15] In short, educational progress has been slow, at best, and shows signs of stagnating at current levels in the absence of concerted policy effort. In 1988 only 8 percent of Mexican-origin persons in the United States had completed four or more years of college, a figure much lower than the 25 percent share of the non-Hispanic white population, but also lower than that of the other major Latino-origin groups.

Some of the limited educational performance of Chicanos can be attributed to Mexican immigration, with immigrants deflating the average figures for the Mexican-origin population. However, immigration alone cannot account for the pattern, when other groups more heavily infused with immigrant members—Cubans and Asians, for example—show only a slight educational deficit. Linda Chávez, conservative commentator on ethnic politics, notes in her recent book *Out of the Barrio* that second-generation people of Mexican origin (those born in the United States of immigrant parents) demonstrate high-school-and-beyond completion levels closer to those of non-Hispanic whites (78 percent versus 90 percent).[16] Still, Chávez's analyses omit mention of another pattern, one showing that third-generation Chicanos (ages 25–34) are less likely to complete high school (30 percent with less than twelve years of education) than second-generation Chicanos (21 percent of whom do not graduate). Clearly, more than immigration status is implicated in the limited achievements of Chicanos in the education system.

While limited English proficiency is often used to explain, in part, the Chicano educational profile, it bears noting that the Latino-origin group with the highest rates of Spanish retention—Cuban Americans— also boasts the highest aggregate socioeconomic status. Limited English skills do reduce economic achievement, but fluent Spanish ability is not synonymous with limited English ability. Indeed, most Spanish speakers in the United States also speak English. Few opportunities exist to evaluate the outcome of truly bilingual Chicanos who have been trained for higher-order linguistic performance and critical skills building in both Spanish and English, but preliminary evidence suggests that just such "additive" rather than "subtractive" curricula, implemented effectively, enhance academic outcomes among Chicano schoolchildren.[17]

LABOR FORCE PARTICIPATION, OCCUPATION, AND EARNINGS. The educational profile outlined briefly above helps place Chicano economic performance in its proper context. Although Chicanos have one of the highest labor force participation rates of all ethnic groups in the United States, their work experiences are most concentrated in job categories and wage ladders offering little hope for a sturdy foothold above the poverty line.

In 1991 Chicano male labor force participation (which includes both employed Chicanos and those unemployed but actively seeking work) stood at nearly 80 percent, versus 74 percent for non-Hispanic white men. In addition, nearly 51 percent of Chicanas were also in the labor force, narrowing the long-standing margin of employment considerably between themselves and non-Hispanic white women (at 57 percent participation).[18] This contemporary Chicano labor force participation pattern tracks well with historical trends. Chicanos, in the past and today, demonstrate high levels of work effort,[19] which, however, does not translate into high occupational or income achievement relative to other groups.

Fewer than one in ten Chicanos worked in managerial or professional specialties in 1991, while this job category held more than one in four non-Hispanic white workers and one in four Cuban workers. Although Chicanos are much more likely to work in manufacturing and service jobs (nearly one-third of Chicanos work as operators, fabricators, or laborers) than in such extractive industries as farming, forestry, and fishing, it is still the case that these latter job categories employ over 12 percent of Chicanos—more than are found in management jobs. Chicanas, like other groups of women workers, are heavily concentrated in clerical and service work, which combined employed two-thirds of Chicana workers in 1991, a departure from the traditional overrepresentation of Chicanas in manufacturing work, as compared to women of other ethnic origins.[20]

Such job profiles do not bode well for Chicano earnings profiles. In 1991 median Chicano earnings fell nearly $10,000 below those of non-Hispanic white men ($12,894 versus $22,207); while Chicanas earned $9,286 at the distribution median, versus $12,438 for non-Hispanic white women. Median Chicano family income stood at $23,240 in 1992, versus $36,334 for non-Hispanic white families. At that same time, the poverty threshold for a family of four was approximately $14,000; thus, Chicano families were much closer to the poverty line, on average, than were non-Hispanic white families.[21]

An overwhelming share of Chicano income (about 90 percent) is derived from wages and salaries, as opposed to public transfer payments or IDR (income derived from interest, dividends, and rents).[22] Thus, analyses of earnings correlates will go far in identifying the important factors contributing to low Chicano earnings.

The earnings prospects of a group of workers vary not only by occupation, but also by individual human capital and labor market characteristics. For instance, multivariate analyses conducted by Bean and Tienda (1987) highlight the income-enhancing effects of education and work in the private sector or self-employment (versus public sector/government employment) for Chicano men. On average, an additional year of schooling yields a 4.6 percent return on earnings; and Chicano men earned 10 percent less in the public sector, other characteristics being equal, than Chicanos who were self-employed in 1980. Chicana earnings profiles respond to some of the same influences, but at more modest rates. Lower rates of return accrue with increased education, longer work experience, and overall wage levels in the community for Chicanas than for their male counterparts. In short, Chicana earnings profiles are flatter across the life course and across different demographic and labor market categories than are the profiles for men, which introduces important questions about the prospects for Chicana economic achievement in the future.

POVERTY STATUS. The earnings profiles outlined above bring us to a more detailed consideration of Chicano poverty. Despite considerable work effort, Chicanos are at high risk for experiencing poverty at least once in their lifetimes. Just over 23 percent of Chicano adults (ages 18–64) fell below the poverty level in 1990, versus 9.7 percent of non-Hispanic white adults. Poverty among the elderly was also more prevalent among Chicanos, with 23.1 percent of the Chicano population over age 65 falling below poverty guidelines, versus one in ten non-Hispanic white senior citizens.[23] Nor was the poverty experience limited to adults. Indeed, it is the Chicano profile of child poverty that is the most disturbing. When earnings in a household fall below poverty guidelines, all household members, adults and children, are counted as poor. Almost half the Chicanos in poverty today in the United States—48 percent—are children under the age of 18.[24]

Poverty hit Chicanos hard at the end of the 1980s. Preliminary data from the 1990 U.S. Census identified one in four Chicano families as poor, versus 9.5 percent of non-Hispanic white families. Despite persistently high levels of work effort, meaningful economic advancement eluded the Chicano population during the 1980s, at least the kind of advancement that led Chicano children out of poverty. By 1989 three of the top ten states in terms of children's poverty rates were Southwestern states with large Chicano populations: New Mexico ranked third with 27.5 percent of its children in poverty; Texas, eighth with 24 percent child poverty; and Arizona, ninth with 21.7 percent child poverty.[25] One in three Latino children lived in poverty in 1990, versus one in eight non-Hispanic white children and two in five African American children.

In sum, the Chicano profile of educational achievement, and ensuing economic achievement, paints a disturbing portrait of human capital investment lost, and economic productivity blunted at a time when it is most desperately needed to avoid a wholesale intergenerational transmission of want. On this serious note, we turn our attention to the explicit policy implications of Chicano demography.

POLICY IMPLICATIONS
OF CHICANO DEMOGRAPHIC TRENDS

Children and Youth

With half the dramatic Chicano population growth of the 1980s owing to natural increase; with nearly a third of the child populations of major Southwestern states comprised of Chicanos; and with a powerful demographic momentum for continued growth through natural increase, it is clear that Chicano children and youth merit special policy attention in any attempt to advance Chicano life chances. The social and economic stakes could hardly be higher when we remind ourselves that half the Chicanos in poverty today are children.

The political stakes in advancing Chicano well-being are high, as well. Opponents of a growing Chicano presence in the United States mince no words in stating their opposition to this growth—as evidenced by the 1988 writings of John Tanton, founding member of Zero Population Growth and creator of both the Federation for American Immigration Reform (an anti-immigration interest group) and U.S. English (an "official English" interest group): "Will Latin American migrants bring with them the tradition of the *mordida,* the lack of involvement in public affairs, etc.? . . . 'Gobernar es poblar'. . . . Can *homo contraceptivus* compete with *homo progenetiva* if borders aren't controlled? . . . perhaps this is the first instance in which those with their pants up are going to get caught by those with their pants down!"[26]

Clearly, Chicano population growth has prompted a powerful political backlash, making it all the more important that scholarship on Chicano populations counter policy suggestions grounded in hysteria with policy proposals grounded in firm demographic evidence. The evidence, reviewed in this chapter, suggests definite directions for policy reform directed toward a young, growing Chicano population. First, no meaningful advancement of Chicano socioeconomic status will take place without a wholesale reevaluation of the relations between Chicanos and the public education system. Rejected by this system through (1) school funding that produces ten-fold differences in per-pupil expenditures (as in Texas, with Latino school districts at the lowest end of the spectrum), (2) half-hearted implementation of instructional programs targeting Chicano children, and (3) tracking systems that disproportionately place Chicano students on nonacademic educational paths, these students reject the system in turn, voting with their feet to the tune of a 50 percent drop-out rate. A logical first priority of federal, state, and local policy reform, then, is public education reform that adapts to the demographic reality of a large Chicano population.

Specifically, these reforms may move in several directions simultaneously. Few would argue that dramatic differentials in school funding produce the egalitarian, meritocratic outcomes most Americans claim they want from a public education system. Judicial and legislative remedies to school funding inequities should continue, for they hold out hope for improving the quality of education for Chicanos. Still, equalizing school finance is not a sufficient remedy. Even in states where finance reform has equalized per-pupil expenditures—California, for example—Chicano educational outcomes lag behind those of other groups.

In addition to receiving sufficient funding, schools must adapt curricula and pedagogical techniques to the realities of their changing demographic composition. In the Chicano case, these adaptations will include varied strategies for expanding English proficiency and varied instructional techniques for keeping limited-English-proficient children apace in such content areas as mathematics, science, geography, history, as they build their English language skills.

The dilemma regarding bilingual education as a pedagogical technique illustrates the challenges involved in implementing such varied strategies. The debate boils down to a conflict between "pure" research on language acquisition and "evaluation" research on actual bilingual education programs. Pure linguistic research, typically based in the laboratory or experimental classroom, has long offered consistent evidence that higher-order thinking skills in two languages develop most fully when the native language, whatever it may be, serves as the principal language of instruction—particularly when the student comes from a disadvantaged environment and enters the learning environment with not only limited English proficiency but also limited Spanish proficiency, measured by extent of vocabulary, for example. This limited linguistic base accounts in part for the differences among Mexican-origin children and the children of such refugee groups as Cubans and Southeast Asians, who include a greater share of immigrants with higher education and higher-status occupational backgrounds, and who fare better in English "immersion" programs than do Chicanos.

Students with limited language skills in both languages respond more favorably to content-area instruction in Spanish—the language they know —and make a more gradual, but more complete, transition to English once the foundation has been laid in their native language. At least, this is the case in "pure" research. Evaluations of real-world bilingual programs, on the other hand, have produced equivocal results, with some showing no significant advantage to bilingual education for later achievement in English.[27] These modest results are not surprising when they are examined more closely in their political contexts. Bilingual education in the United States is synonymous with "remedial" education and suffers from all the stigma, inconsistent implementation, low teacher morale, and low student expectations that come with that designation. Rather than being implemented as a long-term investment in the development of a truly bilingual population, language instruction is more often characterized by intense pressure to "exit" students at the first sign of English usage, whereupon

Spanish is set aside and English becomes the only mode of discourse, in which Spanish-dominant children begin at a significant disadvantage.

When the politics of bilingual education are woven into the broader political debate on educational reform, we see cause for both hope and concern. School-based management, as a technique returning decision making to principals and teachers, offers hope in Chicano-populated school districts so that front-line personnel will have the authority to implement revisions grounded in reality, including bilingual education if student demographics so dictate. However, it is unclear how simultaneous trends toward educational "choice" or a voucher system, allowing parents to shop around for their children's schools, will affect Chicano children. Will the voucher system produce schools that "specialize" in services to limited-English-proficient children? Given the stigmatized nature of language remediation, will parents want to send their children to such schools? And will this kind of specialization exacerbate continuing problems of racial and ethnic segregation? Until answers to these questions have been addressed, the utility of school choice for improving Chicano educational quality cannot be assessed adequately.

Whatever the changes in educational structure (finance reform, management reform, or other), it is clear that the content of education must be examined anew to determine whether or not meaningful communication is taking place between students and teachers. Poor management systems have produced school environments where state-of-the-art technology like computers and stimulating educational software are least likely to filter into those "remedial" classrooms housing a disproportionate number of Chicano students and are channeled instead to academic "excellence" programs where few Chicanos are likely to see them. Such "tracking" begins in the earliest grades, and sets students on a path where their own aspirations and the school system's aspirations for them are modest indeed. Until the lenses through which Chicano schoolchildren's potential is viewed are refocused by parents, teachers, and community leaders, Chicano adults in places like the Silicon Valley will be far more likely to assemble the high-technology products of the twenty-first century than to use or create them. Demographic momentum alone will not reframe educational policy priorities. Demographic power harnessed toward strategic political action will be necessary to implement reform.

The Chicano Labor Force

We have seen evidence of an abiding work ethic in the Chicano community, illustrated by high levels of labor force participation even in the face of
modest wages. Chicanos are a significant share of the "working" poor and,
as such, will benefit from those economic reform proposals that seek to
"make work pay" for all working-class people.[28] Specifically, these reform
proposals include an increase in the earned income tax credit for working
poor families, an expansion of child care allowances, and an increase in the
minimum wage. Together, such reforms reward consistent work effort and
afford Chicano families a firmer footing above the poverty line.

In addition, we see Chicanos continuing to be concentrated in those
sectors of the economy that show the slowest growth: the manufacturing
industries that have experienced the most severe job loss with the changing
structure of the U.S. economy. Coupled with a limited educational back-
ground, a persistent concentration of job experience in a less-remunerative
sector of the economy translates into constrained opportunities for earning one's way out of poverty and a higher likelihood of recurrent unemployment. Therefore, federal, state, and local efforts to retrain unemployed
adults in the wake of changing economic conditions must anticipate that
Chicanos will be heavily represented among their client base. The most
useful efforts to recruit Chicanos into education and training or "E and T"
programs will be those that incorporate the distinct features of the Chicano
population into their curricula. This may include enhanced attention to the
development of communication skills in a population for whom bilingualism is a way of life, and training components that take into account not
only the kinds of jobs clients aspire to, but also the kinds of skill repertoires
and skill deficits that are a function of the sorts of jobs clients come from. In
other words, training Chicano workers for the economy of the twenty-first
century will be more effective in those programs with a firm knowledge of
the Chicano social and economic experiences of the twentieth century.

Single mothers in the Chicano community face a slightly different set
of challenges from the more general challenges facing all Chicanos. Called
upon to be both "provider" and "caregiver" for their children, many single
mothers sacrifice greatly in one area to accommodate the other. The current income support system—Aid to Families with Dependent Children—

does little to enhance Chicana opportunities to combine the work and child-rearing roles in ways that will lead to the successful avoidance of poverty. AFDC, with its complex eligibility rules, is applied selecting against women's ability to earn their way out of poverty by reducing benefits so sharply when women find jobs that working-class jobs become less feasible than continued AFDC receipt, particularly when factoring in the loss of health benefits under Medicaid with the loss of AFDC eligibility. The program, thus, virtually condemns its recipients to rely on it exclusively, or not at all.

Alternatives to this system include an aggressive federal program aimed at collecting child support payments from an absent parent, supplemented by a government stipend if the absent parent has no earnings—Child Support Assurance System.[29] Only about half of the one-parent families in the United States have child support awards mandated by the courts, and only a subset of those actually receive payments. The problem is particularly dramatic among poor single parents, who are far less likely to receive awards and, once awarded, to receive payment. With high levels of employment in the Chicano community and increasing levels of marital breakup, a child support assurance program is likely to tap significant resources currently unavailable to Chicano children. The combination of "make-work-pay" reforms for low-income earners and assured basic child support awards can assist single Chicana mothers in their efforts to escape from and to stay out of poverty as they struggle to both provide for and raise their children.

Finally, health care reform is central to any effort to advance the economic position of the Chicano workforce. Chicanos are dramatically underrepresented in the ranks of the insured and demonstrate health concerns that reflect that status. Furthermore, cost is identified repeatedly as the key barrier to the health care system for Chicanos. Whatever form it may take, meaningful expansion of the health care system to include Chicanos will not only improve health status, but contribute to an improved overall economic position in the twenty-first century.

Mexican Immigrants

With half its demographic growth emerging from immigration, the Chicano population has a strategic advantage in leading the way on immigration and immigrant policy issues. The distinction between "immigration" policy and "immigrant" policy is an important one. Immigration policy represents that exclusively federal realm of policy making that determines who is admitted to the United States and what procedures are implemented to determine admission. Much has been accomplished in the past decade in immigration policy: the 1986 Immigration Reform and Control Act legalized nearly three million undocumented immigrants, most of whom were of Mexican origin,[30] and the 1990 Immigration Act is clearing out staggering backlogs of Mexican applicants waiting to come to the United States. The influence of advocacy groups in the shaping of immigration policy has grown, particularly in the courts, where Latino advocates have won clearer adjudication standards and have often checked the excesses of immigration law enforcement agencies like the U.S. Border Patrol.

Immigrant policy, on the other hand, addresses the questions: What do we do with immigrants when they get here? To what benefits are they entitled as U.S. residents? These questions are answered at the federal, state, and local levels and will likely be more important questions in the twenty-first century. Two issues loom large on this agenda: immigrant political rights and immigrant access to public services.

As a group, Chicano advocates are divided on the issue of encouraging the naturalization of Mexican immigrants. While such advocacy groups as the National Association of Latino Elected Officials (NALEO) see Mexican immigrants as a potential augmention to Chicano voting strength, other groups view naturalization drives as efforts to cut immigrants off from the community of origin and impede the freedom of people to choose a more bicultural, binational lifestyle. Still, there is no disputing that the franchise is a necessary condition for political action on behalf of a constituency, and low naturalization rates minimize Latino voting numbers that could be strengthened in order to improve Latino living conditions. Where administrative barriers exist to the naturalization effort, they can be lowered. As long as advocates realize that the adoption of citizenship imposes not just benefits but also imposes costs on immigrants in many arenas of life, these service organizations can marshal their resources to assist immigrants in dealing with those costs.

Perhaps the most challenging front facing Mexican immigrant advocates is in defining the boundaries of eligibility for public services, including those of health, education, and welfare. Immigration restrictionists claim that immigrants drain the public coffers and depress wages and working conditions in the communities where they settle in large numbers. Often Chicanos agree, at least as is evidenced by data in public opinion polls. While much evidence suggests that these fears are grossly exaggerated, evidence does exist that local governments—cities and counties—face increased health and education costs owing in part to large, impoverished immigrant communities, whose workers—both legal and undocumented—are more readily exploited by employers than are U.S. citizens.[31]

The "first-instinct" policy solution to such problems is a redoubled effort to restrict further immigration. However, restrictionism is not the only solution. Many of the workplace violations that commonly victimize immigrants are violations of U.S. wage and hour laws that can be mitigated with greater enforcement resources targeting employers, particularly when the workforce is legally authorized to work, as is the case in much of the garment-manufacturing industry in the Southwestern United States. Mitigating the wage-depressing effects of immigration can be accomplished by ensuring that employers do not exploit desperate workers.

The costs of educating immigrants and serving their health needs can only be met with more realistic allocations of these resources based on true population composition. An example of refusal to face such reality can be found in the recent decision not to adjust 1990 U.S. Census Bureau figures, which disproportionately omit U.S. Latino residents and, thus, understate the population bases on which congressional representation and a host of program-funding decisions are made. This resistance to facing demographic change has produced a reactive, incomplete policy agenda time and time again. Until policymakers think ahead and seek to both manage and accommodate demographic change, they will be unable to construct an agenda that will improve global competitiveness and economic productivity.

As the U.S. population ages, it relies more and more heavily on minorities and on immigrants to sustain the elderly. As we enter the twenty-first century, the economic success of Chicanos and Mexican immigrants will be tied more intimately to the economic fate of the nation than ever before. The demographic patterns already in place ensure that Chicanos will form a greater part of the labor force and a greater proportional contributor to the nation's wealth than in the past. All observers, from the harshest critics of ethnic diversity to the strongest Chicano advocates, realize that the Chicano population cannot be ignored when envisioning a twenty-first-century United States. The critical issue in the next decade for demographers will be to continue bringing demographic evidence squarely into the center of the debate and affording policymakers and advocates the opportunity to build their cases on a firm, informationally sound foundation. By knowing what the Chicano population looks like and where it is headed demographically, those policymakers and advocates who aspire to create the conditions for Chicano prosperity may hold a stronger hand in advancing their agenda in a time of rapid political change.

NOTES

1. Frank D. Bean and Marta Tienda, *The Hispanic Population of the United States* (New York: Russell Sage Foundation, 1987).
2. William P. O'Hare, "America's Minorities: The Demographics of Diversity," *Population Bulletin* 47 (1992): 1–47.
3. Ibid.
4. Ibid.
5. Ibid.
6. Antonio L. Estrada, Fernando M. Treviño, and Laura A. Ray, "Utilization Barriers among Mexican Americans in the Southwest," *American Journal of Public Health* 80 (1990): 27–31.
7. Bean and Tienda, *Hispanic Population*.
8. Ibid.
9. National Council of La Raza, "Child Poverty Up Nationally in 33 States, and in 84 Major Cities," NCLR *Poverty Project Newsletter* 4 (1992): 1.
10. Rafael Valdivieso and Cary Davis, *U.S. Hispanics: Challenging Issues for the 1990s,* Population Trends and Public Policy, vol. 17 (Washington, D.C.: The Population Reference Bureau, 1988).
11. Alejandro Portes and Rubén G. Rumbaut, *Immigrant America: A Portrait* (Berkeley: University of California Press, 1990).
12. Bureau of the Census, *The Hispanic Population in the United States: March 1991* (Washington, D.C., 1991).
13. Bean and Tienda, *Hispanic Population*.
14. Rogelio Saenz and Alberto Dávila, "Chicano Return Migration to the Southwest: An Integrated Human Capital Approach," *International Migration Review* 24 (1992): 1248–66.
15. Bureau of the Census, *The Hispanic Population in the United States: March, 1988 — Advance Report* (Washington, D.C., 1988).
16. Linda Chávez, *Out of the Barrio* (New York: Basic Books, 1991).
17. James Crawford, *Bilingual Education: History, Politics, Theory, and Practice* (Trenton: Crane, 1989); Kenji Hakuta, *Mirror of Language: The Debate on Bilingualism* (New York: Basic Books, 1986).
18. Bureau of Census statistics, 1991.
19. Bean and Tienda, *Hispanic Population*.

20. Bureau of Census statistics, 1991.
21. Ibid.
22. David Hayes-Bautista, Werner O. Schink, and Jorge Chapa, *The Burden of Support: Young Latinos in an Aging Society* (Stanford: Stanford University Press, 1988).
23. Bureau of Census statistics, 1991.
24. Ibid.
25. National Council of La Raza, "Child Poverty."
26. Quoted in L. Chávez, *Out of the Barrio*.
27. Rosalie Pedalino Porter, *Forked Tongue: The Politics of Bilingual Education* (New York: Basic Books, 1990).
28. David Ellwood, *Poor Support: Poverty in the American Family* (New York: Basic Books, 1988); John Schwarz and Tom Volgy, *The Forgotten Americans: Thirty Million Working Poor in the Land of Opportunity* (New York: W. W. Norton, 1990).
29. Robert I. Lerman, "Child Support Policies," in *Welfare Policy for the 1990s,* eds., Paul Cottingham and Daniel Ellwood (Cambridge: Harvard University Press, 1989).
30. Susan González-Baker, *The Cautious Welcome: The Legalization Programs of the 1986 Immigration Reform and Control Act* (Washington, D.C.: Urban Institute Press, 1990).
31. George Borjas, *Friends or Strangers* (New York: Basic Books, 1990); Charles Keely, "Population and Immigration Policy: State and Federal Roles" in *Mexican and Central American Population and U.S. Immigration Policy,* eds. Frank Bean, Jurgen Schmandt, and Sidney Weintraub (Austin: Center for Mexican American Studies, 1989).

MEXICAN IMMIGRATION IN THE 1980S AND

BEYOND : IMPLICATIONS FOR CHICANAS/OS

Leo R. Chávez and Rebecca G. Martínez

The 1980s were greeted with a great deal of anticipation and, in some quarters, dread, as the "Decade of the Hispanics."[1] However, the expected major increases in educational attainment, economic strength, social status, and political power for Latinos failed to appear to any significant degree.[2] One area in which significant change has occurred for Latinos is in population growth, much of it fueled by immigration. This growth, however, raised some concern among the American public and its policymakers. As a consequence, in the 1980s a number of public policies were designed to reduce the influx of immigrants, especially undocumented immigrants from Mexico and other Latin American countries. These immigration-related policies, together with the ongoing population shifts, will have long-lasting effects on Chicanos.[3] Indeed, the continuing debate over immigration presents profound challenges to Chicano membership in the larger community and identity, with access to opportunities that underlie economic gains. Far from settled, these issues will be debated well into the 1990s and even into the twenty-first century.

This chapter attempts to delineate these issues by first examining the demographic shifts that have occurred because of population growth and immigration. We then examine some key issues for Chicanos that emerge from policies to control immigration, especially employer sanctions regulations. Other policies, such as defining undocumented students as foreign students for tuition purposes, restricting the number of persons allowed per room in apartments, and taking away the right to citizenship of U.S.-born children of undocumented parents, only indirectly attempt to regulate the flow of undocumented immigrants. And yet, such policies have significant implications for Chicanos because they place limits on economic and educational opportunities and strike at the very essence of who is a member of the "community."

A DECADE OF DEMOGRAPHIC CHANGE

Since 1970, the Latino population in the United States has experienced considerable growth. Between 1970 and 1980, the number of Latinos grew from 4.5 percent of the U.S. population to 6.4 percent, with immigration accounting for almost half this growth.[4] By 1990, Latinos accounted for 9 percent of the nation's population, with immigration again accounting for about half the increase.[5] Between 1980 and 1990, the Latino population grew by 53 percent whereas the total U.S. population grew by 9.8 percent.

Among Latinos, the Mexican-origin population witnessed major gains during the 1980s (figure 2.1). The 1990 census counted 13,393,208 persons of Mexican origin, 61.2 percent of all Latinos. The Mexican American population increased by approximately 7.75 million persons, a 54.4 percent increase over the decade. Puerto Ricans and Cubans experienced gains as well. The "other Hispanics"—Central and South Americans—made impressive gains, increasing 66.7 percent over the same period.[6] Political and economic upheavals in Central America, in particular, have contributed to the increasing presence of Guatemalans, Salvadorans, and Nicaraguans.

Latinos are geographically concentrated, with a majority living in just two states, California (34.3 percent) and Texas (19.4 percent). New York and Florida, however, each have over a million Latinos. The five contiguous Southwestern states of Arizona, California, Colorado, New Mexico, and Texas had, in 1990, approximately 13.7 million Latinos, 61.3 percent of all Latinos in the United States.[7] Growth rates varied over the decade, with California's Latino population growing by 69 percent, Florida's by 83 percent, Texas's by 45 percent and New York's by 33 percent.[8]

The Mexican-origin population is even more geographically concentrated (figure 2.2). California alone accounts for 45 percent of Chicanos. Six states—California, Arizona, Colorado, Texas, New Mexico, and Illinois—have 88.2 percent of all persons of Mexican origin.

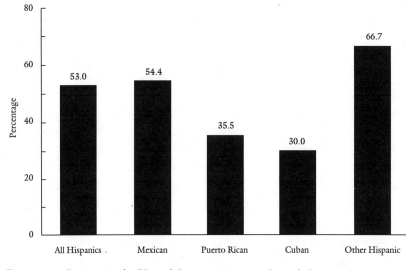

Figure 2.1   Latinos in the United States, 1980–1990 Growth Rates in Percentages. *Source:* Census 1991, Table 1

Figure 2.2   Mexican-Origin Population, 1990. Total Population in U.S. 13,393,208. *Source:* Census 1990: 1–7

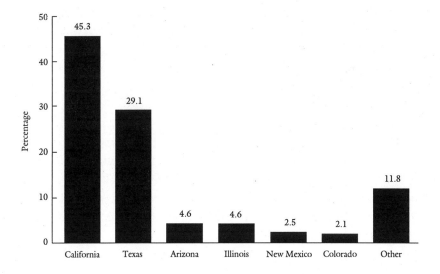

IMMIGRATION AND CHICANOS

The dramatic growth in the Latino population is, to a significant degree, due to immigration. Between 1980 and 1988, 625,690 Mexicans legally immigrated to the United States, more than from any other Latin American country. In 1981 alone, 101,268 Mexicans legally immigrated, almost double the number of the year before and after (figure 2.3). Since 1984, the number of legal Mexican immigrants entering the United States has continued to rise steadily, with a new peak reached in 1988, when 95,039 Mexicans legally immigrated. Mexicans accounted for 14.8 percent of the 643,025 immigrants admitted in 1988.

The years of 1989 and 1990 were unusual due to the large numbers of Mexicans admitted as legal immigrants under the legalization program authorized by the 1986 immigration law—the Immigration Reform and Control Act (IRCA). Fully 405,172 Mexicans were admitted as legal immigrants in 1989, and another 679,068 in 1990.[9]

Legal Mexican immigrants live in much the same geographic area as Latinos generally. An exception, however, is New York, where Mexican immigrants are generally less likely to reside. More than half (56.4 percent or 53,622) of the 95,039 legal Mexican immigrants in 1988 chose California as their state of intended residence. Mexican immigrants that year also intended to reside in Texas (23.9 percent), Illinois (6.2 percent), Arizona (3.6 percent), New Mexico (1.8 percent), and Colorado (1.2 percent).[10] Most (80.7 percent) legal Mexican immigrants in 1988 intended to reside in one of the Southwestern states of California, Texas, Arizona, New Mexico and Colorado. Thus, the Southwest is both the region with the largest Latino population and the area that attracts most legal Mexican immigrants.

Almost 90 percent of immigrants choose to reside in a metropolitan area.[11] The municipality of Los Angeles–Long Beach attracted one out of three (33.6 percent) legal Mexican immigrants in 1988. Other key urban destinations for Mexicans were Chicago, San Diego, El Paso, and Houston. San Diego in particular has seen an increase in the number of Mexican immigrants. Immigrants from Mexico were more likely to settle in San Diego during 1986 and 1987 than in 1984 and 1985.[12]

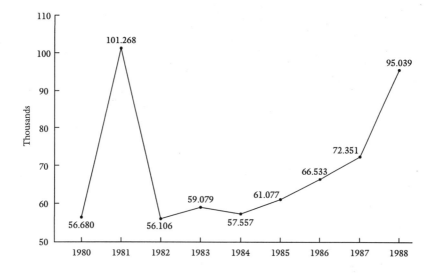

Figure 2.3   Legal Mexican Immigration, 1980–1988. *Source:* INS 1991

FEMALE IMMIGRANTS

The traditional picture of the Mexican immigrant was of a young, single male who migrated for a few months to work in agriculture and then returned home. This characterization was an accurate reflection of many Mexican migrants during the early part of the twentieth century, and well into the forties, fifties, and sixties, when thousands of men migrated as temporary contract laborers under the Bracero Program.[13] After the Bracero Program was terminated in 1964, the flow of Mexican men to agricultural jobs in the United States continued, only the flow was now an undocumented migration.

Although men may have predominated in these earlier migration flows, Mexican women also migrated to the United States, where they helped establish Mexican communities throughout the Southwest and Midwest. Currently, many more Mexican women are crossing the border as both legal and undocumented immigrants than had done previously.[14] For example, women made up 43.9 percent of the legal immigrants from Mexico in 1988.[15]

Mexican women are immigrating for economic as well as social reasons.[16] In the past, the migration literature characterized women as appendages to their migrating husbands; women migrated to reunite with their husbands who were already in the United States. Today, single women also migrate from Mexico to find "a better life," seeking employment in the rapidly growing service sector, especially in domestic work. They often have family in Mexico who rely on the money they send back.

Some Mexican women are single parents who leave their children with parents or siblings when migrating to the United States. In some cases, these women may have intended to work in the United States for a short time, but their stay became extended. As a consequence, they often return to bring their children from Mexico to live with them in the United States.

Research has shown that undocumented Mexican women are more likely to be on their first trip to the United States than are undocumented men, who often have experienced many migrations.[17] Mexican women often migrate once and then stay in the United States, whether they originally came to join husbands or came on their own. Why this is so probably has to do with many factors, but three seem to stand out. If they form a family in the United States, either by having children or bringing their children from Mexico, then they are more likely to settle. The jobs Mexican immigrant women obtain are typically year-round jobs. Although Mexican immigrant women are employed in agriculturally related jobs, which tend to be seasonal, many more work in domestic work, in hotels, restaurants, and manufacturing. Economic and cultural trends among Americans generally are reinforcing this pattern of employment. The number of relatively low-paying jobs in the urban and suburban service sector, the types of jobs Mexican immigrants frequently take, is increasing. In addition, American women continue to work outside the home, which also creates a demand for domestic labor. Finally, undocumented women often fear recrossing the border clandestinely. Crossing the border at night, over hillsides and through ravines, is a dangerous undertaking, one that many undocumented women would rather avoid, even if it means not returning to Mexico as often as they would like. If current trends persist, women will continue to make up a significant proportion of the Mexicans who immigrate to the United States in the 1990s and beyond.

UNDOCUMENTED IMMIGRANTS

Many people migrate to the United States without documentation from the U.S. Immigration and Naturalization Service. Popularly called "illegal aliens," these undocumented immigrants often come to the United States for relatively brief periods of time. Some, however, do settle and add to the existing population. Because undocumented immigrants are a clandestine population, it is difficult to make accurate estimates of their numbers. Some reasonable assessments are, however, available. For example, analysts used data from the 1980 census to estimate the number of undocumented immigrants in the country during the early 1980s at between 2.5 and 3.5 million.[18] More than 80 percent lived in five states: California, New York, Texas, Illinois, and Florida.

California attracts the largest proportion of undocumented immigrants of all nationalities. For example, Cornelius found that in 1987, California had approximately half (1.74 million) of the nation's undocumented immigrants.[19] Although undocumented immigrants accounted for only 1.4 percent of U.S. residents in 1980, they made up 6.3 percent of California's total population.[20] Not surprisingly, most undocumented immigrants from Mexico also choose California as their state of residence. California alone absorbs at least half the total flow of both documented and undocumented Mexican immigrants, "averaging about 67,000 legal immigrants per year since 1981, with an additional net flow of perhaps 100,000 undocumented migrants per year."[21] Understandably, therefore, of the approximately three million people legalized under IRCA, most (55 percent) live in California.[22]

The number of undocumented immigrants who settled in the United States was about the same at the end of the 1980s as it was at the beginning of the decade. Based on the 1980 census, Passel and Woodrow estimated that between 200,000 and 300,000 undocumented immigrants settled in the United States each year.[23] Later, they examined data from the Current Population Survey and estimated that during the late 1980s about 200,000 undocumented immigrants settled annually in the United States.[24] The similarity between the two estimates is important because it suggests that the monumental 1986 immigration law, which Congress designed to stem the flow of undocumented immigrants, had little effect on the number who settle in the United States each year. These estimates also suggest that

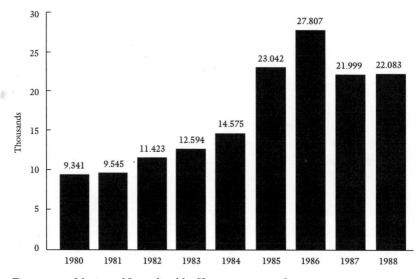

Figure 2.4   Mexicans Naturalized by Year, 1980–1988. *Source:* INS 1991

the number who settle is much less than the millions of illegal aliens often said to come and, by implication, stay in the country.

Legalization of immigration status is an important step for undocumented immigrants who want to work and live in the United States in relative security. It also has implications for Chicanos in the political arena. With legalization comes the opportunity to naturalize and obtain U.S. citizenship. Since immigrants are such a vital part of the growth of the Chicano population, their rate of naturalization is thus an important indicator of potential political—that is, voting—strength.

Mexicans historically have had low naturalization rates for several reasons. Mexican immigrants often believe that gaining U.S. citizenship would create obstacles to their dream of returning to Mexico someday, possibly to retire. For others, it is the emotional issue of nationalism, of losing one's national identity.

Examining the data on naturalization rates (figure 2.4) reveals, however, that larger numbers of Mexicans are naturalizing. Between 1979 and 1988 there was an increasing trend in the number of Mexicans who became naturalized citizens, reaching a peak in 1986 and then decreasing somewhat before stabilizing. These trends reflect a positive movement toward becoming a U.S. citizen, perhaps a result of the efforts of groups such as the Southwest Voter Registration program. The widespread debate over passage of IRCA may also have raised interest in the Latino community concerning the benefits of citizenship.

IMMIGRATION AND CHICANOS

The increasing proportion of the population that is foreign born provides evidence for the importance of immigration for Chicanos. Eighteen percent of the Mexican-origin population in the United States was foreign born in 1970.[25] In 1990, in contrast, 33 percent of the Mexican-origin population was foreign born.[26] Because of immigration, the proportion of immigrants among Chicanos in the nation almost doubled during the last two decades. In California, the state that receives most immigrants, the foreign born accounted for 41.7 percent of the Mexican-origin population in 1990.[27]

Latin American immigrants bring with them the language, values, and behavior that reinvigorate Latino culture in the Southwest and in communities throughout the United States. Without immigration, Chicanos would retain some of their immigrant parents' (figuratively speaking, also included here are grandparents, great-grandparents, etc.) culture, which would be combined with local variations of U.S. culture to create distinctive cultural patterns in their communities. However, research has shown that although immigration from Mexico and other Latin American countries keeps Spanish alive, by the third generation, U.S.-born Chicanos are dominant in English rather than Spanish.[28] Latino immigrants also bring with them values of family solidarity, religion, and hard work that sometimes stand in sharp contrast to American values of individualism and secularism. Behavior patterns among Latino immigrants are also relatively healthy. For example, Latino women born outside of the United States have few babies of low birth weight. Only 5 percent of the babies born to Mexican-born mothers and 5.7 percent of babies born to Cuban-born mothers were of low birth weight.[29] Newly arrived immigrant women are less likely to drink, smoke, or abuse other drugs. Moreover, they are particularly unlikely to do these things during pregnancy.[30] This behavior promotes positive pregnancy outcomes. Immigrants continue behaving in these ways in the United States, but eventually fall victim to acculturation. In short, it appears, as Hayes-Bautista has noted, that acculturation may be bad for your health.[31] But at the very least, Latino immigrants provide examples to the larger Chicano population of the value of alternative behavior.

THE PUBLIC'S CONCERN OVER IMMIGRATION

The 1980s not only witnessed high levels of immigration, they also experienced high levels of public concern about the effects of immigration. A heated public debate on immigration raged throughout most of the decade. The economic downturn of the early 1980s fanned the flames of discontent over immigration, as a small sample of stories from the popular press suggests. On 7 March 1983, *U.S. News & World Report*'s feature story was "Invasion from Mexico: It Just Keeps Growing." The cover of the magazine was a photo of three men carrying two women and a man across some shallow water. The image reinforces the popular characterization of undocumented immigrants as "wetbacks." Two weeks later, on 21 March 1983, *U.S. News & World Report* ran another story on immigration. The cover featured a scattering of signs in Chinese, Arabic, and Vietnamese lettering, as well as a sign in Spanish. Above this bewildering display was the title "English Sometimes Spoken Here: Our Big Cities Go Ethnic." Scribbled above the title was the word "sometimes," with an arrow pointing to where it should go in the sentence. The conclusion suggested by the cover is that English may not actually be spoken in our big cities after all.

Time magazine soon followed suit on 13 June 1983 with its own feature story on "Los Angeles: America's Uneasy New Melting Pot." Its cover consisted of several hand-drawn Asian and Latino faces in various shades of brown. Inside, Los Angeles was proclaimed "The New Ellis Island." The November 1983 issue of *Atlantic* weighed in with its own influential article by James Fallows entitled "The New Immigrants: How They're Affecting Us." The cover featured a round globe on which a weary face was drawn over the continents. Two legs and two arms loaded down with suitcases protruded from the globe. Clearly the world was on the move to the United States. On 25 June 1984, *Newsweek* featured on its cover a man carrying an older woman with a cane across some shallow water, with the title: "Closing the Door? The Angry Debate over Illegal Immigration." This cover was reminiscent of the earlier *U.S. News & World Report* cover, again striking at the "wetback" image.

One of the more persistent issues raised in this public discourse over immigration is the effect of immigration on citizen workers, especially Chicanos and African Americans. Research by academics and the government tend to conclude that immigration results in positive economic outcomes for the United States.[32] One study on Los Angeles, for example, found that immigration did result in Chicanos earning a little less than comparable workers in other parts of the country. The study also found, however, that workers in the area also experienced steady job growth.[33] In other words, they may have made slightly less money, but more people were working. The same study also found that African Americans did better economically in areas that experienced immigration compared to areas with little immigration. However, because the evidence is inconclusive, and because the presence of undocumented immigrants complicates data collection, public concerns about the effects of immigration remain high.

CONFRONTING IMMIGRATION: THE IMPLICATIONS FOR CHICANOS

Persistent media reports on immigration and the public's concern about the negative effects of immigration put pressure on policymakers to "do something" about the situation. In fall 1986, Congress responded by passing the Immigration Reform and Control Act (IRCA), whose purpose was to reduce undocumented immigration. Toward this end, IRCA had provisions that would (1) fine employers for hiring undocumented immigrants, and possibly jail repeat offenders; (2) legalize some undocumented immigrants already living and working in the United States; (3) bolster the enforcement capabilities of the Border Patrol and Immigration and Naturalization Service; and (4) expand the temporary labor program for agricultural workers, if and when needed.[34]

It is not the purpose of this work to evaluate the various provisions of IRCA, or its successes and failures. The question of concern here is, how do the attempts "to do something" about immigration affect Chicanos? IRCA is but one, albeit a dramatic and significant one, policy to control immigration. Others are less direct—for example, charging undocumented students non-resident tuition—but just as important in their implications for Chicanos.

IRCA contained provisions to fine and possibly jail employers who hired undocumented workers. Congress believed that these employer sanctions provisions would attack the problem of illegal immigration at its root cause: jobs. By making it illegal to hire undocumented workers, undocumented immigrants would go back to their country of origin, and others would consider it futile to even consider migrating to the United States.[35]

A great deal of research has focused on the effectiveness of employer sanctions.[36] The general conclusion is that employer sanctions have not been effective in stopping undocumented immigration. Employers and workers have managed to find ways—especially the use of fraudulent documents—to circumvent the law. With little disruption, other than increased paperwork, most businesses that used Mexican labor before IRCA continue to do so today; despite IRCA, it's "business as usual." As the personnel manager at a luxury hotel said, if the new law had worked it would have caused "severe damage. A lot of properties would have a terrible situation. A majority of your staffing would suffer tremendously. Your food service industry would shut down, your hospitality [hotels] would suffer tremendously. Your pricing [would] go up. You'd see in this industry alone a lot of rooms closed. You'd see a lot of permanently closed properties. [But] no one has really suffered an impact other than creating additional paperwork flow."[37]

Although employer sanctions have been ineffective in curtailing undocumented immigration, evidence suggests that the law has increased discrimination against Chicanos and other Latinos. Some of the most important evidence has come from the federal government. The U.S. Congress mandated that the General Accounting Office (GAO) investigate any possible discriminatory effects of employer sanctions. The GAO conducted a survey of employers to assess their hiring practices after the employer sanctions went into effect. In 1990, the GAO concluded that national origin discrimination resulting from IRCA, while not pervasive, does exist at a level that amounts to more than "just a few isolated cases" and constitutes a "serious pattern of discrimination." As the GAO noted, the "results are sufficient to conclude that a widespread pattern of discrimination has resulted against eligible workers." Moreover, "we believe that it is more reasonable to conclude that a substantial amount of these discriminatory practices resulted from IRCA rather than not."[38]

The problem for Chicanos and other Latinos arises when employers decide that they will not hire anyone who "looks foreign" in order to "play it safe" with the employer sanctions provisions against hiring undocumented workers. Unfortunately, what some employers may consider foreign-looking phenotypes (facial structure), skin color, or clothing, may have little correlation with actual immigration status. Consequently, the GAO found that some employers were refusing to consider qualified Chicano and Latino job applicants who are U.S. citizens and legal residents but who may, in their perception, "look foreign."

The findings of the GAO have disturbing implications for Chicanos and other Latinos. Additional research is needed to verify the GAO's findings and to examine if discriminatory hiring practices persist. These findings do raise the reasonable concern that employer sanctions will prove to be an institutionalized set of constraints on economic opportunities for Chicanos and other Latinos. When it is considered that many undocumented workers manage to find work, this outcome of employer sanctions is a truly pernicious contradiction.

Employer sanctions affect Chicanos and other Latinos in another important and unanticipated way (unanticipated, at least, by the framers of the law). Many Chicano and Latino families are complex in the sense that they consist of members with various statuses. The same family may consist of U.S. citizens by birth, legal immigrants, and undocumented immigrants. They are "binational families."[39] Two children in the same binational family, one a U.S. citizen and one undocumented, may both attend school in the United States. If they should both seek work after graduating from high school, however, one sibling cannot be hired legally because of employer sanctions. Not only has society spent money on the undocumented sibling's public education, but it will now miss out on the taxes that would have been paid by the sibling who is, technically, locked out of the job market. Since it is unlikely that the undocumented sibling will now leave the country because of employer sanctions, the obstacles to economic opportunity placed in his or her way appear short-sighted. Of course, the law paints in broad strokes its definition of "illegal alien," leaving little room for the nuances found in the everyday reality of people's lives. As a result, cases such as this hypothetical one abound. Young Chicanos and other Latinos find themselves caught in a legal web that constrains their economic mobility and, perhaps even more problematic, their perception of their possible mobility.

In the post-IRCA period, the battle over immigration has shifted to many fronts since passage of the 1986 immigration law, or IRCA. This shift has occurred because IRCA has proven ineffective at curbing undocumented immigration. Therefore, new strategies have developed to make living in the United States more difficult, and thus less appealing for undocumented immigrants. However, just as employer sanctions affected the lives of Chicanos and Latinos who were citizens and legal residents, these new strategies also have detrimental implications for Chicanos in the 1990s and beyond.

THE BATTLE OVER HOUSING DENSITY

Some communities, particularly in Southern California, have attempted to limit the number of people who can live in a residential dwelling. For example, the cities of Santa Ana, Dana Point, and Orange have passed such ordinances.[40] City officials in these communities complain that overcrowded housing units have become "hotbeds of crime, and health and safety hazards, and claim an occupancy ordinance is necessary to control the problems."[41] The restrictions range from the simple to the complex. Santa Ana's limit of four to five people per bedroom is relatively simple. In contrast, Orange's limit of no more than two people per bedroom plus one additional occupant, no more than one person per 120 square feet of living space, and no more than seven people per bathroom is complicated.

Although the concern for housing density may, at first glance, appear to have little to do with immigration, "housing density" and "overcrowding" are actually part of the discourse on immigration. The communities passing occupancy laws also have attracted low-income immigrants from Mexico, Central America, and Indochina. Residency ordinances would disproportionately affect immigrants. As the assistant director of the state Department of Housing noted in a friend-of-the-court brief supporting a lawsuit against the Santa Ana ordinance: "Santa Ana's ordinance would have an unfair and disproportionate impact on low-income residents, many of whom are Latino immigrants."[42] Quite often, these communities serve as bedroom communities for immigrants who work in more fashionable areas, where little affordable housing is available. By passing laws mandating lower housing density, city councils are indirectly attempting to discourage immigrants from staying and moving into their communities.

The immigrants who would be most affected by such housing laws are those in the most vulnerable stage of their migration. Research has shown that the immigrants most likely to live under crowded conditions have been in the United States for only a short time.[43] They have few economic resources, have low-paying jobs, and live with relatives or friends as a strategy for overcoming these constraints. In short, crowded living conditions are a result of necessity, not choice.

Moreover, immigrants live under crowded conditions only for as long as it takes to become adjusted to U.S. culture and to establish an economic base. Many of these immigrants will return to their country after saving enough money to do so. Housing laws that contain draconian occupancy restrictions would make both establishing a foothold in the United States and saving money more difficult, thus forestalling a move into less crowded housing or return migration. Such laws would thus have the ironic effect of making it more difficult for immigrants to behave in ways that might actually help reduce overcrowding.

Laws restricting occupancy have hit an important snag: they are unconstitutional, at least in California. In May 1992, the California Supreme Court issued a strongly worded ruling that local communities cannot set a limit on the number of people who can live in a residence that is lower than that already established by state law, which allows ten people in an average-size, one-bedroom apartment. In its opinion, the court said that Santa Ana's ordinance "would criminalize a level of occupant density which the state has determined safe."[44] For Chicanos and other Latinos, policies such as housing ordinances target their communities in order to find solutions to problems associated with immigration. However, such "solutions" may also lead to further problems as large Latino families are forced out of their homes and into other communities. As the court noted, "This could only result in increased homelessness and exacerbate housing shortages statewide."[45]

CLOSING THE DOOR TO EDUCATION FOR IMMIGRANTS

The issue of education for undocumented children is at the center of a debate over who should have access to the benefits of society. At issue is an attempt to define who is a "resident" and a member of the "community." Such concepts are never static. They are always contested, especially for less powerful members of society, for example, the homeless, migrant workers, gays, and immigrants. Attempts to limit educational opportunities for a segment of the Latino population have important implications for Chicanos. To illustrate this, we examine the issue of higher education for undocumented immigrants.

The initial battle over access to education was fought in the early 1980s, when the U.S. Supreme Court ruled on the state of Texas's policy of excluding undocumented children from public elementary and secondary schools. The Supreme Court ruled that it is not in the public's interest to deny an education to any member of society. Since then, the law of the land has allowed undocumented children to attend public schools.[46]

The battle then shifted to higher education. In 1985, California's universities and colleges sought to implement a policy that defined undocumented students as nonresidents of the state who must pay foreign student tuition, a considerable amount above regular fees. For example, at the University of California, fees for 1991 amounted to about $3,000, while foreign student tuition added another $7,700 to the cost of a year's education. In the California State University system, the difference was between $1,308 in fees and $8,688 for nonresident tuition for the same year. These fees have since risen dramatically.

The premise of this policy was that because undocumented students are illegally in the country, they cannot establish legal residency in the state. However, the issue of a "resident" of California is not a fixed legal concept. The legal definition of a resident is contested through court cases, and it may actually change under different circumstances. Moreover, the rationale for treating undocumented students in this way is based upon assumed characterizations and misconceptions of undocumented students, most notably the public stereotype of the "illegal alien" as a temporary adult worker who does not pay taxes.

In 1985, legal advocates for immigrant rights went to court to block the implementation of this policy. The Alameda Superior Court heard the case, which was brought under the name of Leticia A. (a student who attended the University of California at the time). Lawyers for Leticia attempted to portray the social context in which undocumented students live.[47] In the course of court testimony, the following points were made:

— Undocumented immigrants rarely come to the United States to go to school. They come to work.
— Rather than adults, it is the minor children of undocumented immi-

grants that are commonly labeled as foreign students. These young people have spent much of their youth in the United States. Defining them as nonresidents penalizes them for a decision their parents made about migrating years ago, and it punishes them for the failure of federal policies to control illegal immigration.

— The financial burden of foreign resident tuition is particularly onerous to undocumented students. Most undocumented students are from Mexico and other Latin American countries, and their parents toil at low-paying jobs. In addition, their parents, despite being undocumented, do pay taxes. They pay taxes directly through sales tax and payroll withholding tax, and indirectly through the portion of their rent that pays the landlord's property taxes.[48] When it comes to paying taxes, the question of undocumented immigrants' legal residency does not exist. They, like all residents, pay taxes.

— To be good enough to be admitted into California's universities and colleges, these students have to be bright. Undoubtedly, they have become steeped in American culture. The University of California takes the top 12.5 percent of students in the state, and the California State University system admits the top 25 percent.

Having grown up in the United States and in American culture, undocumented students are not likely to return to their parents' country of origin.[49] Because they have lived in California for many years, accounting for most of their young lives in many cases, these students bear little resemblance to foreign students who arrive shortly before classes begin from their homes in Paris, Mexico City, Buenos Aires, or Kuwait. Their homes are in California. After so many years of living in the United States, these students are likely to stay the rest of their lives. Therefore, it is highly improbable that policies limiting access to education will function as indirect mechanisms for reducing the number of undocumented immigrants in the country.

Undocumented students will probably legalize their status someday. For young people raised in the United States, an undocumented status is not a permanent, unchanging condition of their lives. There is a high probability that they will become legal residents and citizens either by marrying legal residents and citizens, by acquiring enough years of residency to adjust their status, or by a brother or sister who is a citizen by birth sponsoring their legal immigration.[50] In addition, an undocumented student may have a parent who is a legal immigrant or citizen, or who is in the process of becoming a legal resident or citizen, who will eventually help the student legalize his or her status. But because they are undocumented at the time they are to begin college, some students will be forced to delay their education until acquiring legal residency; others will merely stop short their education.

Placing obstacles to the education of these young people does not solve the immigration problem; it merely creates an underclass of people ill equipped for our modern economy. It creates a class of discontented, smart individuals. Ironically, the tax base of college-educated individuals is higher than that of non-college-educated individuals. By placing obstacles to higher education, society is actually diminishing future tax revenues.

On 3 April 1985, the judge ruled in Leticia's favor. He found the policy of classifying undocumented students as nonresidents for tuition purposes too broad and unconstitutional under the state's constitution. In his ruling, the judge noted that "even if the clear and convincing evidence of the value of postsecondary education had not been shown by plaintiffs, the public policy encouraging an improved and dynamic society is sufficient to find that higher education is an 'important' interest in California."[51]

After the decision, California's universities and colleges treated undocumented students as residents for tuition purposes. The decision was contested, however, when a former UCLA employee, David Bradford, brought a lawsuit claiming that this policy discriminates against legal immigrants and citizens. In 1990, a Los Angeles Superior Court judge ruled in Bradford's favor, thus compelling the University of California, against whom Bradford had brought suit, to treat undocumented students as nonresidents for tuition purposes. An appeals court subsequently upheld the Bradford decision.

The matter was still not settled. In 1991, California Assemblyman Richard Polanco introduced a bill (AB 592) that would have invalidated the Bradford decision and allowed state universities and colleges to consider undocumented students as residents for tuition purposes. Although the California legislature passed the bill, Governor Pete Wilson vetoed it. Advocates for Leticia then brought their case back to court in order to block the California State University system from following the Bradford decision. In May 1992, the same Alameda Superior Court judge that ruled in the original Leticia case again ruled in Leticia's favor. Another lawsuit was quickly filed by a coalition of taxpayer, immigration reform, and conservative groups, which included the Federation for American Immigration Reform, the American Association of Women, Citizens for Law and Order, and Kathleen Brown, California's state treasurer. The coalition argued that undocumented immigrants take precious class seats from citizens and are unfairly subsidized by taxpayers.[52] On 8 September 1992, a Los Angeles Superior Court judge ruled in the coalition's favor; undocumented students in the California State Universities again face paying nonresident tuition.

Quite likely, we have yet to see the final resolution of this issue. The battle over who is a resident for tuition purposes may continue to be fought in the courts and legislatures. Also, anti-immigration activists may also attempt to challenge the earlier Supreme Court decision to allow undocumented students in public primary and secondary schools. Early indications that this may be forthcoming came out of San Diego, California, where a report commissioned by California State Senator Craven presented data on the cost to taxpayers for educating undocumented children in San Diego County's public schools.[53] Academic researchers have attacked the report for exaggerating the numbers of undocumented immigrants in the county and for reducing the reported tax contribution by that population. Despite these criticisms, the report has played a major role in the campaigns for reelection of many California politicians, especially Governor Pete Wilson. It has also helped fuel the "Save Our State," anti-immigrant initiative (Proposition 187) placed on the November 1994 election ballot in California. A key provision of Proposition 187 bars undocumented children from attending public schools. At the very least, these challenges to the right of undocumented children to an education serve as a reminder that rights are subject to change as the political leanings of the U.S. Supreme Court shift.[54]

The battle over who is a resident and therefore deserving of a place in public higher education has important implications for Chicanos and other Latinos. Undocumented young people are not easily separable from other young people in the Chicano/Latino population. Although one child in a family, typically the oldest, may be undocumented, younger children are often born in the United States and are therefore U.S. citizens. Consequently, policies based on residency limit educational opportunities, and thus economic mobility, of some members of a family and not others. Although society may feel justified in treating undocumented students as "outsiders," as people who reside here and are "nonresidents," it does so at a cost. These young people will be adult members of the Chicano/Latino community who will likely attain legal immigrant status and yet may find it difficult to overcome the internalization of a marginal status, of being treated as unworthy members of society.

THE ATTACK ON CITIZENSHIP

Not only is the definition of a "resident" increasingly being narrowed, but the notion of "citizenship" is also being questioned. In October 1991, Representative Elton Gallegly, a Republican from Simi Valley, California, introduced legislation to amend the U.S. Constitution to deny citizenship to a child born in the United States if neither of the parents are citizens, and if the child's mother is not at least a legal resident.[55] His argument is that even though this is a nation of immigrants, we must reduce immigration—both legal and undocumented: "We must recognize, however, that the United States is also a nation of finite resources and opportunities which must be available to and shared by all its citizens. Today, in many parts of this country our cities and towns are being overrun with immigrants, both legal and undocumented, who pose major economic and law enforcement problems for local governments and place an added burden on their already strained budgets."[56]

The ostensible purpose of disallowing citizenship to young Latinos born in the United States, and thus defining them as illegitimate members of the community, is, once again, "to do something" about immigration. Although Gallegly's legislation focuses on the children of undocumented immigrants, his statement clearly makes little differentiation between legal and illegal immigrants. He views immigrants generally as a "problem," as outsiders, regardless of immigration status. Thus, his attempts to stop conferring citizenship on the children of undocumented immigrants appears as but one part of a broader agenda to rid the country of all "outsiders," that is, immigrants and their U.S.-born children. Moreover, the debate over citizenship for immigrants comes at a time of increasing levels of naturalization among Mexican immigrants, as discussed above.

Gallegly's proposal would disproportionately affect Latino children, because most undocumented immigrants are from Latin American countries. The result would be to disfranchise the least powerful members of the Chicano/Latino community. It would create a group of Chicano/Latinos whose marginality went well beyond second-class citizenship. Their marginality would derive from their status of U.S.-born noncitizens. Their status as outsiders would be complete, especially since their birth outside their parents' country of origin would also make their citizenship there questionable. This is a different situation from that of their parents who decided to migrate and enter into an undocumented status. We would now be conferring a status of essentially "no status" on a group of Chicano/Latinos from birth. U.S.-born noncitizen Latinos would be stamped, in castelike fashion, as exterior to the society they were born into, and into which they will grow, marry, work, and have children. A daunting idea.

FINAL THOUGHTS

For both Chicanos and the larger society, immigration during the 1980s was of monumental importance. Chicanos are more numerous and more diverse because of immigration. Nationwide, one out of three Chicanos is foreign born, and in California it is four out of ten. But perhaps even more profoundly, Latinos other than those of Mexican origin are increasingly moving into the Chicano heartland. These patterns, which will undoubtedly continue into the 1990s, offer a number of challenges to Chicanos.

It is possible that because of increased immigration from Central America and other Latin American countries, the term "Chicano" will become more inclusive. As Latino immigrants from countries other than Mexico enter the United States and establish roots, many of their children will grow up in Mexican American neighborhoods and may even grow up calling themselves Chicanos. They will confront many of the same social, economic, and political barriers as Chicanos, some of which have been addressed here, and many others that are discussed in other chapters. It is critical to recognize that when we speak about Chicano issues, we are really talking about issues that affect a larger, more diverse group of people than was true in the 1960s, when the word Chicano took on its current meaning. For example, Leticia A. could be the daughter of an immigrant from Mexico, El Salvador, Guatemala, or any number of countries. Policies aimed at immigrants that restrict housing or citizenship affect Chicanos and other Latinos alike.

For the larger society, the 1980s represented a decade in which the border gave way to uncontrolled immigration. The 1986 immigration law (IRCA) was an attempt "to reestablish control" of the border and immigration. As we have shown, attempts to control immigration, either directly through employer sanctions or indirectly through policies that place limits on housing density, access to education, and citizenship, have important implications for Chicanos and other Latinos. Quite often, the attempt to control undocumented immigration results in discriminatory actions toward Chicano and Latino citizens and legal residents.

Not surprisingly, the 1970s and the 1980s witnessed the important role played by a myriad of national and local organizations in defense of immigrants' rights. Even an incomplete list reflects the many organizations that have brought litigation to protect immigrants' rights: the Mexican Legal Defense and Education Fund (MALDEF), the League of United Latin American Citizens (LULAC), the American GI Forum, the National Center for Immigrants' Rights, Inc., Multicultural Educational, Training, and Advocacy, Inc., poverty and law programs, the Legal Aid Society, Centro de Asuntos Migratorios, Hermandad Mexicana, and the Chicano Federation. The proliferation of such organizations attests to the growing concern over civil rights in the United States during this same period. It has special significance for Chicanos, who run or staff many of these organizations. Rather than feeling threatened or hostile to the newcomers, the activities of the many Chicanos in these organizations suggest a sense of concern and solidarity with Mexican and other Latin American immigrants. It also reflects the level of education and expertise Chicanos have attained, which allows them to actively challenge issues of immigrants' rights. This is a different situation than that which prevailed earlier in this century, when trampling on the rights of immigrants faced much less formally organized opposition, especially from members of the immigrants' same ethnic group.

The focus on distinctions in legal status raises an important issue for Chicanos: Who is defining the "community"? Policies that attempt to limit employment, housing, education, and citizenship do so on the assumption that undocumented residents are not part of the community. And yet, as we have argued, especially when considering young people and families, such an assumption is mistaken at best, and at worst is an attempt to drive a wedge between members of the Chicano/Latino community, often between members of the same family. The divide-and-conquer approach to social control is an old one, and Chicanos must be particularly sensitive to its use in the debate over controlling immigration.

We have focused on but a few of the attempts to control immigration to illustrate how such attempts directly and indirectly affect Chicanos and other Latinos. We believe, however, that these few examples are both salient and illustrative of contemporary social theory concerning power relations. They fit well Michel Foucault's notion of the "micro-physics of power."[57] The public discourse on limiting employment, housing, education, and citizenship for undocumented immigrants, especially Mexican and other Latin American immigrants, does more than merely promote immigration policy, it also serves to discipline the Chicano/Latino community. It reminds Chicanos and other Latinos that they, too, can be defined as outsiders, as illegitimate members of the community. In this way, the public discourse serves as a mechanism of control by instilling in Chicano/Latinos the power relationships which exist in society, relationships that subject Chicano/Latinos to a less powerful status vis-à-vis the dominant social groups. In short, the debate over immigration and the policies to control undocumented immigration wind up controlling not only undocumented immigrants but Chicanos and other Latinos as well.

This discourse on immigration is not simply a discourse about the need to control the "immigration problem." We suggest that it is a manifestation of what Balibar calls a "neo-racism" in which "the category of immigration" has replaced the notion of race. In other words, rather than speaking in terms of biological differentiation and genetic inferiority, Balibar argues that the neo-racism is cloaked in a language which talks about the "insurmountability of cultural differences," "the harmfulness of abolishing frontiers," and "the incompatibility of lifestyles and traditions."[58]

"Foreign-looking" immigrants become threats to American culture, as if we could speak of one exclusive heritage. In our society it is much more acceptable to talk about "cultural differences" and the "uneasy melting pot" than it is to express racist notions of superiority in terms of biological differences and genetic purity, which was quite common when discussing immigrants during the early years of the twentieth century.[59] Rather than talk about race, the discourse on immigration today treats mixing cultures as a problem in much the same way that mixing gene pools was presented as a problem in the past.

Should the debate over immigration continue along similar lines in the 1990s and into the twenty-first century, the challenge will be to critically examine future policies that aim to "do something" about immigration. If the past is any guide to the future, policies that seek to control the presence of unwanted "foreign-looking" people, whether legal immigrants, undocumented immigrants, or even citizens by birth, will create burdens carried by all Latinos.

NOTES

1. "It's Your Turn in the Sun," *Time,* 16 October 1978, 48–55.
2. Henry Flores, "The Selectivity of the Capitalist State: Chicanos and Economic Development," *Western Political Quarterly* 42 (1989): 377–95.
3. We use the terms "Chicano" and "Mexican American" interchangeably throughout the text. We are, however, aware that the term Chicano carries with it political connotations.
4. Bureau of the Census, *Race and Hispanic Origin, 1990 Census Profile* (Washington, D.C., 1990), 1–2; Frank D. Bean et al., "The Spanish-Origin Population in the American Southwest," in *Mexican and Central American Populations and U.S. Immigration Policy,* eds. Frank D. Bean et al. (Austin: University of Texas Press 1989), 72; Sidney Weintraub, "Implications of Mexican Demographic Developments for the United States," in Bean et al., *Mexican and Central American Populations,* 179.
5. Bureau of the Census, *Race and Hispanic Origin,* 1–2; Bureau of the Census, *Census Bureau Press Release* (Washington, D.C., 1989), 2; Bureau of the Census, *Persons of Hispanic Origin for the U.S.* (Washington, D.C., 1990).
6. Bureau of the Census, *Census Bureau Press Release, CB91-215* (Washington, DC, 1991), 4.
7. Bureau of the Census, *Race and Hispanic Origin,* 8.
8. Ibid.
9. U.S. Department of Justice, Immigration and Naturalization Service, *Statistical Abstracts* (Washington, D.C., 1994).
10. Ibid.
11. James P. Allen and Eugene J. Turner, "Where to Find the New Immigrants," *American Demographics* 10 (1989): 23–60.
12. Ibid.
13. Richard B. Craig, *The Bracero Program: Interest Groups and Foreign Policy* (Austin: University of Texas Press, 1971).
14. Wayne A. Cornelius, "From Settlers to Sojourners: The Changing Profile of Mexican Immigration to the United States," in *U.S.-Mexican Relations: Labor Market Interdependence,* eds. Jorge A. Bustamante, Clark W. Reynolds, and Raúl A. Hinojosa Ojeda (Stanford:

Stanford University Press, 1992), 155–95. See also Leo R. Chávez, "Paradise at a Cost: The Incorporation of Undocumented Mexican Immigrants into a Local-Level Labor Market," in Bustamante, Reynolds, and Hinojosa, *U.S.-Mexican Relations,* 271–301.

15. Bureau of the Census, *Race and Hispanic Origin,* 27.

16. Leo R. Chávez, *Shadowed Lives: Undocumented Immigrants in American Society* (Fort Worth: Harcourt Brace Jovanovich, 1992); Leo R. Chávez, "Outside the Imagined Community: Undocumented Settlers and Experiences of Incorporation," *American Ethnologist* 18 (1991): 257–78.

17. Leo R. Chávez, "Settlers and Sojourners: The Case of Mexicans in the United States," *Human Organization* 47 (1988): 95–108.

18. Jeffrey S. Passel and Karen A. Woodrow, "Geographic Distribution of Undocumented Aliens Counted in the 1980 Census by State," *International Migration Review* 18 (1984): 642–71.

19. Wayne A. Cornelius, "The Role of Mexican Labor in the North American Economy of the 1990s" (paper presented at the 4th annual Emerging Issues Program for State Legislative Leaders, San Diego, Calif., 1988).

20. James C. Raymondo, "How to Count Illegals, State by State," *American Demographics* 10 (1988): 42–43.

21. Cornelius, "From Settlers to Sojourners," 4.

22. CASAS (Comprehensive Adult Student Assessment System), *A Survey of Newly Legalized Persons in California,* prepared for the California Health and Welfare Agency (San Diego: Comprehensive Adult Student Assessment System, 1989).

23. Passel and Woodrow, "Geographic Distribution."

24. Karen A Woodrow and Jeffrey S. Passel, "Post-IRCA Undocumented Immigration to the United States: An Assessment Based on the June 1988 CPS," in *Undocumented Migration to the United States,* eds., Frank D. Bean, Barry Edmonston, and Jeffrey S. Passel (Washington, D.C.: Urban Institute Press, 1990), 57.

25. Bureau of the Census, *Persons of Spanish Origin. 1970 Census of the Population* (Washington, D.C., 1973), 46.

26. Bureau of the Census, *Census Bureau Press Release,* 26.

27. Bureau of the Census, *Foreign Born Population by Place of Birth for the U.S.* (Washington, D.C., 1990).

28. Kevin F. McCarthy and R. Burciaga Valdez, *Current and Future Effects of Mexican Immigration in Callifornia* (Santa Monica: Rand Corporation, 1986).

29. Fernando Mendoza et al., "Selected Measures of Health Status for Mexican-American, Mainland Puerto Rican, and Cuban-American Children," *Journal of the American Medical Association* 265 (1991): 227–32.

30. Mario de la Rosa, "Health Care Needs of Hispanic Americans and the Responsiveness of the Health Care System," *Health and Social Work* 14 (1989): 104–13; Mendoza et al., "Health Status."

31. Karen Winkler, "Researcher's Examination of California's Poor Latino Population Prompts Debate over the Traditional Definitions of the Underclass," *The Chronicle of Higher Education,* 10 October 1990, A5–8.

32. Julian L. Simon, *The Economic Consequences of Immigration* (Cambridge, Mass.: Basil Blackwell, 1989).

33. Thomas Muller and Thomas J. Espenshade, *The Fourth Wave: California's Newest Immigrants* (Washington, D.C.: Urban Institute, 1985).

34. U.S. House, *Immigration Reform and Control Act of 1986,* Conference Report. 99th Cong., 2nd sess., 1986, H.R. 99-1000.

35. Leo R. Chávez, Estevan T. Flores, and Marta López-Garza, "Here Today, Gone Tomorrow? Undocumented Settlers and Immigration Reform," *Human Organization* 49 (1990): 193–205.

36. See Bean, Edmonston, and Passel, *Undocumented Migration,* for a number of studies on the effectiveness of IRCA.

37. Chávez, *Shadowed Lives,* 19.

38. General Accounting Office, *Immigration Reform: Employer Sanctions and the Question of Discrimination* (Washington, D.C., 1990), 71.

39. Chávez, "Settlers and Sojourners."

40. Mary Helen Berg, "City of Orange Approves 'Strict' Occupancy Law," *Los Angeles Times,* 28 May 1992, p. A1.

41. Ibid.

42. Catherine Gewertz, "Appeals Court Voids Santa Ana Occupancy Law," *Los Angeles Times,* 29 May 1992, p. A1.

43. Leo R. Chávez, "Coresidence and Resistance: Strategies for Survival among Undocumented Mexicans and Central Americans in the United States," *Urban Anthropology* 19 (1990): 31–61; Leo R. Chávez, "Households, Migration, and Labor Market Participation: The Adaptation of Mexicans to Life in the United States," *Urban Anthropology* 14 (1985): 301–46.

44. Gewertz, "Occupancy Law."

45. Ibid.

46. Alien Children Education Litigation, Brief of the Appellants. In Re: Alien Children Education Litigation, *State of Texas and Texas Education Agency (Appellants) v. United States (Intervenor-Appellee) and Certain Named and Unnamed Undocumented Alien Children (Appellees).* Sup. Ct. 80-1538 and 80-1934 (1980).

47. *Leticia A. et al., v. The Board of Regents of the University of Californi, et al.,* Statement of Decision (May 30). Case no. 588-982-5. Alameda: Superior Court for the State of California for the County of Alameda (1985).

48. For studies on the characteristics of undocumented immigrants, including their tax payments, see Simon, *Economic Consequences;* Chávez, Flores, and López-Garza, "Here Today"; McCarthy and Valdez, *Current and Future;* Muller and Espenshade, *Fourth Wave;* Wayne A. Cornelius, Leo R. Chávez, Jorge A. Castro, *Mexican Migration to the United States: A Summary of Current Knowledge, Research Report Series # 36* (San Diego: Center for U.S.-Mexican Studies, University of California, 1982).

49. Chávez, Flores, and Lopez-Garza, "Here Today"; Chávez, "Coresidence and Resistance."

50. Alejandro Portes and Robert L. Bach, *Latin Journey: Cuban and Mexican Immigrants in the United States* (Berkeley: University of California Press, 1985).

51. *Leticia A. et al. v. The Board of Regents,* 8.

52. Larry Gordon, "Immigrants Face Fee Hikes from Cal State System," *Los Angeles Times,* 9 November 1992, p. A3.

53. Louis M. Rea and Richard A. Parker, "A Fiscal Impact Analysis of Undocumented Immigrants Residing in San Diego County" (San Diego: Rea & Parker, 1992, mimeographed).

54. Gregory Gross, "Critics Pan Study That Claims Migrants a Burden on County," *San Diego Union,* 18 August 1992, p. A1.

55. Elton Gallegly, "Gallegly Seeks to End Automatic Citizenship for Illegal Alien Children," press release of 22 October 1991, Office of Congressman Elton Gallegly, Washington, D.C., 1991.

56. House, Representative Gallegly of California speaking for the Time to Amend Our Birthright Citizenship Laws (22 October 1991).

57. Michel Foucault, *Discipline and Punish: The Birth of the Prison* (New York: Vintage Books, 1979).

58. Etienne Balibar, "Is There a 'Neo-Racism'?" in *Race, Nation, Class: Ambiguous Identities,* eds. Etienne Balibar and Immanuel Wallerstein (New York: Verso, 1991), 20–21.

59. Stephen Jay Gould, *The Mismeasure of Man* (New York: W. W. Norton, 1981).

CHICANAS/OS IN THE ECONOMY : ISSUES AND
CHALLENGES SINCE 1970

Refugio I. Rochín and Adela de la Torre

As we move into the twenty-first century, Chicano scholars must revisit the economic landscape that positions Mexican-origin people within the United States. Even without solid data on this population, characterizations of Chicanos, both ideological and political, abound in print. During the last four decades alone, Chicanos[1] have been characterized as social activists during the 1960s and early 1970s, lauded in the 1980s as the emerging "sleeping giant" that would alter electoral politics in the Southwest, and labeled by neoconservatives as the "ambivalent minority" during the 1990s.[2] Yet beneath these social descriptors are economic indicators that provide a profile of where Chicanos were and where they are headed. By disentangling the literature on Chicanos, we hope to provide a reference point for developing an economic agenda that provides direction to those concerned about integrating Chicanos into the economic mainstream.

This chapter starts with an assessment of the status of Chicanas/os beginning in 1970. Our intent is to examine their relative economic progress from this benchmark year as we approach the twenty-first century.[3] The economic indicators selected for our assessment are demographic statistics; income and poverty; employment, wages, and occupations; and entrepreneurial activities in the business sector. The following questions are central in developing this economic assessment:

— What are the most significant developments in the socioeconomic status and experience of Chicanas/os since 1970?
— What are the emerging issues and lessons for Chicanas/os, given the past trends?

— What are the most significant national and international developments that influenced and will influence the future well-being of Chicanas/os?

THE BENCHMARK

During the 1960s the notion that Mexican Americans were a minority group within the larger U.S. society was a novel concept both for Chicanos as well as for the larger society. Until the Chicano Movement, school textbooks ignored Chicanos as a significant ethnic group because national attention had shifted to the more volatile race question. Although some Chicano scholars wrote extensively about Mexican Americans, none of their publications had the scope, significance, and recognition of Gunnar Myrdal's *An American Dilemma*[4] or E. Franklin Frazier's *The Negro in the United States*.[5] Perhaps the only comparable work on the economic experiences of Mexican Americans during this period that reached a wider audience was Carey McWilliams's *North from Mexico: The Spanish-Speaking People of the United States*.[6] Unfortunately, McWilliams's works were often dismissed in the academy as social action or "reform" literature, not empirically sound social science research.

In 1970, however, the Free Press published *The Mexican-American People: The Nation's Second Largest Minority,* an opus of 775 pages, compiled by Leo Grebler, Joan W. Moore, and Ralph C. Guzmán and many others working out of UCLA.[7] Five years in production, this major work blended a large interdisciplinary team that legitimated research on Chicanos. *The Mexican-American People* included an extensive and detailed analysis of Chicanos in the Southwest, with a special focus on the cities of Los Angeles and San Antonio. It provided a detailed portrait of socioeconomic problems, as well as an inquiry into family traits, relations, and assimilation of Chicanos as an ethnic group. In addition, it assessed the role of the Catholic church and that of the government in the Chicano community.

A major contribution of *The Mexican-American People* was the challenge the analysis posed to ethnic stereotypes of Mexican Americans. It also provided compelling evidence that the 5.6 million Chicanos in the United States were the largest concentration of people of Latin American descent in the world outside of Latin America. The issue of the regional concentration of Chicanos in the Southwest was also articulated with "hard" data, and the thesis of the new ethnic group "majority/minority" subsequently evolved from this study. This was particularly significant in the Southwest where 87 percent of all Chicanos resided in the states of Arizona, California, Colorado, New Mexico, and Texas. Moreover, California and Texas held the overwhelming majority of Chicanos, with the future prospect of even faster population growth due to higher rates of fertility and migration.

The Grebler et al. study on the Chicano population of the 1960s initiated the process by which sociologists and economists have scrutinized how this group would integrate into the larger society. The authors' major research findings, which are still relevant today, were the following:

— Mexican American people were as urbanized as Anglos or nonwhites (16).
— Mexican Americans, fourteen years of age and older, in 1960 averaged about four years less schooling than Anglos and one and a half years less than nonwhites (18).
— Mexican Americans averaged only forty-seven cents for every dollar of Anglo income, and they were worse off than nonwhites (19).
— Mexican Americans bore a heavy share of poverty in the Southwest (20).
— The employee selection process resulted in a large number of Mexican American job aspirants seeking employment in highly competitive industries, with generally non-union employers, and characteristically in small firms (22).
— The percent of Mexican Americans living in overcrowded and in substandard housing units exceeded not only the Anglo share, as one would expect, but also the nonwhite share (23).
— Mexican Americans were disadvantaged, based upon ample evidence that American society at large had acted by omission or commission to hinder them in the development of their individual abilities (24).
— The closing of the border to braceros at the end of 1964 reduced labor-market competition that affected Mexican Americans with particular force (28–29).
— In both education and economic condition, the natives [U.S.-born], regardless of parentage, were far better off than the foreign born (30).

In the 1960s the lack of effective labor-market integration of Mexican-origin people, particularly of more recent immigrants, combined with the high-risk factors associated with poverty, sowed the initial seeds of relative economic disadvantage for a significant proportion of the Mexican American community. Without targeted public-policy measures to reverse the trends, increased polarization within the Mexican-origin community, as well as between it and the dominant majority population, would be exacerbated in the 1970s. *The Mexican American People* ends with this prophetic conclusion:

> These [Mexican American] people themselves have become far more aware of their disadvantage, their social aspirations have been immeasurably heightened, and they insist on more rapid and more effective remedial action. Hence, the past in this case is not a prologue to the future in any deterministic or probabilistic sense. Rather, *the challenge* [emphasis added] is to impart a new thrust to the future—to create the conditions in which the Mexican American people can become ever more active participants in our society, can develop their individual abilities without hindrance, and are free to make personal choices with regard to their cultural identity. (30)

THE SEVENTIES[8]

"The challenge" was met initially by a growing body of research and a rush to diversify academic and political positions. The realization of increasing economic deprivation and a growing gap between Anglos and Chicanos provided Chicanos with the fuel needed to define themselves as a national "minority." Against this backdrop, Mexican Americans became characterized as "nonwhite," although the U.S. Census of Population showed that as a group about 50 percent classified themselves as white and less than 2 percent as black. The remainder of Chicanos, 47 percent, marked the census form "other."[9]

An examination of changes in median family income and the poverty rate during the 1970s suggested no improvement for Chicanos. The occupational and unemployment figures continued to show economic distress in the community, and the real earnings of Chicanos pointed to a declining situation. According to U.S. census reports, the number of families living in poverty in the Southwest grew from 915,790 in 1970 to 1,038,695 in 1980. Chicano families represented 37 percent of the total poor families in the region. As figure 3.1 indicates, the highest net increase in poverty

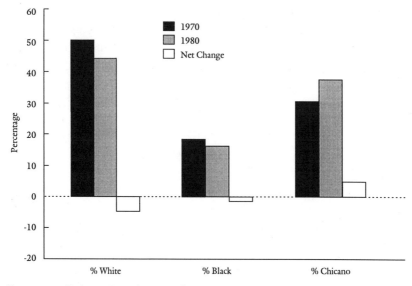

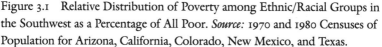

Figure 3.1   Relative Distribution of Poverty among Ethnic/Racial Groups in the Southwest as a Percentage of All Poor. *Source:* 1970 and 1980 Censuses of Population for Arizona, California, Colorado, New Mexico, and Texas.

levels between 1970 and 1980 (the clear bar) was experienced by Chicano families. While the number of impoverished Chicanos showed an increase of 6 percent, the distribution of black families below the poverty level decreased by 1 percent, and whites realized a decrease of 5 percent. This trend signaled a growing shift of the poverty burden to the Chicano community.

Average family size in the Chicano community decreased slightly from 4.89 members in 1970 to 4.26 members in 1980. However, these families remained larger than their black and white counterparts and included more related children under the age of eighteen in each house. Thus, real per capita income (in 1967 dollars) for Chicano family members averaged $406 per anuum in 1980, compared to $412 for black families and $450 for white families. Consequently, real per capita income declined for Chicanos by $20 from 1970 to 1980. Black per capita income declined $4 during the same period. White households, however, experienced an increase in per capita income of $16 (see table 3.1).

Data for 1970 to 1980 also confirmed the UCLA observation of occupational segregation. However, we should add that empirical data reflecting labor market segregation are limited and difficult to assess. Nonetheless,

Table 3.1   Major Characteristics of Poor Persons in the Southwest, 1970 and 1980

	White		Black		Chicano	
	1970	1980	1970	1980	1970	1980
Mean Family Income	$1,962	$3,561	$2,162	$3,800	$2,392	$4,314
real 1967 $	1,708	1,428	1,882	1,524	2,082	1,730
Number of poor persons	1,807,812	2,354,219	783,876	877,538	1,380,606	1,945,572
Mean size of family	3.93	3.17	4.52	3.70	4.89	4.26
Income per capita	$499	$1,123	$478	$1,027	$489	$1,013
(1+3) real 1967 $	434	450	416	412	426	406
Mean number of related children under 18	2.98	2.29	3.41	2.45	3.45	2.69

Sources: 1970 Census, General Social and Economic Characteristics, table 58, State Reports: Arizona, California, Colorado, New Mexico, and Texas.
1980 Census, General Social and Economic Characteristics, table 104, State Reports.
1980 Census, Detailed Population Characteristics, table 250, State Reports. California Almanac, 1984–85, table 15.2.

figure 3.2 shows an increasing concentration of Chicanos in primarily blue-collar and service-sector jobs. Furthermore, unlike the trend for blacks and whites in the Southwest, there was virtually no increase in Hispanic participation in white-collar, professional, or managerial employment.[10]

Thus by 1980, all the indicators reflecting Chicano conditions were about the same as they were in 1970. One explanation posited for the stagnation in mobility was linked to residence and workplace location. Job concentration was found to be correlated with geographic concentration, and this relationship appeared to affect the poverty status of Chicanos. Tienda and Lii discovered that geographic concentration of minorities inhibited economic advancement of minority groups. Accordingly, the net beneficiaries from large numbers of minorities in geographic areas were whites. In determining the extent to which race and education affected income of diverse groups, they concluded "that college-educated whites gained most from minority concentration emphasizes how both ascribed [race] and achieved [education] identifiers must coincide to generate white earnings advantages. Considered by themselves, neither racial nor educational divisions

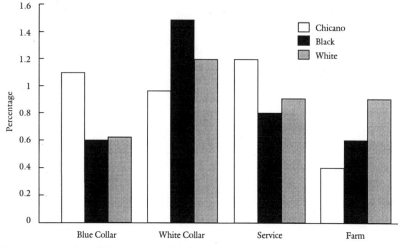

Figure 3.2   Index of Occupational Shift between 1970 and 1980 by Race/
Ethnicity in the Southwest. An example of how the occupational shift index
was calculated: Blue-collar index = (Total Number Blue Collar/Total Experienced
Labor Force) 1980 divided by (Total Number Blue Collar/Total Experienced
Labor Force) 1970. Blue-collar, white-collar distinctions are defined in the 1970
Census of Population.

explain fully how earnings disparities are accentuated by the ethnic composition of labor markets."[11]

During the 1970s more women became "head of household" in the
Southwest (see figure 3.3). De la Torre and Rochín calculated poverty
differences by ethnicity and race with respect to the proportion of poor
women in each group (see figure 3.4).[12] This graph shows that over 40 percent of all Chicana and black female-headed families were poor in 1980,
whereas only 18 percent of white female-headed households in the Southwest were poor. But considering all the poor female-headed households (as
shown in figure 3.4), there was a 17 percent net decrease of white female-
headed households in poverty between 1970 and 1980. On the other hand,
there was a net increase of 10 percent for Chicanas and 7 percent for black
women living in poverty during the same ten-year period of 1970 to 1980.
Therefore, Chicana and black female-headed households in the Southwest experienced disproportionately high rates of poverty relative to white
female-headed households. This finding also pointed to the need for more
studies on the effects of changing family structure among Chicano families

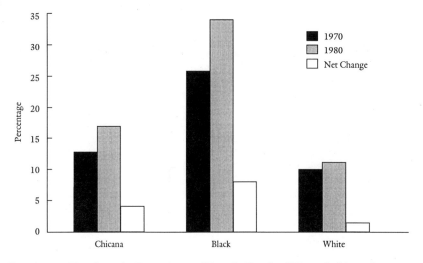

Figure 3.3   Trends in the Percentage of Female Heads of Households in the Southwest, 1970 and 1980. *Source:* 1970 Census, General Social and Economic Characteristics, table 58. State Reports: Arizona, California, Colorado, New Mexico, and Texas. 1980 Census, General Social and Economic Characteristics, table 104, State Reports. 1980 Census, Detailed Population Characteristics, table 250 State Reports. California Almanac, 1984–85, table 15.2.

and of the relationship of these effects to the increased levels of Chicano poverty in the Southwest.

Timely research by Cordelia Reimers suggested that the most important single reason for lower Chicano and black family incomes during the 1970s was the lower wage rates, even after differences in age, education, and geographic distribution were taken into account.[13] Reimers also found that Chicanas had lower returns in proportion to work experience than white non-Hispanic women because most of them were foreign born. Also, on average, Reimers found that these women work less time for pay during a year, thus limiting their earnings. Lack of English fluency did not have a significant effect on wages for any female group, taking into account differences in levels of education. For Mexican men, Reimers concluded that discrimination may result in about 6 percent of the wage differential in comparison with non-Hispanic men but that education could account for as much as 34 percent of the wage gap.

In the early 1980s, Mellor and Haugen examined wage trends and came

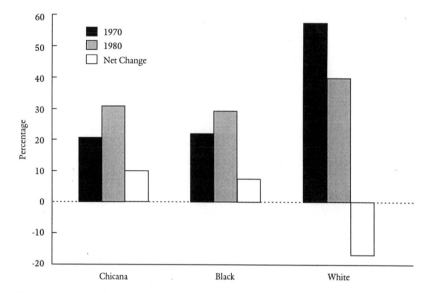

Figure 3.4   Distribution of Poor Female-Headed Households by Racial/Ethnic Groups in the Southwest, 1970 and 1980. *Source:* 1970 Census, General Social and Economic Characteristics, table 58. State Reports: Arizona, California, Colorado, New Mexico, and Texas. 1980 Census, General Social and Economic Characteristics, table 104, State Reports. 1980 Census, Detailed Population Characteristics, table 250, State Reports. California Almanac, 1984–85, table 15.2.

to the conclusion that wage differentials played an important role in Chicano deprivation.[14] Specifically, they found disparate earning ratios among Hispanic, black, and white workers between 1979 and 1984. The Hispanic-white earnings ratio was lower than the black-white earnings ratio, holding gender constant. Furthermore, the overall Hispanic and the black earnings relative to whites earnings never achieved parity. In fact, the ratio of median hourly wage earnings (Hispanic and black over white) experienced a steady decline. Thus, according to the seminal studies on the Mexican-origin population that examined wages, employment, and poverty status during the 1970s, the economic prognosis remained bleak. As the group remained "hidden" in the labor market with limited labor mobility, the fears of increased immiseration for a significant proportion of the Mexican-origin population became a reality by the end of the decade.

THE EIGHTIES

The first in-depth studies of Chicano conditions appeared in the 1970s, followed in the 1980s by several studies and new developments, which added further insights on the economics of Chicanas/os. These developments included a pronounced increase in Chicana scholarship focusing on gender issues, the demise of the Chicano/Mexican American in the national political arena, a unprecedented rise in the number of legal and undocumented Mexican workers in the Southwest, and an increased appearance of Latino enterprises.

Chicanas in the Economy

Scholarship on Chicanas in the workplace and the economy became the focus of ethnographic studies by both sociologists and anthropologists during the 1980s. Researchers such as Baca-Zinn, Zavella, Melville, and several other Chicana social scientists explored women's roles beyond the macho stereotype of the docile housewife and mother.[15] The emergence of Chicana scholars interested in the "politics of work and family" took root in the area of Chicano Studies, where the heated intellectual climate and heightened discussion provided fodder in the 1990s for anthologies on Chicana women and their place in the workforce.

Two important anthologies that bring together an array of Chicana feminist scholarship are: *Building with Our Hands: New Directions in Chicana Studies,* edited by Adela de la Torre and Beatriz M. Pesquera; and the special issue of *Aztlán: A Journal of Chicano Studies,* edited by Vicki L. Ruiz.[16] Each text goes beyond the socioeconomic conditions that define the Chicano/Mexican-origin community to a broader analysis that includes cultural as well as gender factors that mold the lives of Chicana women. In *Building with Our Hands,* the authors maintain that in order to understand the condition of Chicana women, an interdisciplinary approach must be used to understand the role of Chicanas as both cultural subjects and economic actors in forging their own destiny. The inherent contradictions that these women face as active agents in history, as well as their struggles to overcome the perceptions of the dominant male culture, are disentangled through the lens of Chicana scholars, who reinterpret the experience of the Chicana subject through the visual arts, history, economic migration, home, and workplace. Thus, the significance of this book is to make visible the once "invisible" Chicana in feminist scholarship and traditional textbooks on working women. For example, contributions in the de la Torre and Pesquera anthology, by researchers such as María de los Angeles Crummett, illustrate how class analysis plays a critical role in understanding the uneven impact of migration on gender.[17]

Similarly, the *Aztlán* anthology edited by Ruiz provides texture in and meaning to the lives of Chicana women in both contemporary as well as historical periods. Through the use of case studies, poetry, and interviews, the struggles and successes of Mexican-origin women are differentiated by class, gender, and ethnic identity. In a manner similar to what was done in the de la Torre and Pesquera anthology, these Chicana scholars collectively build a profile of Mexicana/Chicana women who not only mediate conflict in their personal lives, but balance work and family in ways that differ from those followed by their white sisters and that vary by immigrant status. Thus this anthology provides further evidence of the rich heterogeneity of the Mexicana/Chicana experience. These studies, and others identified by Segura in her study on Chicanas in the workforce,[18] are at the forefront in fulfilling a growing need to know about the contributions and expanding involvement of Latinas in the labor force. The field is complex, vast, and open for more research.

The Spotlight on "Hispanics"

During the 1980s, "Chicanos" faded from federal records as "Mexican-origin" Americans and were subsumed into the "Hispanic" classification, a concept fabricated by the U.S. Bureau of the Census to include American residents who identified themselves as Mexican, Puerto Rican, Cuban, Central and South American, and "other" (Spanish descendants). No doubt the rising importance of Chicano leaders in the national arena led other "Hispanic" groups to claim minority status, based upon arguments that they too were subordinated peoples who had long suffered exclusion and discrimination because of their origins. They also illustrated how their conditions differed substantially from those common to other groups in the United States. As a result of the collapsing of "Chicanos" into the catch-all category "Hispanics," Chicanos lost a particular avenue for requesting that government meet their specific needs. In the quest for complete ethnic solidarity across all Hispanic subpopulations, Chicanos gave up the richness of their own identity as well as the ability to target specific "Chicano" public-policy issues.

In a thematic issue (entitled "The Politics of Ethnic Construction: Hispanic, Chicano, Latino?") of *Latin American Perspectives,* the editors note that "economic survival is, of course, a powerful reason for accepting the label [Hispanic]; for the very poor, it ensures entitlement to public assistance, while for those with skills and educational credentials, whatever their national origin, it opens the possibility that affirmative action will increase their chances of finding employment." However, they also point out that "data about Hispanics are at best meaningless (as meaningless as data about Whites in general, for example) and at worst only create and reinforce racial stereotypes."[19] Culturally and ideologically, the label creates a misleading image of the historically evolved cultures of the different aggregates to which it is applied, giving a European veneer to a widespread "culture-of-poverty" interpretation of the social problems afflicting a large proportion of this population.

Unfortunately, constant use of the term "Hispanic" has institutionalized this ethnic identifier, resulting in the term "Chicano" becoming almost meaningless in statistical analyses of this subpopulation. In response to criticism that "Hispanic" does not capture the indigenous roots or mestizaje of Chicanos, the term "Latino," is sometimes used as a substitute for "Hispanic," in order to lessen the implied European bias of the latter. Those who use the term "Chicano" do so for political reasons to illustrate the need for further differentiation of the Mexican-origin population.

Immigrants and Chicano Demographics

Another major development of the 1980s was the phenomenal growth in size and influence of the Latino population. More Latinos were added to the U.S. population in the decade than all other minorities combined, and they made up one of the fastest-growing worker groups in the United States. At the same time, persons of Hispanic descent also had a major impact on the ethnic, socioeconomic, and demographic features of the U.S. population. The median income and median age of Latinos (save Cubans) were lower than those indicators of other population groups; and these factors combined to have a great impact on the labor force, because of the relative decline in the number of young Anglo workers competing for jobs and the greater influx of Latino immigrant workers.

During the first half of the decade, immigration surged from Mexico, as the Mexican economy experienced its worst downturn since the 1930s. Although Latinos accounted for approximately one of every three legal immigrants between 1980 and 1986, as many as 1.3 million other Latinos (almost all from Mexico) entered the United States as undocumented aliens.[20] Persons of Puerto Rican, Cuban, or other Latino origin experienced a net loss among Hispanics as their numbers decreased or stayed the same, as was the case with Cuban Americans.

In 1986 the Immigration Reform and Control Act (IRCA) instituted a legalization program by which longtime undocumented aliens were granted amnesty and were able to apply for legal residence between 1987 and 1989. Over 1.5 million aliens applied, about 70 percent of whom were Mexican. Moreover, IRCA had special provisions for documenting immigrant "seasonal agricultural workers" (SAWs). Approximately 1.5 million workers applied for SAW status, nearly 90 percent were Mexican immigrants.[21] Post-IRCA studies all concluded that the SAW program was flawed and easily overcome by applicants who used false documents. IRCA officials did not come close to anticipating the size of the enrollment for amnesty and SAW status and were overwhelmed in their investigations to exclude false claimants. As a result, very few SAWs were rejected, and by default, they obtained legal rights for U.S. employment.

In just three years, the Latino population increased by at least 2 million, from 18.8 million in 1987 to 20.8 million in 1990 (see table 3.2).[22] Latino family size had declined somewhat since 1970, but with an average of 3.82 persons per Latino family in 1990, their number was still high compared to the 3.09 persons of the non-Latino family.[23] Unlike in the past, however, the number of Latino single-parent families and the number of children in such households reached alarming proportions. In 1992, 24.4 percent of Latino families had a female head, with no husband present; 7.4 percent had a male head, with no wife present; and 68.2 percent of Latino families were headed by a married couple compared to 78.9 percent for non-Latino families. Respective figures for single parent non-Latino female- and male-headed households were 16.8 and 4.3 percent. Despite the increase in single-parent households, Latinos remained less likely than the general population to be divorced and more likely to have households with multigenerational clustering.

As one of the fastest-growing worker groups, Hispanics increased 65

Table 3.2   Number of Latinos by Ethnic Origin, 1987–1990 *

| | 1987 | | 1990 | | |
Origin	Number	Percent of Total	Number	Percent of Total	Change in No. 1987–90
Mexican	11.8	62.8	13.3	64.0	+1.5
Puerto Rican	2.3	12.2	2.2	10.5	−0.1
Cuban	1.0	5.3	1.0	5.9	0
Central & South America	2.1	11.2	2.9	13.7	+0.8
Other Latino	1.6	8.5	1.4	6.9	−0.2
Total	18.8	100.0	20.8	100.0	2.0

*Numbers are in millions

Source: U.S. Bureau of the Census, *Current Population Reports,* No. 449, 1991.

percent to 10.1 million from 1980 to 1992, a rate of growth four times that of the non-Hispanic workforce.[24] Mexican Americans remained, by far, the largest group, accounting for 63 percent of all Hispanics in the labor force in 1992. The numbers grew by 28 percent from 1980 to 1992. Far outstripping the growth (but not the number) of all Hispanic groups was that of Central and South American workers, with a growth rate of 61 percent, to become 16 percent of all Hispanic workers. With origins in 15 different countries covering a vast geographical area, this latter group numbered 1.6 million of the U.S. workforce in 1992.[25] Over half the Latinos in the labor force (made up of persons over sixteen years of age who are working or "looking for work") live in California, with the highest concentration in Los Angeles.

As growth of the Hispanic workforce soared, California's economy faced a slump in 1988, which became a severe economic depression by 1990. Unfortunately, labor market problems were increasingly attributed to the large numbers of immigrant workers from Mexico, who would take any job even for lower pay. Indeed, the demographic profile of this group reflected a younger median age, with few years of schooling, and desperate for employment. With this profile of young working Latinos in the United States came concern from native-born citizens that job competition was increasing. It became an even more sensitive topic as the Latino population was increasingly divided between documented and undocumented workers. The loss of quality jobs due to the prolonged recession, and perceived use of public services by the undocumented, set the groundwork for the immigrant backlash that emerged in the 1990s. Despite weak evidence pointing to the use of public services by "illegals," the immigrant backlash became the rallying cry for the struggling middle class. This adverse reaction resulted in Proposition 187, the "Save Our State" initiative that scapegoated undocumented adults and children as a major cause for the economic demise of the state. This four-page initiative denied undocumented individuals access to publicly subsidized medical care, public education, and other public services. Although conservative Republicans such as former Secretary of Education William Bennett and former Secretary of Housing and Urban Development Jack Kemp publicly opposed the initiative as racist and divisive, many state conservative Republican leaders, such as California Governor Pete Wilson, strategically used the initiative to counter the increased voter frustration and anger voiced by the struggling middle class. The success of Proposition 187 in California in 1994 can be linked to the delayed economic recovery in the state combined with the continued decline in real wages and loss of employment security. Another issue that surfaced during the 1994 California campaign was a general uneasiness among the dominant Anglo electorate regarding the increased "Latinization" of the state.

Latino Entrepreneurs and Hispanic Business

The 1980s were also the decade of Latino entrepreneurs in the private sector. According to economic census reports published every five years, there were 219,335 Latino-owned firms in 1977, compared with 117,000 in 1972. Latino companies numbered 248,141 in 1982 with sales of $15 billion.[26] Latino-owned businesses are defined by the Census Bureau as sole proprietorships owned by Latinos, as well as partnerships and corporations in which at least half the shares are owned by Latinos.

California had the largest number of Latino-owned firms in 1982: 74,998. These companies generated gross receipts of $4.2 billion. Texas was second with 61,540 companies and gross sales of $3.4 billion. Miami alone had 24,898 Latino-owned businesses in 1982, and the New York City–New Jersey MSA (Metropolitan Statistical Area) was fourth with 12,292 firms reporting $881.6 million in sales. Latino-owned firms with paid employees (totalling 190,000 people) accounted for 16.1 percent of the total number of U.S. companies. Latino retailers topped the list, employing 65,000 workers, followed by service companies with 52,000. Furthermore, about 58 percent of the 248,151 Latino-owned firms were held by Mexican Americans (143,177 firms). Cubans owned 15 percent of the firms (36,631) and Puerto Ricans owned 6 percent (14,690).[27]

More recent information from the U.S. Census of Economic Business (various reports) showed that in 1987 the number of Hispanic-owned service-oriented businesses increased to 184,372 (from 98,279 in 1982). In retail trade there were 69,911 Hispanic-owned businesses in 1987, and there were 55,516 in construction. The greatest increase in Hispanic-owned businesses was in transportation and public utilities, rising by 750 percent, from 3,155 in 1982 to 26,955 in 1987. Hispanic-owned businesses in finance, insurance, and real estate doubled from 11,123 in 1982 to 22,106 in 1987. Also in 1987, 31 percent (132,212) of all Hispanic-owned businesses were located in California, as compared to 74,998 in 1982. Hispanic-owned businesses continued to increase in number in Florida and Texas, as noted above.[28]

Tracking these developments since 1979, the journal *Hispanic Business* has presented information on the important role of Latino entrepreneurs. For years it has identified the top 500 companies owned by Latinos, a sector of the population that has proven to be dynamic and diverse, with businesses in a wide cross section of fields. Although *Hispanic Business* has monitored the economic successes of Latinos in a variety of businesses, we still know relatively little about Latino entrepreneurs and enterprises; and despite the fact that Latinos will soon pass the 10 percent threshold of the U.S. population, a milestone which signals a significant "Latinization" of the U.S. economy, they remain underrepresented in key management positions in both national and multinational firms.

With the exception of recent research in San Antonio by Chapa and Cárdenas,[29] very little research has been carried out recently on the flow of funds, the institutional sources of credit, and the levels of investments in Latino businesses. Gilberto Cárdenas et al. began work on Chicano ethnic enterprise formation,[30] but little is known about the more complex issues of corporate finance and large-scale enterprises. Domínguez's study on Latinos in capital/financial markets is one of the few research studies in this area.[31] His analysis of small business capital formation includes the following distressing findings: (1) Mexican minorities, because of their poverty status, seldom go beyond the lowest tier of credit, the stratum that plays host to pawnbrokers, loan sharks, and ghetto merchants; (2) Mexican Americans have made very limited inroads into the banking industry; and

(3) "Due to undercapitalization, many Mexican American firms are unable to start with a paid staff and as a result of this smallness, they continue to operate with limited help, even though positive incremental revenues may be realized by increasing their workforce. Consequently, those that are able to have paid employees manage to enjoy greater per capita revenues."[32] The evidence to date suggests that similar financial problems plague many Mexican-origin small-business entrepreneurs.

THE NINETIES

In the two decades after 1970, Latinos became an important part of the general economy, achieving inroads into a broad spectrum of enterprises. However, their most notable achievements were in the labor market, where their numbers grew rapidly. By 1992, there were about nine million employed Latinos in the United States, making up 7.6 percent of all workers. Latinos had higher rates of labor-force participation than Latinas and non-Latinos in general. At least nine out of ten Mexican men (sixteen years of age and older) participated in the labor force in 1992, regardless of educational attainment. On average, six out of ten Mexican-origin women participated in the labor force, but Chicanas with high school and college degrees participated at rates of 75 percent and 80 percent, respectively.[33] Overall, Latinos were as likely to be in the labor force as non-Latinos.

Nevertheless, occupational disparities between Latino and non-Latino workers still prevailed into the 1990s. There was no noticeable improvement in Latino occupational mobility within the last twenty years. Latinos were still less likely than non-Latinos to be managers and professionals, 14 percent to 28 percent, respectively. Moreover, Latinos, and especially Chicanos, were highly concentrated (56.4 percent) in operator, fabricator, and laborer positions; 62.3 percent of these jobs were held by Chicanos compared to 42.1 percent by non-Latino men.

In 1970 Chicano researchers focused little on patterns of employment segmentation. In addition, gains from education that segmented the Chicano population were not significant issues in these early studies. However, in the nineties Chicano researchers learned that the disparity in managerial and professional employment could be reduced somewhat among college graduates. Fully 60 percent of Latino college graduates were employed as managers and professionals, versus 65 percent of non-Latinos. The impact of new immigrants on the occupational profile of Chicanos acted to counter real gains in occupational mobility by native-born Chicanos; that is, the proportion of Mexicans/Chicanos employed in blue-collar and service occupations increased due to new Mexican-origin immigrants, whose arrival acted to buffer real changes in Chicano occupational levels.[34]

Furthermore, the concentration of Mexican-origin workers in these lower-paid occupations partially explained why median weekly earnings for Latinos who worked full time were approximately one-third lower than those for non-Latinos: $345 per week for Latinos and $516 per week for non-Latinos.[35] During the calendar year 1991, the median income of Latino households was $22,688; for Chicano households, it was $22,477. Although these earnings were higher than ever before, they were only 70 percent of the median income of non-Latino households, which had reached $32,311.[36]

During the nineties women in general continued to have different occupational patterns than men. Both Latinas and non-Latinas were still occupationally concentrated, at 64.2 percent and 61.3 percent respectively, in technical, sales, administrative support, and services. However, only 16.3 percent of Latinas held managerial and professional positions, whereas 28.2 percent of non-Latinas were in these jobs. Concomitantly, the median weekly earnings of Latinas was nearly $100 less than the earnings of non-Latinas in 1992: $299 for Latinas versus $393 for non-Latinas.[37]

Latino poverty in the nineties increased more than in earlier decades. With the average poverty threshold for a family of four at $13,924 in 1991, 28.7 percent of all Latinos lived in poverty that year, compared to 9.4 percent of non-Latinos. From another perspective, Latinos represented nearly 10 percent of the nation's population in 1991; however, they represented almost 18 percent of all persons living in poverty.

The distribution of poverty within the Latino community was even more alarming as it was disproportionately borne by the youth. About half (40.4 percent) of Latinos under eighteen years of age were poor in 1991. In comparison, only 13.1 percent of non-Latino children under eighteen were living in poverty. Overall, Latino children represented about 11.6 percent of all children in the United States but represented 21.5 percent of all children living in poverty in 1991.[38] Latino children in poverty reached alarming proportions, with little relief in sight.

DECADES OF INEQUALITY IN EMPLOYMENT

Almost all economic indicators show that Chicanas/os live under conditions of persistent inequality. Two examples are the inequalities in wages and occupational level, which are in part governed by a host of economic conditions. Despite Latinos' high rates of labor-force participation, unemployment still remains a significant problem.

In 1982 the average annual rate of unemployment for all Chicanos, sixteen years of age and older, in the civilian labor force was 13.3 percent, compared to 9.5 percent for non-Hispanics; it was 13 percent for Chicanos and 13.9 percent for Chicanas.[39] During 1986, the year of IRCA, 125.8 million persons held jobs, a significant improvement over the 123.5 million persons employed in 1985; however, the same was not the case for the Chicano community. Most of the over-all growth represented an increase in the full-time employment of the majority population year round. White Americans experienced a substantial decline in unemployment; joblessness among that group fell from 15.6 to 15 percent between 1985 and 1986. On the other hand, the proportion of Latinos experiencing unemployment was very high, an almost unchanged 22 percent during this same period. When unemployment eased, the decline was first experienced by white Americans and later by Chicanos. In March 1992, the unemployment figures were 11.3 percent for Latinos and 7.5 percent for non-Latinos; the average annual unemployment rate for Chicano males was 12.4 percent, while for Chicana females it was 10.5 percent.[40]

Some researchers have suggested that the aggregate rate of unemployment among Chicanos is both higher and more sensitive to downturns in the economy than it is for white Americans.[41] Consequently, there is concern that Chicanos are restricted to sectors inherently high in unemployment, experiencing higher rates of persistent poverty within communities that are increasingly populated by Latinos.

MIDDLE-CLASS SQUEEZE

The eighties did not end without attention to affluent Latinos. Increasingly, researchers have focused their interest on more closely analyzing income gaps across ethnic and racial subpopulations. The issue of closing economic gaps within and across Latino subpopulations, between ethnic groups, and across different populations was of particular interest and became fertile ground for research.[42] One fact was clear: the number of "higher-income" Latino households had increased dramatically over the past twenty years. Yet, it remains the case that the increase in Latino affluence has not been enough to counteract the income decreases experienced by larger segments of the Latino community.

According to an August 1990 report in *American Demographics,* the number of Latino households with incomes of $50,000 or higher (in 1988 dollars) increased 234 percent between 1972 and 1988, from 191,000 to 638,000. Despite this increase, upscale households constitute only 12.9 percent of all Latino households. Furthermore, downscale households (those with incomes of less than $25,000) represent 56.1 percent of Latino households but only 45.9 percent of non-Latino households—a full 10 percent difference.[43]

Both Latinos and non-Latinos are accounted for in Karoly's study entitled "The Trend in Inequality Among Families, Individuals, and Workers in the United States."[44] Karoly used a variety of measures to assess the inequality question. Every measure revealed the same trends: the rich increasing their wealth, the poor becoming poorer, and the middle class becoming smaller. According to Karoly, "The rise in inequality cannot be dismissed as a statistical aberration [as some critics have charged], it is real and represents a significant break with historical patterns." Looking only at median income, which rose during the entire study period for all families (1970–1987), Karoly found that Latino families fared much worse than any other group. While the median income grew by 24.8 percent for white families and 20.1 percent among African-American families, it grew by only 8.6 percent for Latino families. For those families at the low end of the scale (10th percentile), both African Americans and Latinos experienced a decline in family income since 1973, while white families showed real income growth over that period. At the same time, income increased for high-income families in all categories, which contributed to greater inequality overall. Karoly found that for all families with children, real income dropped by 22 percent for the low-income 10th percentile, while the high-end 90th percentile showed a 23 percent rise in real incomes.[45]

In contrast to the devastating trends for male workers, Karoly discovered that inequality actually lessened for women through about 1980, though it increased thereafter. In fact, Latinas are the only group of low-income women (10th percentile) to show an improvement relative to the median in every five-year period since 1970. The rise in Latinas' income probably reflects, at the low-income end, women working more weeks per year, and at the high-income end, more women entering professional careers. At both levels, however, the average income of Latinas is but a fraction of that of Latinos: weekly 1987 wages for Latinas in the 10th percentile, for instance, were 67 percent of those of their Latino counterparts. Although studies of income distribution do not look into population dynamics among Latinos (such as the influx of immigrants), some of the growing distribution towards the low end of the income scale might be explained by immigration.[46] Recent immigrants traditionally start at the bottom of the economic ladder, and most Latino immigrants are members of families with children. Moreover, recent immigrants earn less and have higher jobless rates than do earlier post–World War II immigrants (including naturalized braceros) and U.S. natives.[47]

There is also a gap in English fluency between Latinos (from the Caribbean Islands, for example) and non-Latino immigrants; this places them at a disadvantage for better-paying jobs, regardless of years of schooling. And, as surmised by Meisenheimer,[48] the existence of large and numerous Spanish-speaking enclaves in this country may help to explain the lower level of English fluency among Latino immigrants.

At last count, about half of all Latinos were foreign born, with the majority born in Mexico.[49] Today's Latinos include both large numbers of recent immigrants and first-generation offspring who not only experience new and different economic and cultural surroundings, but often speak Spanish as a first language.

THE EFFECTS OF IMMIGRATION ON CHICANAS/OS

Before this decade ends, it would be particularly important to assess the impact of the 1986 Immigration Reform and Control Act, given the increased number of immigrants from Mexico who constitute a growing portion of the poor Chicano community.[50] Such an assessment would probably shed light on the potential effects of NAFTA (North American Free Trade Agreement) and other areas of expansion in global trade.[51]

The extent and duration of poverty for Chicanos has been no doubt influenced by the implementation of IRCA section 121, which amends the

Social Security Act by imposing a verification-of-immigration-status requirement in order for applicants to qualify for Aid to Families with Dependent Children, Medicaid, Unemployment Compensation, and Food Stamp programs. Financial assistance for housing, under Section 214 of the Housing and Community Development Act of 1980, and the program of grants, loans, and work assistance, under Title IV of the Higher Education Act of 1965, were amended in a similar fashion by various IRCA provisions.

The Systematic Alien Verification for Entitlement program (SAVE) tracks individual use of social services by immigrant status.[52] This provides the basis for limiting services not only to documented individuals, but also to selected individuals who have entered the United States under the amnesty provision of IRCA. Thus, the requirement of immigration-status verification has the effect of restricting access to certain public services by non-U.S. citizens and favoring those who choose to enter the legalization process.

Prior to the passage of IRCA, entitlement programs serviced an array of settled, legal and undocumented individuals relying on means testing as a basis for entitlement to most programs. With its passage, a major concern of IRCA was to dissuade possible public charges from becoming citizens. Thus, in order to eliminate the possibility of increasing the welfare rolls with new immigrants, the law included a provision that excluded those individuals under the amnesty program from using specific health and social service programs. Specific federal programs that were targeted under IRCA were Aid to Families with Dependent Children under Part A of Title IV of the Social Security Act, Supplemental Security Income, the Medicaid under Title XIX of the Social Security Act, and the Food Stamp Program under the Food Stamp Act of 1977. With the exception of Medicaid for pregnant women and children, each of these federal programs was amended to disallow participation for five years by those individuals who chose to become "eligible legalized aliens" (ELAs) under the IRCA amnesty provision. The success in limiting ELA entitlement to public programs based on poverty status could only occur if final citizenship status was linked to limited entitlement use.

Federal exclusion of need-based programs shifted financial responsibility for the new immigrant population to county governments. Although assistance to local providers was available through state legalization assistance funds (SLIAG) from the federal government, county providers with ever dwindling revenues were not able to provide the level of high-quality services needed to effectively integrate this new immigrant group into local communities.

In a study by de la Torre, Hunter, and Rosenzwieg, which focused on the impact of eligible legalized aliens (ELAS) on the utilization of medically indigent services in Southern California, they found that counties such as San Diego were unable to provide adequate services under the county's medically indigent services program. Additionally, because of cuts in state funds, San Diego is under constant threat of closure of such programs; and as recently as March 1991, the San Diego Board of Supervisors voted to suspend the program due to inadequate funding sources. Fortunately, such actions were temporarily prevented.[53] Despite such threats of closure of medically indigent services, uninsured eligible legalized aliens were forced to rely on these programs for medical services. Currently in California, Republican legislators have introduced a state bill, Assembly Bill (AB) 154, that will allow counties to move from threats to direct action on closing county medically indigent programs. Clearly, with the breakdown of the county-based medically indigent programs, i.e., the health care providers of last resort, immigrant Latinos without health insurance will have no source of emergency care except that provided by benevolent societies and/or private hospitals willing to treat clients without health insurance. The public health consequences , should AB 154 pass, would be devastating not only to Latinos but to the health status of all Californians.

A "catch-22" situation exists for eligible legalized aliens who rely on public assistance. On one hand, short-term use of public assistance programs may be essential to their traversing the poverty line. At the same time, however, their use of cash-based programs could signal to the INS that they are potential public charges possibly jeopardizing citizenship under IRCA. Unless these eligible legalized aliens are able to distinguish between cash and non-cash need-based programs, they are not likely to take full advantage of health, education, and welfare programs available to them under SLIAG funding. As a result, programs available under IRCA may be significantly diminished. Thus, it is important to assess the adequacy of these programs and whether they meet the needs of the impoverished immigrant population. However, as long as eligible legalized aliens are fearful or misinformed of their entitlement rights, accurate assessment of these programs will be difficult.

COLONIAS AND UNDERCLASS ECONOMIES

Another aspect of the nineties is the increase in impoverished Latino communities throughout the Southwest. California, for example, contains over one hundred communities in which Latinos are the majority population. In rural California there are approximately seventy communities ranging in population from 3,000 to 20,000 where Latinos represent from 50 to 98 percent of the population. The concern over these communities (known as "colonias") is that they show signs of becoming centers of rural underclasses of Latinos, populated by impoverished working people laboring to support themselves via the agricultural economy. These communities have a relatively low tax base and hence lack many of the amenities needed to provide adequate health, schooling, and safety.[54] In addition, colonia residents continue in a subordinate position, which is sustained by agribusiness and compounded by immigration. The overwhelming dominance of large farms and their dependence upon low-skill labor means a political alliance of the agribusiness firms in order to support a liberal immigration policy. There is and has been little enforcement of immigration laws in agricultural areas, which also means that farmers can take advantage of the massive population growth in Mexico, assured of an abundant supply of workers. Under these circumstances, farmer and agribusiness interests are well positioned to dictate wages and working conditions and hence impact the welfare of rural colonias.

BEYOND THIS CENTURY

The economic trajectory has altered little since 1970. Indicators of Chicano entrepreneurs and business investments have improved relative to the indicators for non-Latinos in the economy. However, indicators of employment, occupation, and income distribution appear to have falling trajectories, especially for Chicanas/os, now under the rubric "Hispanic." Schooling and educational attainment are better than before, and Chicano natives (citizens and documented residents) are more empowered than two decades ago, but the gap between Chicanos and others continues to widen.

Given the emerging demographics, economic conditions, geographic concentrations, poverty, and rapid growth of the Hispanic community, it is not likely that we will witness significant improvements within the lower economic strata of the Chicano population without immediate and major policy interventions to ameliorate these trends. Solutions to reversing rising poverty and unemployment are complex, especially so with the increasing role of the United States in NAFTA and the global economy. Major initiatives in health-care delivery, education, and job training must target Chicano working poor in order to prevent the emergence of a true cycle of poverty. However, Chicanas/os are not the only ones fighting for attention from the federal government. In today's political arena, the politics of economic development are more difficult than in the decades before.

The emergence of new underclasses of legalized Chicano poor and the continual flow of more oppressed and hidden groups of undocumented workers are almost inevitable with current immigration policies and patterns of residential clustering. The impact of immigration is not fully known, but there appears to be a link between Mexican immigration and high Chicano poverty rates.

Activities aimed at developing the employability of the growing population of Latino workers should be pursued. The youthfulness of the Latino population and its burgeoning size are major factors influencing employment strategies for the future.[55] Without substantial adjustments, in tune with changes in the labor market, Latinos will have a smaller fraction of the jobs by the year 2000 than they have today, while they will form a large proportion of those seeking work.

It is apparent that more attention needs to be given to developing Latinas/os as positive resources and not as burdens on society. Each year of delay in significantly and successfully attacking the problems of Latino earnings and employment makes it more difficult to turn things around. By the year 2000—in the worst case scenario and without support for new programs aimed at helping them—Latinos will be left largely to low-wage, limited-skill jobs, a category of positions whose numbers will continue to decline. Yet, at this time, few policies are being designed and coordinated to handle the upcoming displacement of Latino laborers from the fields and plants. Centers for career planning and placement could be mobilized to support educational goals and English language training. Business and government could adopt strategies to make schooling more effective and help Latinos attain proficiency in English. If anything, such measures should be explored before the next century.

Traditional job training and employment programs by themselves are unlikely to have a profound impact on the future success of Latinos. If new efforts to train and employ Latinos are to succeed where earlier efforts have failed, both individual attitudes and social institutions must also change. Radical changes may be required in the public educational system for it to succeed with Latinos. If anything, the added Latino numbers will require a flexible school system for educating a more diverse student body. In school districts with the most serious retention problems, experiments with government-supported vouchers, which allow students to shop for the educational programs that suit them best, could be considered, thereby forcing school districts to improve their offerings. Schools could also be more directly linked to employers who will hire graduating Latinos. The reason for establishing a formal link between school and work is to improve the initial employment experience, because less than favorable early experiences in the labor market usually lower lifetime earnings.

The complex interconnections among family structure, education, work, income, and living environments make it evident that problems cannot be solved by government fiat or decree. Issues of individual initiative and entrepreneurship must also be considered. More support and research are needed on programs that could promote the entrepreneurial capabilities of Latinos, in order to develop their capital formation skills and to promote business role models for others. Business programs that are usually left to business specialists of the private sector and financial institutions tend to bypass Latino communities. Latinos should be encouraged to pursue education with an eye to private business careers and to thus develop a cadre of private-sector business leaders.

The result of extenuated problems, poverty is a condition that must be addressed in order to raise the economic aspirations and opportunities of Latinos. There is insufficient research addressing the correlates, trends, dimensions, and implications of Latino poverty, including specific attention to Latino single-headed households, children, and elders. In particular, research and information on Latina female-headed households and the opportunities for different occupations and employment for them is critical for developing sound labor market policies. Is child care or family planning needed? Are the issues facing Latinas related to culture, customs, and family ties?

Finally, it is apparent that more attention is needed for developing a positive Latino self-image. Numerous studies and reports tend to portray a negative, self-inflicted condition facing Latinos. Relatively little has been reported on the economic contributions of Latinos to society. Clearly their entrepreneurial activity in the small-business sector, as well as their strong immigrant labor-force participation, must be recognized as major contributions to the U.S. economy.

NOTES

1. In this chapter "Chicanas" and "Chicanos" are terms used interchangeably with "Mexican American females" and "Mexican American males," respectively. Also, the terms "Latinas" and Latinos" are used instead of "Hispanic females" and "Hispanic males," respectively.
2. Peter Skerry, *Mexican Americans: The Ambivalent Minority* (Boston: Free Press, 1993).
3. For a view back to 1939, see Martin Carnoy, Hugh Daley, and Raúl Hinojosa-Ojeda, *Latinos in a Changing U.S. Economy: Comparative Perspectives on the Labor Market since 1939* (New York: Inter-University Program for Latino Research, Hunter College, 1990).
4. Gunnar Myrdal, *An American Dilemma: The Negro Problems and Modern Democracy* (New York: Harper & Row, 1944).
5. Franklin E. Frazier, *The Negro in the United States* (New York: Macmillan, 1949).
6. Carey McWilliams, updated by Matt S. Meier, *North from Mexico: The Spanish-Speaking People of the United States* (New York: Praeger, 1990).
7. Leo Grebler, Joan W. Moore, and Ralph C. Guzmán, *The Mexican-American People: The Nation's Second Largest Minority* (New York: Free Press, 1970).
8. For more detailed accounts of the changing socio-demographics of Chicanas/os in this decade, see Frank D. Bean and Marta Tienda, *The Hispanic Population of the United States* (New York: Russell Sage Foundation, 1987); George Borjas and Marta Tienda, eds., *Hispanics in the U.S. Economy* (Orlando: Academic Press, 1985); and Rodolfo de la Garza et al., eds., *The Mexican American Experience: An Interdisciplinary Anthology* (Austin: University of Texas Press, 1985).
9. Bureau of the Census, *Persons of Spanish Origin by State: 1980* (Washington, D.C., 1982).
10. Ibid.
11. Marta Tienda and Ding-Tzann Lii, "Minority Concentration and Earnings Inequality: Blacks, Hispanics, and Asians Compared," *American Journal of Sociology* 93 (1987): 141–65.
12. Adela de la Torre and Refugio Rochín, "Hispanic Poor and the Effects of Immigration Reform," *Chicano Law Review* 10 (1990): 1–13.
13. Cordelia Reimers, "A Comparative Analysis of the Wages of Hispanics, Blacks, and Non-Hispanic Whites," in Borjas and Tienda, *Hispanics in the U.S. Economy,* 27–75. See also Cordelia Reimers, "Sources of Family Income Differentials among Hispanics, Blacks and White Non-Hispanics," *American Journal of Sociology* 89 (1984): 889–903.
14. Earl F. Mellor and Steven E. Haugen, "Hourly Paid Workers: Who They Are and What They Earn," *Monthly Labor Review* 109 (1986): 20–26.
15. Maxine Baca-Zinn, "Employment and Education of Mexican American Women: The Interplay of Modernity and Ethnicity in Eight Families," *Harvard Education Review* 50

(1980): 47–62; Patricia Zavella, *Women's Work and Chicano Families: Cannery Workers of the Santa Clara Valley* (Ithaca: Cornell University Press, 1987); and Margarita Melville, ed., *Mexicans at Work in the United States* (Houston: Mexican American Studies, University of Houston, 1988).

16. Adela de la Torre and Beatriz M. Pesquera, eds., *Building with Our Hands: New Directions in Chicano Studies* (Berkeley: University of California Press, 1993); and *Aztlán: A Journal of Chicano Studies* 20 (1993).

17. María de los Angeles Crummett, "Gender, Class and Households: Migration Patterns in Aguascalientes, Mexico," in de la Torre and Pesquera, *Building with Our Hands.* Other studies in this same volume also illustrate how the intersection of ethnicity, gender, and class differentially affect women in their homes and in the labor market.

18. Denise A. Segura, "Walking on Eggshells: Chicanas in the Labor Force," in *Hispanics in the Workplace,* eds. Stephen B. Knouse et al. (New York: Sage Publications, 1992), 173–93.

19. Martha E. Giménez, Fred A. López III, and Carlos Muñoz, Jr., introduction to *Latin American Perspectives* 24 (1992), 24.

20. Peter Cattan, "The Diversity of Hispanics in the U.S. Work Force," *Monthly Labor Review* 116 (1993): 3–15.

21. Phillip L. Martin et al., *Immigration Reform and U.S. Agriculture* (Oakland: University of California, Division of Agriculture and Natural Resource Publications, 1994).

22. The adjusted 1990 census counted 23.5 million Hispanics, about a 50 percent increase from the previous census.

23. Bureau of the Census, *The Hispanic Population in the United States* (Washington, D.C., 1993).

24. Cattan, "Diversity of Hispanics," 6.

25. Ibid., 8.

26. Refugio Rochín, "Latinos in the Economy: Current Realities and Future Expectations," in *Readings for Teachers: Latinos in the Making of the United States of America: Yesterday, Today and Tomorrow,* ed. New York State Department of Education (Albany: New York State Department of Education, 1992), 10–23.

27. Juan Guedella, "A New Benchmark," *Hispanic Business* 12 (1987): 12, 16.

28. Ibid.

29. Jorge Chapa and Gilberto Cárdenas, *The Economy of the Urban Ethnic Enclave* (Austin: Lyndon Baines Johnson School of Public Affairs, University of Texas, 1991).

30. Gilberto Cárdenas, Rodolfo de la Garza, and Niles Hansen, "Mexican Immigrants and the Chicano Ethnic Enterprise: Reconceptualizing an Old Problem," in *Mexican Immigrants and Mexican Americans: An Evolving Relation,* eds. Harley Browning and Rodolfo de la Garza (Austin: Center for Mexican American Studies, University of Texas, 1986), 157–84.

31. John R. Domínguez, *Capital Flows in Minority Areas* (Lexington, Mass.: Lexington Books, 1976).

32. Ibid., 140.

33. Cattan, "Diversity of Hispanics," 10.

34. Douglas S. Massey, *The Demographic and Economic Position of Hispanics in the U.S.* (Washington, D.C.: National Commission for Employment Policy, 1992), 19–21.

35. Cattan, "Diversity of Hispanics," 12.
36. Jesús M. García, "The Hispanic Population in the United States: March 1992," in *Current Population Reports,* Series P20-465 RV (Washington, D.C.:Bureau of the Census, 1993).
37. Cattan, "Diversity of Hispanics," 12.
38. Phillip García, "An Evaluation of Unemployment and Employment Differences Between Mexican Americans and Whites: The Seventies," *Social Science Journal* 20 (1983): 51–62.
39. Bureau of the Census, *Persons of Spanish Origin in the United States,* March 1982 (Washington, D.C., 1985).
40. Bureau of the Census, "The Hispanic Population of the United States: March 1988," in *Current Population Reports,* Series P-20, no. 438 (Washinton, D.C., 1989); and J. García, "Hispanic Population 1992."
41. P. García, "Unemployment and Employment," 55.
42. Rebecca Morales and Frank Bonilla, eds., *Latinos in a Changing U.S. Economy: Comparative Perspectives in Growing Inequality* (Newbury Park: Sage Publications, 1993).
43. For additional citations, see Refugio I. Rochín, *Middle-Class Squeeze* (Claremont, Calif.: The Tomás Rivera Center, 1992).
44. Lawrence A. Karoly, *The Trend in Inequality among Families, Individuals and Workers in the United States: A Twenty-Five Year Perspective* (Santa Monica, Calif.: Rand Corporation, 1992), 22.
45. Ibid.
46. George J. Borjas and Marta Tienda, "The Economic Consequences of Immigration," *Science* 235 (1987): 645–51.
47. Joseph R. Meisenheimer III, "How Do Immigrants Fare in the U.S. Labor Market?" *Monthly Labor Review* 2 (1992): 3–19.
48. Ibid., 8.
49. Cattan, "Diversity of Hispanics," 4.
50. Gregory de Freitas, *Inequality at Work: Hispanics in the U.S. Labor Force* (New York: Oxford University Press, 1991) offers an initial analysis of the situation.
51. Refugio I. Rochín, "Public Proceedings of the North American Free Trade Agreement: Facts and Myths," proceedings of the forum San Diego–Tijuana Borderlands: Problems and Prospects (San Diego: San Diego Mesa College Borderlands Project, 1992), 24.
52. *Immigration Reform and Control Act of 1986,* Public Law 99-603, 204, 100, Stat 3359, 3405-3411.
53. Adela de la Torre, Howard R. Hunter, and Robert Rosenzweig, "SLIAG Funds: Windfall or Band-Aid," *Critical Issues in Progress* 1 (1993): 10.
54. Refugio I. Rochín and Mónica D. Castillo, "Immigration, Colonia Formation and Latino Poor in Rural California: Evolving Immiseration," *Occasional Papers Nov. 93-1* (Claremont, Calif.: The Tomás Rivera Center, 1993).
55. Richard Santos and Patricia Seitz, "School-to-Work Experience of Hispanic Youth," *Contemporary Policy Issues* 10 (1992): 65–73.

PART TWO. CHICANA/O POLITICS:

TRAJECTORIES AND

CONSEQUENCES

Politics has been the strategy by which Chicanas/os have sought to improve their socioeconomic and political standing in the United States. During the 1980s Chicanos' increasing reliance on politics was accompanied by speculation about the agenda and trajectory of Chicano political development. Observers associated with the "English Only" movement, for example, alleged that Chicanos were pursuing a separatist agenda detrimental to the national security of the United States. Other observers claimed that Chicano political activism had made a right turn, reflecting a thrust towards conservatism. John A. García examines the evolution of Chicano political development since 1980, using the Chicano Movement as a benchmark. García argues that the movement left a legacy that has influenced post-1980 activism, organization, and politics. Nevertheless, there have been significant changes in Chicano political activism. Among other things, the agenda of Chicano politics has broadened; moreover, group identity has been expanded beyond national group boundaries. These and other developments of the 1980s and 1990s pose numerous challenges to Chicano political activism.

Isidro D. Ortiz examines the responses of four major national Chicano advocacy organizations to the political developments of the 1980s, in particular to the advent of Reaganomics in the context of the claims regarding the anticipated political effects of Reaganomics and Chicano leadership strategies. He documents the pursuit of accommodation rather than confrontation on the part of Chicano advocacy organizations. More specifically, according to Ortiz, in the early 1980s the four advocacy organizations pursued a new strategy, the corporate grantsmanship and partnership strategy, which enabled the organizations to survive, but which also redounded to the benefit of corporations. The consequences for corporations were of such significance that in retrospect it may be more appropriate to label the 1980s as the "Decade of the Corporation" rather than as the "Decade of the Hispanics."

Chicano-Mexicano relations in contemporary times have been complex and intense. Relying on conceptual models of public policy and extensive original research, María Rosa García-Acevedo provides a succinct interpretative analysis of the political links established by both Mexican-origin communities since 1970. During this period Chicanos and Mexico made significant attempts to form policies aimed at a closer political relationship. The accomplishments and limitations of this era of rapproachement form the basis of her chapter. García-Acevedo concludes with a discussion of possible future trends of Aztlán and Mexico. The essays in this section offer insights into this debate as well as other issues associated with Chicano politics.

THE CHICANO MOVEMENT : ITS LEGACY

FOR POLITICS AND POLICY

John A. García

In the mid-1960s a sense of self-determination and a desire for immediate social change served as catalysts for the Mexican-origin population of the United States. Moving from an "invisible minority" status to this nation's largest ethnic group has resulted in a redefinition by Chicanos themselves of institutional relationships and responses. In a more contemporary sense, the Chicano Movement has left a legacy that has shaped current organizations and politics for the Chicano community. The turn of events in that community and within the larger society during 1965–1975 represents an effort by an economic and political underclass to remove inequities and exclusionary practices. The outward manifestation of *la política* resulted in a variety of adaptive strategies and policy demands, known collectively as "el Movimiento chicano" (Chicano Movement). The primary focus of this chapter is to identify key components of the Chicano Movement, as well as its political impact and the resulting consequences for the Chicano community in the 1990s. Carlos Muñoz and Juan Gómez-Quiñones identified some central features of el Movimiento: (1) self-determination and self-definition of the Chicano experience in American society; (2) the need for indigenous leadership and organizations to carry out the interests of the community; (3) resurgence and positive redefinition of culture and traditions; (4) adoption of direct confrontation politics with unresponsive institutions and political actors; and (5) a strong sense of urgency for immediate social change.[1]

The Chicano community and its political activism of the 1960s and 1970s targeted the political sphere as the area in which to begin their efforts for reform, with a renewed spirit of critical analysis of American society, particularly in terms of equality and collective benefits for all Chicanos.

Although the Mexican-origin community felt a sense of cultural pride despite the negative experiences of conquest and subordination in the 1840s and beyond, their language, customs, beliefs, and values had been made the objects of denigration by the majority population, as too their religious beliefs and phenotypical traits.[2] Therefore, one of the objectives of the Movimiento was to liberate Mexican-origin people from a sense of cultural inferiority. Mexican Americans had been isolated from the dominant American society, except when that society needed Mexican American labor to harvest the crops, work the mines, build the railroads, work in the manufacturing centers, or defend the country from "hostile nations." Even now full and complete participation in political institutions, educational systems, and labor markets has not been realized for Chicanos.[3]

The second part of this chapter will relate the central themes and objectives of the Chicano Movement to the contemporary political development of the Chicano community. The roots of the Chicano Movement took hold immediately following the World War II. The war effort had provided Chicanos with expanded training in technical and organizational skills, more educational opportunities, and new job possibilities. With the increased urbanization of the Mexican American population in the 1940s and 1950s, and relative postwar prosperity, some socioeconomic gains were being made.[4] These factors contributed to the development of a larger skilled and middle-class segment of the population and a greater number of Mexican American leaders and organizations, which began to prepare the groundwork for major sociopolitical demands on U.S. society.[5] With increased mobility and somewhat expanded organizational resources, the Chicano community was reenergized with a more heightened sense of political and cultural activism. The precise order of these developments—increased mobility and heightened political/cultural consciousness—is difficult to determine. The presence of cultural identification and pride has been continuous throughout the Chicano experience; however, at the same time collective orientations and actions toward the political system have not always been a major pattern. Thus, a sense of ethnic consciousness may diminish with succeeding generations. On the other hand, increased social mobility enables the Chicano community to expand its organizational resources (e.g., leadership base, skills, education, financial resources). While we may not be able to present the causal order of Chicanismo, our discussion should indicate the relative importance of culture and socioeconomic mobility on *la política chicana.*

One additional note in our discussion of the Chicano community and the political arena concerns the policy and structural experiences of Chicanos. Chicanos have made specific gains in the sociopolitical system (e.g., job opportunities, GI educational benefits, voting rights); yet contemporary changes in the political and social climates have caused some ground to be lost. For example, the periodic extensions of the Voting Rights Act require significant efforts by Chicano and other Latino leaders and organizations to maintain the bilingual provisions in the legislation. In a more contemporary sense, continued economic recessions, budget cutbacks, and less aggressive affirmative action enforcement translated into lost political ground during the late 1960s and early 1970s. Thus, the discussion of Chicanos in the U.S. political system can be characterized as one of continued Chicano presence and limited gains, marked by institutional resistance and setbacks. The more focused discussion that follows will examine the Chicano Movement's impact on the political system and the Chicano community itself.

CHICANOS, THE POLITICAL SYSTEM, AND EL MOVIMIENTO

A perspective from which to discuss Chicanos and the movement lies with the identification of structural factors that defined power relations and cultural forces that permeate the Chicano experience, as well as changes in the socioeconomic status of Chicanos. We can use the concept of "political culture" as a way to provide some context for our discussion, because it entails people's expectations about the realities of politics and implants in them shared ideals as to what their public life might be.[6] Thus, for Chicanos, "political culture" refers to a system of beliefs about patterns of interactions with political institutions.[7] Implicit in these patterns are the values of equity, equality, and responsive political institutions and representation.

A crucial element in the ideation of Chicanos deals with a sense of their identity both in class and racial/ethnic terms, thus providing a definition of the individual and his/her role within society. This identity represents membership in a complementary community, as well as geographical and ideological loyalties.[8] A sense of national identity with America legitimizes the activities of leadership and allows for the mobilization of support and commitment.

Conversely, the concept of ethnic identity can focus on the divergent political elements within a pluralistic system that tends to be divisive. With a strong sense of ethnic identity (Chicanismo), segregated residential communities, and geographical proximity to Mexico, Chicanos' political activities and system assessment would tend to challenge the central leadership and increase political conflict. In this context, we are defining a political culture among Chicanos, which incorporates some rootedness in American society, and a distinctive ethnic identification, which can emphasize group differences and status.

Milton Esman offers five conditions that are necessary and sufficient to explain the politicization of ethnic groups in the industrialized world: (1) group identity based on objective social distinctions and feelings of solidarity they generate; (2) grievances based on perceived social, economic, or cultural deprivation or discrimination; (3) rising expectations of amelioration; (4) declining authority and effectiveness of the political center; and (5) effective political organization.[9]

Group Identity

For Chicanos, these conditions parallel the political aspects of the Chicano Movement. The development and strengthening of ethnic and cultural identity was based upon a critical analysis of the involuntary inclusion of Mexican-origin people into the United States. Proximity to Mexico, significant numbers of family members living in Mexico, foreign-born status (both as permanent resident aliens and as undocumented workers), and cultural persistence all contribute to the maintenance of a sense of group identity.

Part of the redefinition of group identity involves a reconstruction of how Chicanos viewed themselves and the positive aspects of the Chicano experience. This meant a revitalization of the Mexicano/Chicano cultures and interpreting them through the eyes of *el pueblo mexicano*. The net result was a growing awareness of Chicanos' historical experiences, cultural attributes (i.e., language, customs, value systems), and experiences within American society.

The increase in cultural pride, cultural awareness, and a sense of group consciousness represent the cognitive and psychological aspects of the Chicano Movement. In order to understand the political world of Chicanos, we should examine the psychological realm of the movement. Previous works on ethnic politics have characterized the political activation of first-generation ethnics as resulting from group survival and a strong sense of national origin.[10] Once racial/ethnic groups integrate themselves more fully into American society, succeeding generations lose any real attachment to an ethnic identification. This thesis is discussed in the works of Parenti and Wolfinger regarding voting and other forms of electoral participation.[11] However, in their research in the mid-1960s, Parenti and Wolfinger do acknowledge the persistence of ethnic identification beyond the first generation and its impact on political activities.

As stated before, the Chicano Movement (in a contemporary sense) started in the mid-1960s. Cries for self-determination and justice by the Chicano community and its leadership drew upon the long-standing sense of being Mexicano/Chicano. Chicanismo embodies the persistence of group identity that contained cultural values, symbols, and practices which result in group pride and political mobilization.

Grievances and Discrimination

The second condition applicable to the Chicano Movement deals with grievances based on perceived social, economic, or cultural deprivation or discrimination. Works such as those of Barrera and Gómez-Quiñones portray the socioeconomic conditions of Chicanos at the time of the acquisition of much of the now American Southwest following the Mexican-American war.[12] Economic subjugation and exploitation of Mexican-origin people rapidly became the norm; and during the Manifest Destiny period in the latter half of the nineteenth century, this pattern continued with an open border that facilitated the importation of labor from Mexico to aid economic expansion in mining, ranching, agriculture, and railroad construction. Thus the role of the Mexican-origin population was that of a reserved labor pool, an elastic labor source concentrated in working-class occupations.

The pattern of discrimination and prejudice was also made evident by the existence of restrictive covenants in residential areas, separate areas in public facilities, segregated schools and classrooms,[13] differential treatment in the justice system, and societal stereotypes about Mexican-origin people as lazy, dirty, uneducated, and immoral.[14] Thus the focus of the Chicano Movement included attacks directed at the discriminatory practices that many Chicanos encountered on a daily basis. Full and equal protection under the law, and due process rights served as objectives of the movement. In the legislative arena, the Voting Rights Act and Civil Rights Act were prime examples of efforts to remove or prohibit long-standing discriminatory practices in the areas of employment, housing, elections, and public accommodations.

During the first phase of the Chicano Movement, the issue of equal access and opportunity ranged from taking control of neighborhood parks to challenging "English-only" policies in the schools. Much of the effort aimed at overcoming differential treatment and prejudice entailed strategies such as confrontational actions and protests. The experience of school walkouts and "blowouts" were not uncommon among Chicano activists. Mass marches and demonstrations were used by the United Farm Workers Union, Crusade for Justice, the Chicano Moratorium, and the Brown Berets, for example.[15]

Rising Expectations

The third component of the Chicano Movement is that of rising expectations among the politically mobilized community. The winds of social change fueled the sense of impatience and urgency within the Chicano Movement. Chicano activists highlighted the inconsistencies of the American dream and Chicano reality, which had the effect of activating a backlog of frustrations. Critical analyses of American institutions and the capitalist economic system were major foci of Chicano activists. Besides the examination of institutional racism, the ideology of the Chicano Movement included a politics of liberation from the exploitive and subordinate status experienced by Mexican-origin persons north of the Río Bravo. Works by Acuña, Barerra, and Gómez-Quiñones developed many of the central components of the movement's ideology.[16]

With such a strong emphasis on social change, equality, equity, self-determination, and cultural nationalism, rising expectations and a robust energy to take control of the Chicano community's destiny were an integral part of the Movimiento. Improving the Chicano condition translated into greater community control and effective decision making regarding education, neighborhood services, access to social services, responses to abuses of the criminal justice system, and the impact of the escalation of the Vietnam War in the Chicano community.

The rise of indigenous community organizations with local leadership was characteristic of the Chicano Movement. Emphasis on cultural pride and a nationalistic "fervor" were persistent themes espoused by Chicano activists. Forming indigenous organizations with primary interests in the improvement of the Chicano community altered the Mexican-origin people into becoming empowered and proactive.

Declining Authority and Effectiveness

The fourth aspect of the rise of the Chicano Movement lies with the pressures on the American political system to respond to issues of inequities and exploitation of powerless communities. The timing of the Chicano Movement coincided with a myriad of other social actions by underrepresented groups (i.e., African Americans, Native Americans, the disaffected youth, feminists, and the like). The ability of the U.S. political system to be responsive to these demands for access, equality, representation, and self-determination placed economic strains and, at times, resulted in repressive actions of force by the state.

Despite passage of significant legislation like the Civil Rights Act of 1964, the Voting Rights Act of 1965, the War on Poverty initiatives, and the Equal Opportunity Act, the status of Chicanos did not alter substantially. For the most part, the legislation mentioned may have had the effect of raising expectations of change even higher among Chicanos than what the political system could realistically accomplish. An expanding social agenda placed the goals and objectives of the Chicano Movement in constant competition with other competing groups and program initiatives. The goals of the Chicano Movement focused on the economic restructuring of a capitalist system to one of more widely shared ownership and more control by workers. This kind of restructuring was beyond incremental reforms and conflicted with some fundamental values of political and economic elites.

The questioning of authority was endemic to the fervor of the Chicano Movement; political institutions were placed on the defensive and responses proved to be symbolic or were limited to "benign neglect." Chicanos were on the outside, looking into the political system, in their efforts to define a community political agenda and play an active role in its implementation. In many regards, community control and greater political/

economic autonomy challenged the authority of the political system and impaired the ability of institutions to interact in "traditional" ways with the Chicano communities. Minimizing system effectiveness and disputing the legitimate authority of the status quo served as a major context and target of the Chicano Movement.

Chicano Political Organizations

The thrusts of the Chicano Movement were politically and economically oriented toward a change in the American status quo, and accompanying this orientation was a basic distrust of existing institutions and organizations. As a result, the Chicano community looked inward for its leadership and organizational structure. Numerous local and neighborhood-based organizations were formed to empower and "liberate" the Chicano community from exploitation and inequities. The Crusade for Justice in Denver was a good example of a community-based organization that tried to address the powerlessness of Chicanos. Cultural pride and historical interpretations and activities, community self-help projects, and community control couched in a radical ideology were the pillars of this organization headed by Rodolfo "Corky" González.

In a more direct, politically oriented context, the formation of El Partido La Raza Unida (La Raza Unida political party) was an effort in the early 1970s to set up an alternative political party formed by, run by, and reflecting the interests of the Chicano community. This essay is not intended to provide a detailed history of the various Chicano organizations, as other scholars have written extensively about them.[17] The primary intent here is to acknowledge the development of several Chicano-based organizations and the accompanying ideology and objectives that each carried forward. Their constituencies were defined as the working-class segment of the community, which was viewed as the dominant, most unrepresented and powerless sector.

Another important dimension of Chicano political organizations was the insistence upon indigenous leaders. Individuals recruited as leaders or persons who seized the opportunity for leadership roles came from the Chicano experience and had roots in the community. In many respects, Chicano-based organizations developed at the grassroots and local levels and directed their agendas toward empowerment and improving life in their barrios. Central to most of the Chicano political organizations was the inclusion of culture, history, and ethnic pride. Use of cultural symbols (i.e., the Mexican eagle for the United Farm Workers Union, the Virgin of Guadalupe, use of Spanish) was integrated into these organizations' ideology and procedures. An integral part of Chicano empowerment was based on a redefinition of Chicanos past and present. Thus, political organizations served to develop alternative perspectives and interpretations of Chicano history and possible future.

The litany of Chicano political organizations is an extensive one in which most of the activities took place at the neighborhood level, in the schools, and on college campuses. The issues ranged from organizing workers for better pay and working conditions to challenging the educational establishment for its failure to diversify pedagogy and recognize cultural differences. Politics of protest and gaining access to the political process were major goals of these organizations. At times there were ideological differences that related to "working within the political system" as opposed to radical change outside of conventional channels and institutions. In addition, political philosophies varied from a Marxist-Leninist orientation, cultural nationalism, and pluralism to incremental reform. Chicano political organizations served as the articulators and critics for the community in both redefining itself and in advancing its causes.

In the discussion of the basic elements of el Movimiento chicano, we can discern the importance of this period as to the whole of Chicano experience in the United States and the community's political development. At the same time, there is a definite legacy left by el Movimiento with regard to the politics of the Chicano communities in the 1990. The remainder of this essay links that legacy with the contemporary politics of Chicano communities, as well as of the larger Latino community.

THE CONTEMPORARY LEGACY OF
THE CHICANO MOVEMENT

While the Chicano community continues to grow in population and geographical diversity, the themes of community autonomy, activism, and cultural pride remain as part of the Chicano political landscape. The remaining section will examine some contemporary issues for the Chicano community in the 1990s and their ties to the legacy of el Movimiento.

Group Identity

Group identity remains a central feature of the Chicano community, serving to maintain a sense of cohesiveness and a basis for group mobilization. Continuous migration from Mexico and greater "institutionalization" of Chicano culture through the arts, media, and Chicano organizations have fostered an active group identity. One additional development in this community has been the efforts to expand group identity beyond national group boundaries. The continued growth of the Chicano community has been accompanied by the significant growth of other Latino populations. As a result, much of the national media, political organizations and some of the leadership promoted the 1980s as the "Decade of the Hispanic."

The efforts to unite persons of Spanish origin under a "pan-ethnic" umbrella label had the effect of expanding the population and geographical base for Hispanics/Latinos and projecting Chicanos and other Latinos into national arenas.[18] The cultivation of an additional identity for Chicanos has been met with a variety of responses. One perspective sees such attempts to "redefine" Chicanos as part of a larger group configuration to be contrary to the origins of the Chicano Movement. The emphasis on culture and nationalism from Mexican roots seriously erodes when combined with the culture and nationalism of other Latino groups. The distinct historical experiences of Chicanos and their cultural nationalism would be placed in jeopardy by a broader sweep of different histories of twenty-plus Latino-origin groups.

On the other hand, another perspective would be the more expansive characterization of Latinos as a situational identity with specific political goals and ends.[19] In this manner, there is the recognition of some common ground among persons of Latino origin. The linkage between Spanish and indigenous ancestry, Spanish language, religious affiliation and traditions, and general cultural traditions and practices can serve to create a broader community of culture. At the same time, the creation of a Hispanic community can represent a set of common interests and concerns that form a united social and political agenda. The issues of access, empowerment, education, immigration, language policies, and the economy can advance Latinos as a national political community.[20] This perspective takes a more pragmatic view of expanding community resources and population base to be more effectively engaged in national political arenas. There is a recognition of real political utility to expand group identity for very specific political purposes and situations.

This aspect of group identity has some parallels with the earlier Chicano Movement in that distinctive group parameters are defined largely in cultural and historical terms. Cultural nationalism and experiences in the United States can serve to define the realities for Latinos whether located in the Southwest, southern Florida, the New York metropolitan region, or the Midwest. The practical actualities of Central American immigration and that of other Caribbean national-origin groups have caused greater awareness and contact among Chicanos. In some cases, this has meant heightened competition and tensions between Chicanos and other Latinos; while in other situations, more dialogue and cooperative ventures on issues such as immigration reform and discrimination in the workplace serve as examples for all. Nevertheless, the external political dynamics and demographic realities of population trends have had a direct effect on the Chicano community. The current status of group identity for Chicanos is the maintenance of national-origin identity with all the cultural cues and symbols, together with a broader identity as part of a Hispanic/Latino umbrella. The latter development is more of a process than an accomplished community of consensus and single identity. Multiple identities do exist and extend beyond Chicanismo, and "Hispanicity." Yet Chicanos still think of themselves as Mexican-origin people with a long-standing quest for equity and empowerment in American society.

Chicano Issues and the 1990s

The thrust of the Chicano Movement also stressed political and economic empowerment, as well as greater political representation. During the interval between the mid-1970s and the early 1990s, there has been a noticeable increase in the number of Chicano elected and appointed officials, as well as in the number of activities defining and expanding a Chicano political agenda. The Chicano community and its organizations have been able to use several pieces of legislation to improve opportunities for political representation and voter registration/participation.

The political mobilization of Chicano voters has produced steady progress. As a result of the Voting Rights Acts, the U.S. Bureau of the Census has maintained data on voter registration and turnout since the late 1970s. There has been a gap between Chicano voting rates and those of Anglos and African Americans.[21] The primary factors have been the lower socio-economic status of Chicanos, the youthful age structure of the Chicano population, and the significant proportion (approximately 40 percent) of Chicano noncitizens. Organizations such as the National Association of Latino Elected Officials (NALEO) have initiated active citizenship campaigns in order to encourage and facilitate Mexican nationals to pursue naturalization. In addition, organizations such as the Southwest Voter Registration and Education Project have been conducting voter registration campaigns throughout the nation. Their more successful efforts have positive results when such campaigns immediately precede elections. In this manner, important issues are identified and voter interests are heightened. These campaigns also serve to identify prospective candidates and community basis of support for contesting elections. While the voter registration and turnout gap still does exist, gains in socioeconomic status, higher percentages of naturalized citizens, greater proportions of Chicanos over the age of eighteen, and political consciousness should contribute significantly to greater improvements in registration and turnout rates among Chicanos.

With the continued growth of the Chicano population, as well as of other Hispanic groups, there has been increased pressure for greater political representation at all levels. The Voting Rights Act (VRA) of 1965 established a steady federal presence in the monitoring of voter registration and election related activities, but the South was the primary jurisdiction of focus. It was only after passage of the VRA extensions of 1970 and 1975 with their designation of linguistic minorities that Chicanos could make effective use of this legislation. Support for the extension of the Voting Rights Act and continued litigation challenges regarding election systems have served as indicators of activities to expand Chicano political representation.

The use of bilingual materials within a geographic area based on at least 5 percent linguistic minority population brought the matter of voters' rights to many Southwestern counties in which Chicanos resided. The issues of voter intimidation, at-large election systems, annual registration, and historical exclusion of Chicanos from the electorate furthered the cause of and the desire for increased political representation. Organizations such as the Mexican American Legal Defense and Education Fund (MALDEF) and the Southwest Voter Registration and Education Project (SWVREP) initiated litigation to alter election systems, improve access to voter regis-

Table 4.1   Hispanic Elected Officials by Level of Government, 1993

	Number of HEOS*	% of HEOS
FEDERAL		
U.S. Senators	0	0.00%
U.S. Representatives	17	.34%
STATEWIDE		
Governors	0	0.00%
State Executives	8	.16%
State Legislators	156	3.11%
LOCAL		
County Officials	384	7.65%
Municipal Officials	1,358	27.06%
Judicial/Law Enforcement	628	12.51%
Education/School Boards	2,308	45.99%
Special District Offices	160	3.19%
TOTAL	5,019	100.00%

*HEO (Hispanic Elected Officials)

Source: The NALEO Educational Fund, 1993 (as of January 1993).

tration, and challenge redistricting plans. In both 1980 and 1990, the latter proved to have a direct link to assuring competitive Chicano districts at the federal, state, and local levels. Marked gains were evident in the 1982 and 1992 elections with a significant increase in the number of Chicano elected officials. The gains were more evident at the local level, especially in school districts.[22] Although the number of Chicanos and other Latinos at the congressional level had grown to seventeen by 1992 (see table 4.1), the issue of political representation or the inadequacy of it remains a constant item on the Chicano political agenda.

Concomitant with a greater number of Chicano elected and appointed officials comes the issue of effectiveness and outcomes.[23] One development from the period of the Chicano Movement is the "penetration" of Chicanos in decision-making institutions. As a result, the community's anticipation has been raised to expect concrete policies and actions. From a research and policy perspective, there is limited evidence as to the extent of Chicano representatives' impact on policy outcomes and implementation.

Part of the problem lies with the inertia of economic and political institutions, policymakers' disposition toward benign neglect, and the political system's inability to deal with social change in a timely manner. In a parallel fashion, the thrust of the Chicano Movement was a demand for immediate and basic social change. The rate of progress for Chicanos has been slow, with some spurts of noticeable change. Incrementalism has been a pattern for change for Chicanos, yet the initial urgency of social change has served to sustain contemporary efforts.

Language and Education

The strong pattern of Spanish language maintenance serves as another factor influencing the policy arena of education.[24] More recently, anti-immigrant and xenophobic movements that attempt to establish English as the official language view Chicano culture with suspicion. As indicated earlier, the Chicano Movement emphasized cultural pride and maintenance. Thus, there have been long-standing efforts to institutionalize bilingual/bicultural education by Chicanos. In addition, the recognition and promotion of culture in all facets of American life has been a central mission within the Chicano community.

Since the beginning of the Chicano Movement, substantial efforts have been made to adopt legislation to implement bilingual/bicultural education in the K–12 grade levels. While legislation has been enforced, the level of federal funding and the scope of bilingual/bicultural programs have been less than satisfactory for the Chicano community. Also, as a result of financial uncertainty at the federal level, Chicanos have broadened their efforts at the state and local school district levels. Their efforts represent attempts to increase the level of funding for bilingual programs, certification requirements, and expansion of maintenance programs.

One of the consequences of persisting cultural pride has been that some segments of the "mainstream" society view Chicanos and other Latinos as isolationists and unpatriotic to the United States. The theme of ethnic and cultural "balkanization" is often used to characterize, with serious alarm, Chicanos who are seen to be undermining "fundamental" American values and traditions.[25] However, using data from the Latino National Political Survey, the authors of a recent paper demonstrate that there has been a positive incorporation of fundamental American political values in Latino political culture and that there are Chicanos and other Latinos actually living the American dream.[26] In addition, levels of pride and affection for the United States among Mexican-origin persons is very high, regardless of nativity, language use, and class. For many Chicanos, attachment to the United States and a heightened sense of ethnicity are not antithetical nor incompatible.

Efforts at immigration reform and "official English" movements are responses to Chicano culture and pride. Restrictionist policies, patriotic litmus tests, and ethnic hate crimes have served as indicators of contemporary tensions between the Chicano community, which is striving for social change, and mainstream America. This situation has placed some of the leadership and organizations, as a whole, on the defensive to prove Chicanos' loyalty and legitimate right to be part of American society and its overall political agenda. Nevertheless, the challenge to the Chicano community is to effectively use its institutional bases and power accumulated since the inception of the Chicano Movement to improve social and political conditions. It is abundantly clear that culture and politics remain intertwined for Chicanos in the 1990s.

A remaining critical issue relates to social services, employment, and the participation of Chicanos in the economy. Questions of access, substantial job-training program participation, delivery of social services, and Chicanos' vulnerability to fluctuations of the economy (in terms of unemployment, layoffs, out-migration of firms from the United States, and the like) are all key areas of concern. Specific issues include limited access to programs due to language difficulties, legal status (permanent resident aliens and undocumented persons), and the lack of bureaucratic representation.[27] The employer-sanction provision in the Immigration Reform and Control Act placed a greater burden on Chicanos and other Latinos. The occupational distribution and industry location of Chicanos and their regional concentration (the Southwest) have made them subject to more job market discrimination than other groups and to a heavier burden of proof of their legal status.

In addition, Chicano workers are competing in a restructured labor market (high technology, service industries) with fewer human capital skills than other workers, and they are competing with non-minority interregional migrants for jobs that are becoming increasingly scarce.[28] One of the postscripts of the analysis of the Chicano Movement is the crucial yet expendable role that Chicano workers serve in the economy. Chicanos provided critical labor in the development of the Southwest, particularly in mining, ranching, agriculture, railroads, and manufacturing. However, as the economic structure changed after World War II, Chicanos found themselves to be more marginal as workers, serving as a reserve labor pool as fluctuations of the economy determined many Chicanos' labor market status. Contemporary discussions of primary and secondary labor markets and minority worker demographics have served as a relevant frame for analysis; and it is the employment policy area that has become a key battleground for any economic gains among Chicanos.

Social service cutbacks in such programs as food stamps, Aid to Families with Dependent Children, housing assistance, indigent health care, to name a few, have a direct and negative effect on the Chicano community, which contains a high percentage of dependent population (both young and elderly persons). Job-training programs, the range of training options, and access to these are a major concern within the Chicano community. In addition, labor market discrimination and ineffective enforcement of affirmative action policies have been viewed as serious obstacles for Chicanos to overcome in the 1990s.

One more recent area of controversy in employment is that of language. Use of Spanish is viewed by some as detrimental in the workplace; but, at the same time, others see it to be a necessary skill for job performance. The former point concerns trends among employers to impose restrictions on the use of Spanish on the job. Also it has been argued that employers are not able to communicate nor to keep informed as to the activities of workers. The latter point centers around the market value of being bilingual in one's job. MALDEF initiated a class action suit on behalf of bilingual police officers, demanding that they be compensated for this additional skill. A central legal question is whether the employee can be required by a supervisor to use whatever skills are brought to the job (i.e., Spanish language skills). Issues of language and language rights will continue to be a focal point for Chicanos, especially in the workplace. The foregoing represent a core of vital policy areas, as well as national and local political battlegrounds for el Movimiento.

Our discussion of the development of the Chicano Movement involves the continual presence of cultural maintenance and ethnic identity within American society, the growing number of Mexican-origin persons residing in the United States, and the continued institutional neglect and unresponsiveness. The combination of these factors has influenced the political organizations, leadership, voting participation, and political mobilization of Chicanos.

Political Organizations and Leadership

One of the thrusts of the Chicano Movement was the development of indigenous organizations with a cadre of independent leaders critical to their success. As with any movement, the rise of new organizations and ad hoc groups was connected to fast-moving events and situations. In many cases, individuals "came forward" in leadership roles. "Post-analysis" of the Chicano Movement not only acknowledged the youthfulness of many of the activists, but also the significant involvement of Chicanas in leadership roles.[29]

The rise of Chicana feminism within el Movimiento has numerous historical antecedents in the period of Spanish conquests in the New World, in the Mexican Revolution, and in the increased participation of Chicanas in the labor force during world War II. Chicana feminism incorporated the intersection of class, gender, and ethnicity.[30] It was a challenge to existing power relations in terms of patriarchy, sexuality, labor markets, and the family institution. Chicana activists critiqued power relations in all social institutions and prevailing cultural ideologies. The boundaries of the Chicano Movement were expanded such that patriarchy, equality, gender roles, and culture served as crucial areas of discourse and struggle. The rise of Chicana organizations such as Hijas de Cuahtémoc, Encuentro Femenil, and Comisión Femenil Mexicana Nacional served to articulate Chicana perspectives and the Chicana agenda, as well as advancing *la lucha* within and outside the Chicano community.

In a contemporary sense, the goals of Chicanas (i.e., empowerment, equality, and active participation) remain central in the 1990s. The formation of an organization such as Mujeres Activas en Letras y Cambio Social (MALCS) is representative of the continuing analysis and critiques of power relations determined by class, gender, and ethnicity. The maintenance of culture and its interpretation within *la familia* and the workplace are critical arenas for the realization of a Chicana agenda. Issues such as equal pay, affirmative action, reproductive rights, family rights, political representation, and women's health access and rights permeate the Chicano agenda; Chicanas pursue them within existing Chicano organizations as well as

Table 4.2   Female Hispanic Elected Officials by Selected States, 1993

State	Total HEOs[8]	Female HEOs	% Female of HEOS
Arizona	302	82	27.2%
California	687	202	29.4%
Colorado	206	41	19.9%
Florida	69	20	29.0%
Illinois	798	521	65.3%
New Jersey	39	9	23.1%
New Mexico	692	149	21.5%
New York	96	36	37.5%
Texas	2,002	393	19.6%
Other States	128	42	32.8%
TOTAL	5,019	1,495	29.8%

*HEO (Hispanic Elected Officials)

Source: The NALEO Educational Fund, 1993 (as of January 1993).

within Chicana groups. Chicana activism has served to heighten awareness of the impact that social structures (inclusive of class and ethnicity)
have had on Chicanas and the impact that they themselves can have on
social structures. Thus the involvement and the participation of Chicanas
in leadership roles continue to be an important gauge of Chicano advancement and empowerment. To that end table 4.2 illustrates the numbers of
Chicana elected officials as some indication of leadership positions. At the
same time, Chicana perspectives on issues provide additional focus and
emphasis on both policy discourse and specific policy initiatives.

Many of the Chicano organizations and groups were grassroots in nature
and neighborhood in focus. Since the waning of the Chicano Movement,
there has been greater institutionalization of the organizational efforts initiated early on. Older organizations like the League of United Latin American Citizens (LULAC), American GI Forum, and Mexican American Political Association (MAPA) have since broadened their goals and constituency
bases. In addition, Chicano organizations have targeted the national policy
arenas for greater involvement.

The broadening of goals and constituency bases represents a different
stage of political advances for Chicanos. The latter point lies with the larger
definition of community. The 1980s had been designated as the decade for

the rise of Hispanics on the American scene. As a result, a broader incorporation of community meant the inclusion of other Latino-origin groups (e.g., Cubans, Puerto Ricans, Central Americans) as part of a Latino/Hispanic umbrella. This evolvement significantly increased the population base from approximately fourteen million Chicanos to over twenty-two million Latinos. Strategically, it served to legitimate Chicanos as part of a larger, national minority group. At the same time, redefining community has created some cross-pressures and tensions. The basis for a broader community lies with a common language, ancestry, and similar culture and traditions; yet, each Hispanic group's experiences in the United States are not totally parallel to those of other Hispanic groups either chronologically or structurally. While the "Decade of the Hispanic" has passed, the development of a broader-based community is still progressing, although slowly. It appears that more progress has been made at the elite (activist) level than among the masses of Latinos. In many respects, the idea of a broader community base can be viewed as the development of a situational identity. Ethnicity is constructed using some common thread(s) (e.g., culture, common experiences) and a new ethnicity is advocated for political and strategic benefits. The umbrella terms of "Hispanic" and "Latino" foster a more expansive view. For the most part, this idea, when integrated at the personal level, involves a multiple set of ethnic identities. Thus, a person uses a particular identity depending on the situation or desired reaction.

In addition to a broader-based constituency that Chicano organizations and their leaders have sought, there is also the broadening of goals. This has happened in an effort to become a more significant participant in the national arena. As indicated earlier, the primary focus of the Chicano Movement's activities and arenas were the barrio communities. The 1990s has seen a different emphasis on where organizational energies should be placed. Permanent offices in Washington with full-time directors and staff have been established by many Chicano organizations. With the increase in the number of Chicano and other Latino elected officials (especially at the federal level), the development of the Congressional Hispanic Caucus has served to link all Chicano organizations.

For many years, the areas of bilingual education, voting rights, and immigration were seen as the core of the Chicano agenda. During the 1990s, additional policy areas have been added to the core, including health and medical care (access, costs, delivery systems, and utilization); the North

American Free Trade Agreement (NAFTA); urban pollution and the environment; the criminal justice system and crime; economic development and employment policies; and social welfare policy. One underlying theme of all these issues has to do with policy impact on Chicanos. There are direct costs to Chicanos with the restructuring of our economic base, the rise of crime and concentration of toxic waste sites in the barrio, and being an at-risk group for a number of diseases and health conditions.

As a result, a broader agenda and a national arena have become "necessities" for the Chicano leaders and organizations trying to exert influence. The points of contact between Chicano interests and policy implementation lie at the agency level, with congressional committees, and with other interest groups generating data and analysis for the policy-making process. The difference between these patterns and those established during the height of the Chicano Movement lies in access, positioning, and institutional bases. Chicanos during the 1960s and early 1970s were "on the outside looking in" and trying to communicate a sense of urgency about social change to inaccessible and unresponsive institutions. Although limited, the penetration by Chicano leaders and organizations into decision-making bodies has afforded them the opportunity to lobby, advocate, initiate, and influence from different vantage points.

In addition, styles and strategies have undergone some changes. The reliance on direct action, protest, and mass demonstrations has been less prevalent from the mid-1980s to the present. More extensive use of class-action litigation, conventional lobbying of elected officials, use of the mass media, community policy advocacy, and compromise and negotiation by Chicanos in legislative bodies have been more the mode of operation. Leadership styles follow the context and tenor of these kinds of strategies with greater moderation of language, tone, and demands for immediate action. In a real sense, the broader stakes and different arenas have moved Chicano politics toward a more pragmatic orientation with a time dimension that sees progress as a deliberative process.

One other difference in the contemporary leadership (at least the more visible) is a lesser reliance upon charismatic persons in leadership roles. Effectiveness, strategic planning, and concrete outcomes appear to play a greater function in the political dynamics of contemporary Chicano politics. In a way, there is more interelite interaction than relying on a close mass-leader contact within the Chicano community. At the same time, Chicano leaders would be hard pressed to be totally out of touch and synchronization with the Chicano community. Chicano politics is still connected to mass mobilization and resource bases.

One can suggest that the political times may be different and that institutionalization of the movement calls for different strategies and approaches. While the Chicano community has become more diverse economically (i.e., a slightly larger middle and/or professional class) and while a sizable foreign-born (immigrant) segment remains, there are still some common grounds. The articulation between the community and its leadership was an integral part of the Chicano Movement and will continue to be so in the contemporary period. Accountability, representation, support base, community resources, and legitimacy are issues critical to the improvement of the Chicano community. The evolution of leadership within the Chicano community should continue to undergo changes with an ever-widening diversity of styles and personalities. The diversity within the Chicano community, as well as the broader Latino constituency, should enable the infusion of a wide variety of leaders and advocates.

EL MOVIMIENTO AND ITS LEGACY FOR CONTEMPORARY CHICANO POLITICS

One of the major impacts of el Movimiento has been dispelling the melting-pot thesis that has long characterized the fate of all immigrant and indigenous groups. The rise of el Movimiento came about largely due to a strong desire of Chicanos, with the best interests of the Chicano community in mind, to redefine the realities of the Mexican-origin people in the United States.[31] A sense of urgency for significant social change and equality was impressed upon the consciousness of this community by its fervent and ideological activists. In the earlier part of this chapter, I outlined some key dimensions of the Chicano Movement, which included (1) group identity based on objective social distinctions and feelings of solidarity that they generate; (2) grievances based on perceived social, economic, or cultural deprivation or discrimination; (3) rising expectations of amelioration; (4) declining authority and effectiveness of the political center; and (5) effective political organization. I have developed these themes to amplify the range and importance that the Chicano Movement served, both during the 1960s and 1970s and as regards its legacy for contemporary politics.

Group identity, culture, and importance of indigenous organizations were central to the impetus of the Movimiento. At the same time, the less-than-satisfactory ability of the "system" to respond and the condition of "being outside the power centers" accentuated the strategies of protest and direct action by the Chicano community. Its legacy for contemporary Chicano politics lies with the evolution of group identity to maintain a sense of Chicanismo and expand identity to include other Hispanics and Latinos. The importance of cultural heritage, language (real and symbolic), and a sense of a distinctive history in the United States continue to be a viable part of current Chicano politics.

With the evolution of Chicano organizations, there has been a growing institutionalization of structures and activities. In addition, these organizations have targeted national arenas to influence in more conventional ways (e.g., lobbying, advocacy, informational resource). Leadership styles are now less confrontational and more deliberative within key policy-making institutions. Progress and advancement are viewed as incremental and as resulting from a negotiating process in which compromise is an integral part. Chicanos have been able to penetrate political and economic institutions so that they are no longer exclusively outsiders. This has had the effect of altering or expanding strategies to influence the placement of Chicano issues on a national policy agenda.

One other vestige of the Chicano Movement's ideology was an emphasis on the economic system and structure. Chicano activists and intellectuals pursued a critical analysis of capitalism and the role that Chicanos play in that system. Briefly, Chicanos were seen as a reserve labor pool whose elasticity was related to economic fluctuations. Also, Chicanos were placed in a cuing system whereby they were positioned in secondary labor markets. In a more contemporary sense, the economic position of Chicanos has not changed dramatically (i.e., concentrated in blue-collar and/or service occupations, higher rates of unemployment and underemployment, located in declining industries). As a result, Chicano organizations and leaders have directed some of their energies toward the private economic sector as a means improving the economic well-being of the Chicano community. Such efforts have included economic development in the barrio, promoting entrepreneurial activities among Chicanos, aggressive affirmative action programs, and opening access to corporate boards. While the current style and nature of contact with economic institutions is quite different from that of the earlier Chicano Movement, it is also very evident that the economic status of Chicanos is being recognized and that prospects for change are not limited to the political arena alone.

Any discussion of el Movimiento chicano would incorporate the themes of culture and identity, urgency for social change, and the drive for self-determination for and by *el pueblo chicano*. The contemporary politics of the Chicano community may not excite the same degree of fervor and intensity, but the very real issues and the idea of overcoming long-standing institutional arrangements stay as the agenda for change and struggle. I have suggested that the movement has evolved to a more institutional stage with more permanency of structure and functional leadership. Yet the soul of the movement still lies in el pueblo. Thus, the future and the continued legacy of the Chicano Movement lie with the vitality of the soul and spirit of the community and with the sustained and strategic efforts by Chicano leaders and organizations to keep the original goals and issues on the road to resolution.

NOTES

1. Carlos Muñoz, Jr., *Youth, Identity, Power: The Chicano Movement* (London: Verso Press, 1989); Juan Gómez-Quiñones, *Chicano Politics: Realities and Promise* (Albuquerque: University of New Mexico Press, 1990).

2. For a detailed discussion, see Ernesto Galarza, *Merchants of Labor: The Mexican American Bracero Story—An Account of Managed Migration of Mexican Farm Workers in California, 1942-1960* (Charlotte, Calif.: McNally and Loftin, 1964); Anthony Dworkin, "Stereotypes and Self-Images Held by Native-Born and Foreign-Born Mexican Americans," *Sociology and Social Research* 48 (1965): 214-24; and Rodolfo Acuña, *Occupied America: A History of Chicanos*, 3rd ed. (New York: Harper and Row, 1988).

3. Rodney Hero, *Latinos and the U.S. Political System* (Philadelphia: Temple University Press, 1992).

4. For a detailed discussion of this time period, see Elizabeth Sutherland Martínez and Enriqueta Longeaux y Vásquez, *Viva La Raza: The Struggle of the Mexican American People* (Garden City: Doubleday, 1974); Fernando Peñalosa, "The Changing Mexican American in Southern California," *Sociology and Research* 51 (4): 405-17; and Mario T. García, *Mexi-*

can Americans: Leadership, Ideology, and Identity (New Haven: Yale University Press, 1989).

5. M. García, *Mexican Americans.*

6. Lucien Pye and Sidney Verba, *Political Culture and Political Development* (Princeton: Princeton University Press, 1968).

7. Gabriel Almond and Sidney Verba, *The Civic Culture* (Princeton: Princeton University Press, 1963).

8. Charles R. Foster, "Political Culture and Regional Ethnic Minorities," *Journal of Politics* 44 (1982): 560–568.

9. Milton Esman, "Two Dimensions of Ethnic Politics: A Defense of Homeland and Immigrant Rights," *Ethnic and Racial Studies* 8 (1985): 438–40.

10. For an analysis of the dynamics of ethnic politics, see Lawrence Fuchs, *The American Kaleidoscope: Race, Ethnicity and the Civic Culture* (Middletown: Wesleyan University Press, 1990); and Nathan Glazer and P. Moynihan, *Beyond the Melting Pot* (Boston: MIT Press, 1979).

11. Michael Parenti, "Ethnic Politics and the Persistence of Ethnic Identification," *American Political Science Review* 61 (1965): 717–26; Raymond Wolfinger, "The Development and Persistence of Ethnic Voting," *American Political Science Review* 59 (1965): 896–908.

12. Mario Barrera, *Race and Class in the Southwest* (Notre Dame: University of Notre Dame Press, 1979); Gómez-Quiñones, *Chicano Politics.*

13. For a lucid account of these policies, see Guadalupe San Miguel, *Let Them All Take Heed* (Albuquerque: University of New Mexico Press, 1987).

14. Dworkin, "Stereotypes and Self-Images."

15. Acuña, *Occupied America.*

16. Acuña, *Occupied America;* Barrera, *Race and Class;* Gómez-Quiñones, *Chicano Politics.*

17. For an account of the development of Chicano organizations, see Douglas Foley, et al., *From Peones to Políticos: Class and Ethnicity in a South Texas Town 1960–1987* (Austin: University of Texas Press, 1988); Ignacio García, *United We Stand: The Rise and Fall of La Raza Unida Party* (Tucson: Mexican American Studies and Research Center, University of Arizona, 1989); M. García, *Mexican Americans;* Carl Allsup, *The American GI Forum: Origins and Evolutions* (Austin: University of Texas Press, 1982); and Muñoz, *Youth, Identity, Power.*

18. I will use the term "Latinos" and "Hispanics" interchangeably to represent the Spanish-origin population living in the United States.

19. Felix M. Padilla, *Latino Ethnic Consciousness: The Case of Mexican Americans and Puerto Ricans in Chicago* (Notre Dame: University of Notre Dame Press, 1985).

20. John A. García and Sylvia Pedraza-Bailey, "Hispanicity and the Phenomenon of Community of Interest and Culture among Latinos in the U.S." (paper presented at the annual meeting of the American Political Science Association, Washington, D.C., 1990).

21. See Mario Calvo and Steven Rosenstone, *Hispanic Political Participation* (San Antonio: Southwestern Voter Registration and Education Project Monograph Series, 1989); and Raymond Wolfinger and Steven Rosenstone, *Who Votes* (New Haven: Yale University Press, 1980).

22. John A. García, "The Voting Rights Act and Hispanic Political Representation," *Publius* 16 (1986): 49–66.

23. Tatcho Mindiola and Armando Gutiérrez, "Chicanos and Legislative Processes: Reality and Illusion in the Politics of Change," in *Latinos and the Political System,* ed. F. Chris García (Notre Dame: University of Notre Dame Press, 1988).

24. John A. García and Robert Brischetto, "Assessing the Need for Bilingual Elections: Spanish Language Maintenance in the Southwest," in *Bilingual Elections at Work in the Southwest,* ed. Robert Brischetto (San Antonio: Southwest Voter Registration and Education Project/Mexican American Legal Defense and Education Fund, 1982).

25. See Joel Garreau, *Nine Nations of North America* (New York: Avon Books, 1982).

26. See Rodolfo de la Garza, Angelo Falcón, F. Chris García, and John A. García, "The Effects of Ethnicity on Political Culture: A Comparison of Puerto Rican and Anglo Political Values," Harvard University Center for American Studies Occasional Papers 92-2 (August 1992); and Rodolfo de la Garza et al., "Mexican Immigrants, Mexican Americans and the American Political Culture," in *Immigration and Public Policy,* eds. Barry Edmondson and Jeffrey Passel (Washington, D.C.: Urban Institute Press, 1993).

27. Harry Pachon, "Hispanic Underrepresentation in the Federal Bureaucracy: The Missing Link in the Policy Process," in F. C. García, *Latinos and the Political System,* 306–13.

28. John A. García, "Where are They Moving and Why," *Agenda* 2 (1981): 14–17.

29. See Muñoz, *Youth, Identity, Power;* Gómez-Quiñones, *Chicano Politics;* and Christine M. Sierra, "Chicano Political Development: Historical Considerations," in *Chicano Studies: A Multidisciplinary Approach,* eds. Eugene García, Francisco Lomelí, and Isidro D. Ortiz (New York: Teachers College Press, Columbia University Press, 1984).

30. For an extended discussion, see Denise Segura, "Chicanos and Triple Oppression," in *Intersection of Class, Race and Gender,* eds. Theresa Córdova, N. Cantú, Gilbert Cárdenas, John R. García, and Christine Sierra (Austin: University of Texas Press, 1986); Denise Segura and Beatriz Pesquera, "Chicana Feminism: Their Political Context and Contemporary Expressions," in *Women: A Feminist Perspective,* 5th ed., ed. Jo Freeman (Mountain View, Calif.: Mayfield, 1993); and María Apodaca, "A Double-Edge Sword: Hispanics and Liberal Feminism," *Critica: A Journal of Critical Essays* 1 (1986): 76–114.

31. Acuña, *Occupied America.*

CHICANA/O ORGANIZATIONAL POLITICS

AND STRATEGIES IN THE ERA

OF RETRENCHMENT

Isidro D. Ortiz

In the early 1950s sociologist C. Wright Mills set forth a pessimistic, yet influential, thesis about the role of white-collar workers in the struggle for political change. The "rearguarders" thesis holds that white-collar workers will be dependent variables in the struggle for political change.[1] During the early 1980s several analysts and scholars suggested that the thesis did not apply to a segment of the white collar sector in the Chicano population, the leadership of national Chicano advocacy organizations. Analysts associated with the "English-only" movement, for example, alleged that the leadership had adopted and was spearheading the promotion of the strategy of separatism, whose pursuit threatened the national security of the United States.[2] In contrast, other scholars suggested that Mills's thesis might not apply because Reaganomics would serve to politicize the leadership of organizations reliant on federal funding and stimulate them to spearhead an oppositional anticorporate and anti-Reaganomics movement that could contribute to a fundamental realignment in American politics.[3] This suggestion was not illogical because Reaganomics, in part the intellectual brainchild of corporate-funded institutions such as the Heritage Foundation, was anticipated to have a significant effect on the type of federal funding that some of the organizations relied upon for operating programs. Indeed, as a result of the federal cutbacks under Reaganomics from 1981 to 1983, Chicano and other Latino organizations across the country lost over 4,000 staff positions, an average of 20 percent in each.[4]

However, as the 1980s came to a close and the 1990s began, several Chicano scholars implied that the "rearguarders" thesis applied to the Chicano organizational leadership. Rodolfo Acuña argued that the leaders, whom he characterized as the "new brokers," had opted to serve rather than to

challenge corporate interests during the 1980s.[5] In a similar vein, historians Mario T. García and Juan Gómez-Quiñones alleged that the organizational leadership chose to conform to the politically conservative developments of the 1980s rather than to challenge them.[6] Neither documented
the claims, however.

That the leadership of national Chicano advocacy organizations adopted
the strategy of separatism or assumed a leading role in an anticorporate movement is far from the case. Indeed, the leadership of four major
national advocacy organizations, the Mexican American Legal Defense and
Education Fund (MALDEF), the League of United Latin American Citizens (LULAC), the National Council of La Raza (NCLR), and the National
Network of Hispanic Women (NNHW), adopted the strategy of accommodation. They struggled to protect programmatic gains in the face of
Reaganomics; but at the same time, they adapted to the hostile political
environment and to Reaganomics by, among other things, turning to the
corporate sector for funding for organizational activities and creating coalitions with selected corporations. Their adaptations proved significantly
consequential for the organizations and corporations. The organizations
became amplifiers of corporate deeds, which facilitated corporate efforts
to "reshape the prevailing political and intellectual climate of opinion."[7]
Because of these unprecedented developments, it may be appropriate to
designate the 1980s as the decade of the corporation rather than as the
"Decade of the Hispanic," for the activity resulted in the resurgence of at
least one corporation, the Adolph Coors Brewing Company, which had
proclaimed that the decade would be the "Decade of the Hispanic."

ORGANIZATIONAL ACTIVISM:
A REARGUARD DEFENSE

In response to the Reagan Administration's initiatives, the organizations
mounted a rearguard defense of programs important to Chicanos and
other Latinos, as suggested by Mills. For example, MALDEF and NCLR articulated and mobilized opposition to Reagan initiatives and selectively
coalesced with other groups. Their efforts aimed to preserve programmatic gains important to Latinos (such as bilingual education programs in
local school districts), to prevent violations of civil rights and other forms
of discrimination against Latinos, and to enhance Latino participation in

the electoral process. From 1983 to 1984 MALDEF, in conjunction with the National Association of Bilingual Education, developed and implemented a two-year strategy to prevent passage of Reagan-administration-conceived amendments to the Bilingual Education Act. In coalition with groups such as the American Civil Liberties Union, MALDEF lobbied against Reagan administration proposals to limit access of poor people to courts as part of the reauthorization of the Legal Services Corporation Act. With fifty-four groups MALDEF, moreover, conducted a study and submitted a report to Congress documenting and criticizing the impact of the Reagan administration's 1983–1984 budget.[8]

The NCLR lobbied against the Reagan administration's proposed bilingual education measures; it also created the Civil Rights Network to provide community organizations with information on civil rights enforcement topics, in order to enhance the ability of Chicano and Latino groups to participate in governmental hearings and complaints processes as part of an effort to impede perceived Reagan administration relaxation of enforcement of civil rights legislation.[9] LULAC criticized the Reagan administration's cutbacks of federal education programs as it sought to preserve access to higher education for Chicanos and other Latinos. The cutbacks, LULAC's leadership declared, would foster elitism in higher education at the expense of Latinos and other minorities.[10] The NNHW, through its newsletter, drew attention to the federal budgetary cutbacks and urged its supporters to oppose attacks on programs, such as affirmative action, that benefited Latinos. In 1984, moreover, the NNHW advocated increased political participation by Latinas.[11] These organizational responses were not the only adaptations on the part of the organizations, however.

THE NEW STRATEGY

In 1981 over fifteen Chicano and other Latino organizations submitted grant proposals to 135 corporations among the Fortune 500.[12] Fifty-eight percent of the organizations experienced success in having one or more of the grant proposals funded.[13] The Mexican American Legal Defense and Education Fund, the National Council of La Raza, the League of United Latin American Citizens, and the National Network of Hispanic Women were among the most successful of the organizations.

MALDEF obtained approximately $460,000 from a range of corporations.

Large portions of the funding were unrestricted and made it possible for MALDEF to pay basic operating costs and launch new projects. MALDEF also obtained in-kind contributions: for example, in 1981 the organization received data on the results of Levi-Strauss Company's minority recruitment and employment efforts, to be used as part of MALDEF's testimony on affirmative action before the U.S. Congress. MALDEF's pamphlets were printed by Chevron, and it also received critiques on public relations matters from Anheuser-Busch. Moreover, corporate executives, such as Walter Haas, Jr., of Levi-Strauss, recruited "influential leaders" to appear at MALDEF's fund-raising dinners to which corporate peers were also invited, enabling MALDEF to recruit additional corporate support.[14]

In 1982, the NCLR obtained support for its technical assistance project, Project Raíces, from corporations such as Chevron, Coca-Cola, Citibank/Citicorp, Westinghouse, and Tenneco Oil. With the assistance provided by these corporations, the NCLR provided training and technical assistance to the staff of local Latino organizations.[15]

LULAC obtained grants of $5,000 each from Pabst Blue Ribbon and Digital Corporation.[16] LULAC also garnered a $20,000 grant from the Adolph Coors Company, to provide administrative assistance for its national office. In 1982 LULAC also secured support for its scholarship fund. By March 1982, thirteen corporations had contributed $86,000, with CBS as the largest contributor.[17]

In 1982 the NNHW initiated a successful search for annual corporate sponsors for its newsletter. Soon it secured corporate sponsorship for the publication from six corporations; and in 1983 it secured more funding for the newsletter from, among other corporations, Pacific Telephone Company, Wells Fargo Bank, and the Clorox company's foundation, the Clorox Foundation. In addition to funding, the NNHW secured in-kind services from corporations; for example, the NNHW obtained the use of the corporate boardroom of Wells Fargo Bank for a seminar on strategies for the achievement of representation by Latinos on corporate boards. In addition, in 1984 the NNHW secured funding and technical services of various kinds from its corporate sponsors.[18]

After obtaining corporate support, the organizations sought to establish sustained and formal exchange relationships with those same corporations. LULAC took the first steps to elaborate a relationship with the corporate sector. In 1981 LULAC's leadership invited corporations to sponsor events at the organization's annual convention. Moreover, in an attempt to create a forum for the discussion of the desired partnerships, at the 1981 convention, officials of LULAC's National Educational Services organized a breakfast and luncheon with the theme, "Salute to Corporate America toward the Unrealized Hispanic Dream." [19]

To enhance its ability to form the partnerships, LULAC's leadership emphasized the economic advantages to corporations of recognizing Hispanics and collaborating with LULAC. For example, in an editorial after the 1982 Super Bowl, the editor of the organization's magazine declared that advertising firms were "fumbling the ball" when it came to the Hispanic market by failing to incorporate Hispanics into the commercials of clients, such as those who paid for television commercials during the Super Bowl. [20]

The LULAC national president in 1982, Tony Bonilla, advocated Hispanic-corporate cooperation as one answer to the federal budgetary cutbacks in education. Speaking at the Higher Education Conference at Northern Illinois University, Bonilla declared that President Reagan's education policies would foster elitism in higher education at the expense of Hispanics and other minorities. Hispanic-corporate cooperation could mitigate such a development and would occur if corporations recognized that Hispanic buying power had surpassed $50 billion and was rising. He called upon corporations to develop internship programs to train Hispanics in areas traditionally closed to them. [21]

In March 1982, LULAC formally linked itself to the corporate sector through its LULAC National Educational Service Center, to which three corporate officials were appointed as board members. After they assumed office, the editor of LULAC's magazine announced the new working relationship, declaring, "We have now brought corporate America and Hispanic America to the decision-making table." [22]

During the first months of 1982, Bonilla traveled across the country for the purpose of meeting with the presidents and executive officers of major corporations. His meetings with these officials involved "selling the growth of Hispanics as consumers and LULAC as an organization dedicated to advancing the causes of social justice of the underprivileged." The efforts concluded with the receipt of $96,500 in contributions from corporations at the LULAC national convention on 2 July. Two days before the official opening of the convention, Bonilla again called for the establishment of a "full partnership" between LULAC and "Corporate America." In calling for the partnership he reminded corporations of the advantages of such a relationship.

The envisioned partnership was realized at the convention during a luncheon sponsored by the Adolph Coors Company. Billed as "Hispanics and Corporate America: Investing in the Future," the luncheon was the site for the receipt of the contributions from an array of corporations. Constituting the largest contributions made on a single occasion from the private sector in the organization's fifty-three year history, the funding, as mentioned above, was to be utilized to help LULAC establish a national office in Washington.[23]

LULAC's formation of a partnership with the corporate sector was succeeded several months later by the First Corporate/Hispanic Partnership Summit in San Francisco on 23 October 1982. Sponsored by the Forum of National Hispanic Organizations and the independent sector, this day-long conference gave the leadership of major national Latino organizations and corporate officials (a total of approximately 125 persons) an opportunity to meet.[24]

Several months after the summit, the president of the NCLR, Raúl Yzaguirre, promoted the creation of the "new partnerships" between Latinos and corporations at the fifth annual affiliates conference of the NCLR. The private sector, he noted in his annual speech to the affiliates, was "realizing the importance of Latinos." Private-sector executives believed that the private sector had an obligation to offset the federal cutbacks. Moreover, the corporate sector had demonstrated a willingness to provide support to Latino organizations; the participation of the corporate sector in the summit meeting in San Francisco was evidence of such a willingness. The corporate sector and Latinos had a "lot to gain" if a "partnership" between them succeeded. Therefore, Latinos should work to make the partnership succeed, he concluded.[25]

Shortly thereafter, the NCLR, under Yzaguirre's direction, took a formal step to create the partnerships. The NCLR formed a Corporate Advisory Council (CAC) composed of top-level officials of selected corporations, whose mission was to advise and assist NCLR in obtaining foundation and corporate funding and increased access to financing for NCLR-assisted projects. The CAC was also to serve as a source of technical consultation on the improvement of NCLR operations, projects and products, such as its publications.[26]

In the wake of NCLR's action, LULAC took a step aimed at enhancing its ability to establish partnerships. It coalesced with organizations in the African American community that had experience in negotiating with corporations. In March 1983, its president, Tony Bonilla, traveled to Atlanta. At a press conference there, in conjunction with the Reverend Joseph Lowery of the Southern Christian Leadership Conference and with Coretta Scott King, Bonilla announced the intent to build a Hispanic-Black coalition. During the LULAC national executive board meeting in Atlanta, he and the Reverend Jesse Jackson, founder of People United to Save Humanity (PUSH), announced the formation of just such a Hispanic-Black coalition. The coalition would monitor the nation's corporations to achieve equity with whites in the free enterprise system and would seek to negotiate contracts and services for minority firms, franchises for minorities, better employment representation, especially in middle- and high-management positions, and improved representation in the media.[27]

Shortly after the announcements, Bonilla and the Reverend Jackson initiated discussions with the Southland Corporation, the owners of the 7-Eleven chain of convenience stores, and Chief Auto Parts stores. On 30 July 1983, Bonilla, acting on behalf of LULAC and the National Hispanic Leadership Conference and in conjunction with the leaders of Operation PUSH, signed a five-year trade agreement with the Southland Corporation. After the signing of the agreement, Bonilla announced the new partnership in an article praising Southland Corporation, and declaring that the agreement was historically significant.[28] With this agreement in hand, LULAC, the National Hispanic Leadership Conference, and Operation PUSH began successful negotiations on a second accord. On 1 June 1984, they signed a similar trade pact with the Miller Brewing Company.[29]

As LULAC formalized its partnership, the NCLR acted to capitalize on and augment its corporate relationships. In 1984 the NCLR and its CAC jointly planned NCLR's seventh annual conference, whose theme was "Hispanic Leadership: Impact, Influence, and Involvement." As planned by the NCLR and the CAC, the conference was intended to provide a "showcase for the concerns and accomplishments of NCLR and its network of Hispanic community-based organizations and its corporate and public sponsors." NCLR's president promoted the conference as "a perfect opportunity to bring together and highlight Hispanic leaders, both for the Hispanic community and the nation, and to present them to corporate leaders.

This stimulates the sharing of ideas and information, and more productive cooperation within the community and potential private-sector funding sources."[30] As a result of the efforts of NCLR and CAC, over thirty-five companies agreed to participate through financial contributions, exhibit booths, and sponsorship of special events in the conference. Moreover, the NCLR obtained financial support for the conference from Sears, Roebuck and Company, the Nestle Company, Coca-Cola, and General Motors Corporation.[31]

On 29 October 1984, the leadership of NCLR and five other national Latino organizations built upon the steps taken in the preceding two years. In Los Angeles the leadership of the organizations and the Adolph Coors Company signed a five-year agreement. Under the terms of the agreement the Coors Company agreed, among other things, to hire more Latinos and to donate a minimum of $2.5 million to Chicano and other Latino organizations between 1985 and 1990, provided that sales of its products increased among Latinos. The agreement was signed by the leadership of NCLR, National Image, United States Hispanic Chamber of Commerce, American GI Forum, National Puerto Rican Coalition, and the Cuban National Planning Council. In accordance with the agreement, the leadership of the organizations and Coors formed a committee to monitor the progress of the company's commitment by meeting on a quarterly basis in 1985 and semiannually every year thereafter.[32]

NNHW's founder, Sylvia Castillo, originated the organization as a "link" between Latinos and the corporate sector. Specifically, its role was to act as "a broker between the talented Hispanic women and the needs of corporate America."[33] The sponsorship of conferences and seminars, which brought together Latinos and representatives of the corporate sector, served as the principal mechanism by which the NNHW fulfilled the broker role.

In the fall of 1984 the NNHW organized a conference for Latina businesswomen and corporate officials, with the theme "An Investment in America's Future." The organization proposed to bring together 200 mid- to senior-level Hispanic women from across the country "to participate in a variety of roundtable discussions covering such topics as corporate appointments, first time entrepreneurship and career development." The NNHW also sponsored a symposium "to bring together Hispanic scientists with leaders from industry, education and government."[34]

Three years later the NNHW elaborated the broker role through the publication of its newsletter *Intercambios Femeniles* in magazine format. Such a format was adopted in order to enable the NNHW "to offer recruitment advertising and corporate image advertising opportunities" to the NNHW's "corporate sponsors' patrons." Corporations could "now communicate their opportunities" to NNHW "directly."[35] The NNHW, in turn, would communicate them to Latinas.

THE STRATEGIC RESPONSE: AN EXPLANATION

Why did the organizations opt to pursue the strategy of accommodation? An answer to this question can be provided by relying upon the framework developed by Jo Freeman in 1979 for the analysis of social movement organizational decision making.[36] According to Freeman, one major reason why this strategy was chosen is that the organizations possessed the expertise and experience necessary to make the strategy work. This experience was gained over a period of time in the organizations' development units. For example, MALDEF's development and public relations department had been and remained the most sophisticated and developed of all Latino organizations. It was directed by a vice president for development and was staffed by six professionals whose primary responsibility was the development and implementation of fund-raising strategies as well as public relations strategies conducive to the enhancement of MALDEF's image and visibility.

A second reason was that the organizations lacked personal funding bases sufficient to sustain their operations. MALDEF's funding problems are typical: since 1973 the organization had unsuccessfully pursued the creation of such a base; and in the 1980s, it found itself having to continue to seek funding from foundations and corporations. The budgetary cutbacks initiated by the Reagan administration worsened MALDEF's fiscal conditions and increased its need for funds by depriving all the organizations of critical resources. In 1981, as a result of the cutbacks, MALDEF lost $600,000 in federal funds, 20 percent of its 1981–1982 budget. Because of the loss of funds, MALDEF's leadership had to undertake a "painful staff reduction" that concluded in the elimination of about one-fourth of the staff positions in 1982–1983. The reductions disrupted MALDEF's program activities in the areas of urban crime prevention, equal employment, and immigration.[37]

The budgetary cutbacks evoked pessimism within the ranks about the possibility of regaining federal funding. Among Latino organizations only 11 percent of the survivors of the budgetary reductions thought they would regain federal funding in the succeeding two years. By 1983, 56 percent had concluded that the federal government would not be a viable source of funding for their operations in the future.[38]

Despite the lack of resources sufficient to sustain the organization, the leadership of the organizations was nevertheless committed to the integration of Latinos into American life. This pragmatic orientation of the leadership was reflected in LULAC's admonition to its members at the beginning of the 1980s: "We Hispanics have got to start practicing pragmatic politics."[39]

The leadership had never seriously regarded separatism as a possible option. It is not too inaccurate to say that they had never even been inclined to subscribe to the idea of separatism. As a group, the leadership may be best described as American liberals whose worldview does not include a scenario of a separate Latino society or state. They headed organizations that have deep roots in American liberalism. LULAC, for example, was created by the generation of political activists now known as the Mexican American Generation, a generation that subscribed to liberal pragmatism. The founders and the initial leadership of MALDEF and NCLR came from the ranks of LULAC.[40] The NNHW's ideological roots lay in the variety of feminist theory known as liberal feminism.

Additionally, the organizations did not have a membership base from which to generate funding to compensate for the federal budgetary cutbacks. They lacked this base, in large part, because at least two of them, MALDEF and NCLR, were created as social movement organizations.[41] Such organizations do not rely on members for the performance of their tasks or for their support. They consist largely of professionals who carry out the organization's activities and rely upon contributions for the resources necessary to maintain the organization.[42]

Lastly, the organizational leadership was highly optimistic that corporations would respond to the utilization of the corporate grantsmanship and articulation strategy. The roots of this optimism lay in part in the findings of a survey carried out by the Council of Foundations in the early 1980s. The study sought to determine the "giving attitudes" of the chief executive officers of major corporations. The results of the study were deemed to be "very promising" by the leadership of the Latino organizations, in particular the president of NCLR. The leadership recognized that there was no guarantee that Latinos would "receive a fair share" of corporate support; However, they were optimistic that the potential could become a reality through work and cooperation with the private sector.[43]

The optimism was also rooted in a perception that the orientation of corporations toward Chicanos and other Latinos was undergoing change in the 1980s. As a former high officer of MALDEF noted in 1984, "Corporations are changing themselves. They are also undergoing change. They are becoming more sensitive to the issues presented by the Hispanic community. They are trying to improve their standing within the community. They are making very positive efforts in their minority representation at all levels. Those kinds of corporations really are, in essence, investing in themselves—which is good. Part of that investment is to the Hispanic community."[44]

THE CONSEQUENCES OF ACCOMMODATION: TRANSFORMATION OF ORGANIZATIONS

The late 1970s and 1980s witnessed "the resurgence of corporate political power in the United States," according to Vogel.[45] The resurgence was, in large part, a function of the efforts of business "to increase the political effectiveness and reshape the political and institutional climate of opinion" toward business. To achieve the latter, corporations adopted a variety of strategies. Among other things, corporate executives became more visible in order to improve the public image of business; corporations also launched extensive advocacy advertising campaigns to appeal to the public. Through philanthropy, they sponsored programmatic initiatives, research, and projects ranging from programs on the public broadcasting system to endowed chairs on campuses to funding of scholarships favorable to business.[46]

Francis Fox Piven and Richard Cloward have noted that "the occasion of giving vitally needed assistance can easily become the occasion of inculcating the work ethic . . . of enforcing work itself, for those who resist risk the withdrawal of that assistance."[47] In pursuing corporate support and partnerships, the organizations created an opportunity for corporations to expect and demand that Latino organizations engage in activities of "amplification" (the articulation within the minority community of the good will and material achievements of the corporation).[48] Amplification may occur in written form in organizational publications or at organizational events, such as annual conferences, fund-raisers, and banquets. Through the performance of amplification, Latino advocacy organizations became participants in the corporate effort to reshape the climate of opinion toward business.

The performance of amplification by the organizations occurred at a time when strong opposition to "cowboy capitalism" and free-market policies existed among minorities, in particular among Chicanos in the Southwest, as Dolbeare noted in the early 1980s.[49] In addition, Chicano and other Latino elites, in particular, viewed corporations as largely unresponsive to the Chicano population. In a survey conducted by *Hispanic Business* magazine, 86 percent of Latino elites surveyed rated corporations as fair or poor in their responsiveness to the Latino community.[50] Corporations indeed needed to change Latino community opinions toward business in order to gain their favor.

The expectation that the organizations perform amplification was evident in the statement of an official of one of the brewing companies. Shortly after the initiation of corporate relief giving, he declared:

> It's understood that if I'm making a major contribution at a banquet, you will ask me to say a few words. It's like routine now, that is, "It's my pleasure to present $5,000 for a scholarship." Latino organizational leadership is becoming very professional. They know they have to stroke their sponsors.
>
> It's nice when you get it. In fact, the wiser organizations will publish our contributions. When you see that sort of thank you note, I circulate it because it means that we are appreciated. I may not remember if I don't receive this kind of thank you. But I'll remember when the organization approaches again for contributions. If I can't remember any follow-up to our contributions, like a thank you note in our files or some sort of publicity, then it will probably influence me later on.[51]

The demand that the organizations perform amplification was spelled out in the agreement between Coors and the six organizations. In return for Coors's assistance, the organizations had to agree to the following provision: "Each member of the Coalition agrees to cooperate with Coors, including appointing an organization to address ongoing issues and potential political and social difficulties that may occur in the national scene regarding Coors and its products over the life of the agreement."[52] In addition, the organizations were to hold press conferences announcing the signing of the agreement and the termination of the boycott (initiated in the late 1970s to protest alleged discriminatory hiring practices of the Adolph Coors Company).

From 1982 onward, the organizations fulfilled the expectation and demand for amplification. After garnering corporate support, MALDEF, for example, amplified corporate endeavors in its annual reports, newsletters, and events. In its 1981, 1982, and 1984 annual reports, it performed the amplification function through the listing of its corporate supporters for the preceding program year. In its newsletter, *MALDEF,* the organization amplified corporate endeavors as early as 1982 through articles specifying corporate deeds on behalf of MALDEF and Latinos and through publication of photographs of one or more corporate officials involved in activities such as providing support to MALDEF or being honored for the corporation's assistance. In an article entitled "Some Corporate Friends," *MALDEF* declared, "Do corporations owe it to society to pursue anything other than the almighty dollar? Some companies say no. But a growing number believe it's not only good citizenship, but also good business to help minority communities. That turn of mind often means useful advice, lively printed work, cooperative allies, and dependable financial support for MALDEF's work."[53] The article then proceeded to delineate the level of corporate support received by MALDEF, the nature of the support, and the corporations whose support had been exceptional. Lastly, it detailed the diversity of support and noted that each contribution was helpful and encouraging to MALDEF and facilitated organization efforts on behalf of Chicanos and other Latinos.

In another article entitled "Anheuser-Busch Grant Spurs Leadership, Citizenship," MALDEF publicized the receipt of a grant from Anheuser-Busch for the operation of leadership development and citizenship programs. It proclaimed "advancement for Hispanics nationwide through three innovative programs will be the product of a major $200,000 grant to MALDEF from Anheuser-Busch, Inc."[54] *MALDEF* also reported the results and proceedings of a fund-raising dinner and graphically documented acknowledgments and the amplification of corporate support.

The NCLR also amplified corporate efforts in a similar manner; for example, in 1984, at its National Conference Awards Banquet, the organization honored John McNulty, vice president for public relations of General Motors Corporation, by awarding him its President Award for contributions to the philosophy, goals, and mission of the NCLR. According to NCLR's president, McNulty had "played a key role in improving NCLR visibility in the corporate sector." He was deserving of the award because "he had demonstrated an understanding concern and willingness to take action in support of Hispanics and Hispanic issues."[55]

In addition, in a page of its convention program formally acknowledging its appreciation of corporate support, the NCLR listed its corporate supporters. It encouraged members of the NCLR to review the list and express their appreciation to the representatives of the corporations who were attending the conference. It also expressed its hope that when members of the NCLR were purchasing goods or services, they would "remember— and buy from—these friends of the Council."[56]

LULAC preceded its amplification efforts by underscoring the logic and legitimacy of profit-making activities. Its magazine, *LULAC,* published an article offering a rationale for entry into business: "There Is Only One Reason to Go into Business: To Make a Profit." The article quoted Robert J. Gans, president of Gans Ink and Supply Company in Los Angeles, who declared, "Profits are patriotic."[57] In her capacity as LULAC's national director of economic development, Linda Alvarado, in conjunction with Dr. Alicia Cuarón, LULAC national director of Leadership and Educational Development, organized a conference to enhance Hispanic participation in the free enterprise system.[58]

LULAC also highlighted the views of William Coors, chairman of the board of Adolph Coors Company, by reporting in an article in its magazine parts of his speech to a group of Latino businessman. Coors believed, *LULAC* reported, that the United States had "lost sight of the fundamental law of productivity" on its way to success. As a result, "Americans were heavily paying financially for the mistake. But the financial price was exceeded by the loss of freedom." If Americans wanted "to continue to enjoy their freedom," they "had to increase their productivity." Coors offered two suggestions, "getting the government off the backs of the American people" and balancing the federal budget. After delineating the specific details of these suggestions, *LULAC* also noted that Coors had acknowledged that the federal budget cuts had been felt by most Americans. However, the cuts were necessary because the United States could not afford previous levels of funding. Lastly, it noted that Coors realized that free enterprise capitalism was controversial in some circles and was regarded by some as the worst economic system in the world. However, Coors regarded it as "the best" and asked rhetorically what its critics would replace it with if it were "dumped."[59]

At the tenth-anniversary banquet of the its National Education Service Center in February 1982, LULAC awarded Robert W. Brocksbank, manager of College Relations and Recruitment with Mobil Oil Corporation, its first Annual Trustee of Education Award. The award recognized individuals who had made "outstanding contributions to the betterment of American education." Brocksbank was cited for his contributions in helping Hispanic students.[60]

In the September 1982 issue of its magazine, LULAC also amplified the contribution made by Sears, Roebuck to the achievement of LULAC's goal of establishing a partnership. It published a photograph of its president, Tony Bonilla, receiving a check from representatives of Sears during the LULAC annual convention. The caption read as follows: "True corporate-Hispanic partnership is shared between [LULAC and] officials of Sears, who presented a check for $25,000 to Tony Bonilla, LULAC National President, during the League's annual convention. It was the second of three $25,000 contributions made by Sears."[61]

The NNHW's performance of amplification began in 1982. *Intercambios Femeniles,* the organization's newsletter, served as the principal mechanism for the performance of the function. In 1982 the NNHW initiated its regular listing of corporate sponsors and revealed the sponsorship of the organization's newsletter by Atlantic Richfield Corporation, Adolph Coors Brewing Company, Mervyn's, Pacific Telephone Company, Wells Fargo Bank, and Anheuser-Busch. Several months later, in the spring of 1983 issue of the newsletter, the NNHW relisted its corporate sponsors and attributed the publication of the newsletter issue to the benevolence of a different set of corporations and corporate officials.[62] In its 1983 spring/summer issue of *Intercambios Femeniles,* the NNHW specifically amplified on behalf of Wells Fargo Bank by placing a picture of members of the Network "enjoying the corporate boardroom of the Wells Fargo Bank penthouse" while attending a seminar on strategies for the achievement of representation by Latinos on corporate boards. One year later the NNHW again attributed the

existence of the newsletter to corporate sponsorship. The amplification occurred in an editorial urging support of the newsletter.[63] In the succeeding
issue NNHW published a picture of an Anheuser-Busch official presenting
a check to the chair of NNHW for the organization's activities.

The Legitimation of Conservative Corporations

In establishing amplification as a condition for the receipt of assistance,
some of the corporations anticipated that amplification would enhance
their support among Latinos. The expectation was fulfilled for the Coors
Company. Before the signing of the agreement between Coors and the six
organizations, the company had lost a significant portion of the beer market. The loss was, in large part, due to a boycott against the brewery by
Chicano organizations. The boycott was fueled by the Coors family's advocacy of "cowboy capitalism" and Reaganomics. In the aftermath of the amplification by the organizations, Coors's sales increased among Latinos. In
1984 Chicanos and other Latinos accounted for 5 percent of Coors business
and by the end of 1985, 9 percent. Latino sales increased from $56.6 million
in 1984 to $115 million in 1985, an increase of more than $59 million.[64]

The Capacity to Serve Corporate Interests: An Explanation

The pursuit of the strategy of accommodation was not universally ap-
plauded. The action met with criticism from some Chicano political activists. Nevertheless, the organizations were able to pursue the strategy without significant interference. However, we could ask why the organizations
were able to pursue a strategy that served corporate interests as much as
their own. The question can be answered by following the analytical lead
offered by Ira Katznelson, who suggests that the capacity of a group, at
any point in time, is best understood as a function of the group's resources
and of political factors, such as (1) the strength of alternative ideologies,
(2) the type of power relationships existing between a group and authorities, and (3) the heritage of previous decisions.[65]

One reason why the Latino organizations were able to pursue the
strategy was that they enjoyed visibility and legitimacy as advocates for
and leaders of Chicanos and other Latinos. Coca-Cola documented their
prominence in a visibility poll conducted as part of a large study designed
to ascertain Chicano and other Latino attitudes and priorities.[66] The legitimacy, achieved through the organizations' advocacy activities, served to

immunize them from the criticism and enhanced their maneuverability. By the early 1980s MALDEF, for example, had broadened its role as a representative of Hispanic interests; it had expanded its litigation and advocacy work to include Latinos other than Mexican Americans; and it had increasingly advocated for the rights of Latino citizens and noncitizens, legal residents, and undocumented immigrants. Through litigation, MALDEF had successfully defended the educational rights of children of undocumented immigrants; moreover, it had challenged workplace raids by the Immigration and Nationalization Service. In addition it supported labor law protection for undocumented workers and equitable treatment for Central American immigrants seeking political asylum in the United States.[67] Because of these activities it had achieved credibility, visibility, and stature that afforded it the autonomy to act according to its definition of what was in the best interests of Chicanos and other Latinos.

If Chicanos and other Latinos had possessed significant access to the federal government or the ability to control their own destiny, the pursuit of accommodation strategy could have been difficult, if not impossible. However, they did not possess either during the 1980s. The executive branch of the government, as Gómez-Quiñones has noted, was "not only inaccessible, it was generally negative toward the basic social and economic needs of the [Mexican] community, and it undertook specific negative actions concerning immigration and labor."[68] Chicano and other Latino links to Congress were primarily through the Hispanic Congressional Caucus. Throughout the 1980s the caucus lacked cohesiveness, which weakened its effectiveness; and in any case, numerically Chicano and other Latino congressmen were a tiny minority, accounting for only 2.8 percent of all congressmen.

As has been documented, prior to the 1980s Chicanos and other Latinos had made socioeconomic and political advances. Nevertheless, their needs remained unmet and the groups continued to be socioeconomically disadvantaged. As political scientist F. Chris García noted at the conclusion of the 1980s, Chicanos and other Latinos were in "a depressed labor position [that] was reflected in income statistics."[69] Nationally, in short, Chicanos and other Latinos faced what political scientist Roberto Villareal has called the "cruel reality that they remained unable to control their political destiny."[70] The efforts to empower the groups were plagued by a lack of "strong entrenched organizations that possessed large, stable pools of resources." In many communities effective locally based organizations existed to provide service to their communities. Nationally, however, Chicanos and other Latinos "were not effectively organized in many critical areas such as health, education, fair housing, and many other areas addressing basic human needs."[71]

In the presence of a vigorous anticapitalist ideological movement, the pursuit of the strategy may have been difficult. Through the 1980s such an ideological counterweight was absent among Chicanos and other Latinos, as one historian noted at the conclusion of the 1980s.[72] Moreover, the nationalist organizations that critiqued the pursuit of the corporate grantsmanship and partnership strategy lacked the resources sufficient to impede its pursuit. For example, in San Diego, La Unión del Barrio conducted effective consciousness-raising activities against the termination of the boycott and the formation of the partnership with Coors. However, it did not have the funding or personnel to wage a national-level campaign against the pursuit of the strategy.

At the same time, the ascendancy of the radical right served to increase the need for a pragmatic approach but left few places where Latino organizations could find support. As corporations demonstrated a willingness to offer assistance, the resort to corporate support seemed to become logical, if not imperative, to the organizations.

Prior to the 1980s Chicanos and other Latinos, in conjunction with other groups, had struggled successfully for the expansion of a social welfare economy in the United States. Latino organizations were also successful in having concrete segments of their political agenda, in particular the protection of voting rights and bilingual education, endorsed by the courts and legislative bodies. In the early 1980s, they continued to make demands, which together with their achievements provoked a backlash that gained momentum during the decade. From this backlash flowed restrictive policy prescriptions that diminished the prospects that the public sector would be a source of resources to address the needs of the community; it also led some Chicanos and other Latinos to conclude that it was incumbent upon these groups to adopt the strategy of accommodation. The sentiment is captured by F. Chris García who noted that

tactics that were used successfully in the late 1960s and early 1970s probably would bring forth negative reactions from the majority culture in the 1980s rather than produce sympathetic understanding and support. The economic situation has become a tight one with little or no slack to afford majority culture people the luxury of supporting causes which do not serve their own immediate interests. Competition, no cooperation, egocentrism rather than social concern, ethnocentrism rather than toleration of diversity seem to be descriptive of the 1980s. In light of this situation, it seems incumbent for Latinos to use more accommodative and conventional tactics in pursuing their political, social, and economic goals.[73]

CONCLUSION

In summary, during the 1980s the "rearguarders" thesis applied to the leadership of national Latino advocacy organizations. Contrary to the hopes and expectations of analysts such as Piven and Cloward and the claims of advocates of "English-only," the elites eschewed the leadership of an anticorporate oppositional or separatist movement. Instead, they accommodated. As predicted by Mills's thesis, they followed the class that was triumphant during the 1980s; specifically, they garnered resources and formed mutually supportive relationships with corporations, enabling these institutions to make inroads during the "Decade of the Hispanic."

NOTES

1. C. Wright Mills, *White Collar: The American Middle Classes* (New York: Oxford University Press, 1951).
2. See, for example, Rusty E. Butler, *On Creating an Hispanic America* (Washington, D.C.: Council on Inter American Security, 1985).
3. See, for example, Francis Fox Piven and Richard Cloward, *The New Class War: Reagan's Attack on the Welfare State and Its Consequences* (New York: Pantheon, 1992).
4. Kurt Whisler, "How Hispanic Organizations Have Fared with the Cutbacks: A Survey," *Caminos* 3 (1983): 54–55.
5. Rodolfo Acuña, *Occupied America: A History of Chicanos* (New York: Harper and Row, 1989).
6. Mario T. García, *Mexican Americans: Leadership, Ideology, and Identity* (New Haven: Yale University Press, 1989): 301; Juan Gómez-Quiñones, *Chicano Politics: Reality and Promise, 1940–1990* (Albuquerque: University of New Mexico, 1990): 181.
7. David Vogel, *Fluctuating Fortunes: The Political Power of Business in America* (New York: Basic Books, 1989), 11.

8. Joaquín Avila, *Report to the MALDEF Board of Directors* (San Francisco: Mexican American Legal Defense and Education Fund, 1983); Mexican American Legal Defense and Education Fund, "Federal Budget Unfair to Latinos," *MALDEF* 12 (1982): 2.

9. "Seventh Annual NCLR Conference to Focus on Hispanic Leadership," *El Noticiero* 3 (1984): 1–3.

10. "Is It Only for the Elitist?" *Latino and LULAC* 53 (1982): 27–28.

11. Margarita Prieto, "Editor's Note," *Intercambios Femeniles* 2 (1984): 2.

12. "Corporate Money for Organizations . . . Who Gives It? . . . Where Does It Go?" *Nuestro* 6 (1982): 27–31.

13. Whisler, "Hispanic Organizations Cutbacks."

14. "Some Corporate Friends," *MALDEF* 12 (1982): 2.

15. National Council of La Raza, "Council Appreciates Corporate Assistance," 7th annual conference program, Washington, D.C., 1984.

16. "Digital, Pabst Blue Ribbon Make League Donations," *Latino and LULAC* 52 (1981): 23.

17. "1982 Scholarship Fund Post Half-Way Mark," *Latino and LULAC* 53 (1982): 28.

18. The receipt of the support is delineated throughout the issues of the organization's newsletter *Intercambios Femeniles* for 1982, 1983, 1984.

19. "Superbowl Losers?" *Latino and LULAC* 53 (1982): 1.

20. Ibid.

21. "Is It Only for the Elitist?"

22. "Corporate Education Team," *Latino and LULAC* 53 (1982): 17.

23. "Hispanic-Conference Partnership," *Latino* 53 (1982): 19.

24. Herman Gallegos, "Making a Dent in the Corporate Sector," *Nuestro* 6 (1982): 49–51.

25. "Hispanics and the Private Sector: New Partnerships," *Caminos* (1983): 42–43.

26. "Partnership between Corporate Leaders and the Council," *El Noticiero* 6, no. 1 (1987): 1.

27. "Hands of Unity," *Latino* 54, no. 3 (1983): 6.

28. "7-Eleven Does It Right," *Latino* 54, no. 5 (1983): 18–19.

29. Stephen Beale, "Friendly Persuasion: Pacts and Covenants," *Hispanic Business* 9, no. 2 (1987): 20–24.

30. "Seventh Annual NCLR Conference."

31. Ibid.

32. Tomás Díaz, "Coors and Hispanics: A New Business Partnership," *Hispanic Business Review* (1985): 16–21.

33. Julia K. Kilgore, "Of Singular Vision," *Hispanic Business* 10 (1988): 24.

34. Sylvia Castillo, "President's Message to the Network," *Intercambios Femeniles* 2 (1984): 19.

35. Virginia García, "From the Editor: A Step Forward," *Intercambios Femeniles* 2 (1987): 4.

36. "Resource Mobilization and Strategy: A Model for Analyzing Social Movement Organization Actions," in *The Dynamics of Social Movements,* eds. John D. Zald and Mayer N. McCarthy (Cambridge, Mass.: Winthrop Publications, 1979).

37. For a discussion of these effects, see Vilma Martínez, *Report to the MALDEF Board of Directors* (San Francisco: Mexican American Legal Defense and Education Fund, 1981); and Avila, *Report to MALDEF Board.*

38. Whisler, "Hispanic Organizations Cutbacks," 54.

39. Quoted in Charlie Ericksen, "Hispanics Have to Practice Pragmatic Politics in the '80s." *LULAC* 51 (1980): 26.

40. Carl Allsup, *The American GI Forum* (Austin: University of Texas Press, 1982).

41. Christine M. Sierra, "The Political Transformation of a Minority Organization" (Ph.D. diss., Stanford University, 1983).

42. John D. McCarthy and Mayer N. Zald, *The Trend of Social Movements in America* (Morristown, N.J.: General Learning Press, 1973).

43. "Hispanics and the Private Sector," *Caminos* 2 (1983): 42–43.

44. Joaquín Avila, interview by A. Candelaria, Los Angeles, Calif., 22 March 1984.

45. Vogel, "Fluctuating Fortunes," 213.

46. Ibid.

47. *Regulating the Poor: The Functions of Public Welfare* (New York: Random House, 1971): 22.

48. Karen Orren, "Corporate Power and the Slums: Is Big Business a Paper Tiger?" in *Theoretical Perspectives on Urban Politics,* eds. Willis D. Hawley et al. (Englewood Cliffs: Prentice Hall, 1976), 58.

49. Kenneth Dolbeare, *Democracy At Risk* (Chatham, N.J.: Chatham House, 1984), 185.

50. "100 Influentials and Their Assessment of the Critical Issues," *Hispanic Business* 9 (1987): 20–21.

51. Anheuser-Busch official, interview by Marguerite Marín, Los Angeles, Calif., 22 March 1984.

52. "Three Agreements Summarized," *Hispanic Business* 6 (1984): 22.

53. Mexican American Legal Defense and Education Fund, "Some Corporate Friends," *MALDEF* 12 (1982): 8.

54. Mexican American Legal Defense and Education Fund, "Anheuser-Busch Spurs Leadership, Citizenship," *MALDEF* 12 (1982): 1.

55. National Council of La Raza, "GM's John McNulty, Cong. García among Those to Be Honored at 1984 National Conference," *El Noticiero* 3 (1984): 1–2.

56. National Council of La Raza, "Council Appreciates Corporate Assistance."

57. "There Is Only One Reason to Go into Business," *LULAC* 52 (1982): 23.

58. "Workers or Owners," *Latino and LULAC* 53 (1982): 16.

59. "The Law of Productivity," *Latino and LULAC* 53 (1982): 18.

60. "Brocksbank, Bonilla Are Winners of LNESC Award," *Latino* 53:8 (1982): 26.

61. "Hispanic-Corporate Partnership."

62. "Credits," *Intercambios Femeniles* 1 (1982): 2.

63. Sylvia Castillo, "Hispanic Women's Conference to Focus on Executive Level Opportunities," *Intercambios Femeniles* 2 (1984): 22.

64. Janet Simons, "Coors Turns Boycotters into Buyers," *Advertising Age* 57, no. 2 (February 1986): 42–47; and, "Coors Comes Bubbling Back," *Fortune* (1986): 113.

65. Ira Katznelson, *Black Men, White Cities* (New York: Oxford University Press, 1973).

66. "Coca-Cola USA Hispanic Leadership Survey, 1984," (Atlanta: Coca-Cola USA, 1984).

67. Christine M. Sierra, "Latino Organizational Strategies on Immigration Reform: Success and Limits in Public Policy making," in *Latinos and Political Coalitions: Political Empower-*

ment for the 1990s, eds. Robert E. Villareal and Norma G. Hernánez (New York: Green-wood Press, 1991), 61–80.

68. Juan Gómez-Quiñones, *Chicano Politics: Illusion and Reality, 1945–1980* (Albuquerque: University of New Mexico Press, 1990), 185.

69. F. Chris García, "Feedback: Outcomes and Reactions," in *Latinos in the Political System,* ed. F. Chris García (Notre Dame: University of Notre Dame Press, 1989), 463.

70. Roberto Villareal and Norma G. Hernández, "Coalitional Politics as a Strategy for Latino Empowerment: A Developmental Approach," in Villareal and Hernández, *Latinos and Political Coalitions,* 185–92.

71. Raúl Yzaguirre, "Keys to Hispanic Empowerment," in Villareal and Hernández, *Latinos and Political Coalitions,* 178–84.

72. Gómez-Quiñones, *Chicano Politics: Illusion and Reality,* 197.

73. F. Chris García, conclusion to García, *Latinos in Political System,* 498.

RETURN TO AZTLÁN : MEXICO'S POLICIES

TOWARD CHICANAS/OS

María Rosa García-Acevedo

Looking toward the new millennium, the Chicano community is faced with a challenge that goes beyond the U.S. border: the sustainment of links with its homeland, Mexico.[1] This problematic relationship, which began in the mid-nineteenth century with the Treaty of Guadalupe Hidalgo, has had a fascinating but complex evolution. Prior to the advent of the Chicano Movement, few formal ties existed between Mexico and the Chicano community. Chicanos had been too preoccupied with national questions such as civil rights, education, and fair employment practices to turn their attention to foreign policy concerns. Some were also discouraged by the existence of discriminatory Mexican attitudes toward Chicanos. Moreover, for many Chicanos, Mexico was an unknown, uninterested, and distant homeland. This condition, though, would be reversed with the onset of the Movimiento.[2]

During the late 1960s, Chicanos, in their rejection of U.S. institutions, turned to Mexico in a quest for a legacy that had been denied. From the very beginning the Chicano Movement's leadership, students, scholars, and artists looked to Mexico for support for their struggle. In seeking support, Chicanos successfully attempted various kinds of linkages with Mexico, which ranged from cultural to political. Their achievements resulted, in large part, from the evolution of Mexican governmental policy design toward Chicanos. After 1970 Mexican governmental policy toward Chicanos increasingly became more proactive, ambitious, and purposive, as Mexican regimes adapted to changing political developments within the Chicano community, Mexican internal politics, and U.S.-Mexican relations.

Generally speaking, the policies of ancestral countries toward their nationals who reside in another country have not received appropriate attention.[3] Traditional approaches in the fields of Comparative Politics, International Relations, and Public Policy do not acknowledge the importance of either these policies or the proposals or responses of a non-state entity, such as the Chicano community.[4] The Chicano-Mexico relationship is also a rather unexplored area for standard studies on Mexican foreign policy.[5] In addition, although various scholars have made major contributions in Chicano studies, a comprehensive work on Chicano-Mexico relations is still pending.[6]

This chapter applies concepts drawn from public policy literature to carry out the task of exploring Mexican governmental policies vis-à-vis Chicanos during the period 1970–1994. Specifically, certain conceptual categories of policy design,[7] such as goals,[8] political agents,[9] targets,[10] and tools,[11] are used to organize the discussion. These concepts offer the flexibility that can be applied to the study of political ties between governmental policies and a non-state entity such as the Chicano community.

The chapter is divided into five segments that correspond with the examination of the elements of Mexican policy design toward Chicanos. Specifically, each section analyzes the goals, political agents, targets, and the political tools of Mexican policy. The organization of these sections follows the chronological order of the four Mexican administrations during the period 1970–1994. During these years, four Mexican Presidents were in office: Luis Echeverría (1970–1976); José López Portillo (1976–1982); Miguel de la Madrid Hurtado (1982–1988); and Carlos Salinas de Gortari (1988–1994).

Both primary and secondary sources are used in this study. In particular, elite interviewing was utilized to obtain vital data.[12] Interviews were conducted with Mexican officials whom scholarly works on Chicano-Mexicano relations cite as being the most influential during the period 1970–1994.

THE GOALS

The Mexican presidential administrations in power during the period 1970–1994 enunciated five main goals regarding the Chicano community. Three of them had profound historical roots: the defense of the civil rights of the Mexican-origin population in the United States, the enhancement of Mexican culture in the United States, and the acquisition of Chicano political support. The remaining two, the promotion of Chicano participation in U.S.-Mexican relations and the fomenting of business links, had almost no precedents.

During President Luis Echeverría's term, a political discourse that supported the civil rights of the Chicano community was used on various occasions. Before Chicano audiences in Chicago, San Antonio, and Los Angeles in 1972, President Echeverría declared that he favored improved access of Chicanos to health programs, educational opportunities, and equal justice.[13] Moreover, in private talks with President Richard Nixon and other U.S. high officials, he advocated better treatment of Chicanos, specifically in terms of educational opportunities.[14]

President José López Portillo also addressed the importance of Chicano civil rights. Upon his return from a trip to the United States, he declared in a speech at Palacio Nacional: "As a result of a passionate request on behalf of our Chicano brothers, I told the President of the United States [Jimmy Carter] that we observed with much concern that the rights to education, health, and legal protection were denied to them [Chicanos] . . . and this assessment was acknowledged."[15]

However, these examples of presidential statements had no major consequences in terms of improving the defense of the civil rights of the Chicanos. Furthermore, they were portrayed by various U.S. officials as acts of interventionism and used to criticize Mexico.[16] Given this scenario, certain changes in the political discourse on civil rights occurred.

After 1980, the Mexican government intensified its efforts to protect the civil rights of Mexican nationals in the United States. The *política de protección* (policies designed to protect the civil rights of Mexican citizens abroad) received top priority in Mexican foreign policy. The Secretaría de Relaciones Exteriores (Ministry of Foreign Affairs, SRE) sent a directive to all consuls in the United States specifying that consular protection be allocated priority status in terms of budget and staff. Such *políticas* were followed up during the administrations of Presidents Miguel de la Madrid and Carlos Salinas.[17] For example, in 1989 Secretario de Relaciones Exteriores, Fernando Solana, stated that the Mexican consulates in the United States were improving the legal assistance offered to 40,000 Mexican nationals in the United States.[18] Furthermore, in the hostile political environment for the civil rights of the Mexican immigrants, as reflected by the passage of the Simpson-Rodino Law in 1986 and Proposition 187 in California in 1994, Mexican officials restated that the Mexican consulates in the United States would strengthen their *política de protección*.[19]

The enhancement of Mexican culture in the United States was a second goal of the Mexican policy toward Chicanos. From the early 1970s to the present, the four administrations stressed that cultural and educational links with Chicanos were the optimal channel for interacting with the Mexican-origin community.[20] Interestingly, various voices within the Mexican government argued that this was the only goal of Mexican policy toward Chicanos that did not question the principle of non-intervention in U.S. affairs. Thus, for them it was the goal that should receive top priority. President Echeverría stressed the commitment of the Mexican government in providing Chicanos with the resources they needed to preserve their culture and the Spanish language.[21] His successors also committed themselves to this goal.[22]

The development within the Chicano community of political support for the Mexican government became the third goal. The emergence of this goal in the late 1980s was fostered by the activism of the Mexican opposition parties within the Chicano community and the results of the presidential elections of 1988 in Mexico.[23] Although political support was not a publicly stated goal in the crafting of a Chicano policy, various Mexican high-ranking officials acknowledged its existence, as this goal was indeed a critical part of the presidential agenda. According to at least one knowledgeable Mexican policymaker, the pursuit of political support of Chicanos was conceived as a "preventative measure," designed to avoid any conditions that would enable the Mexican leftist opposition to "take advantage of the situation" as had occurred during the electoral process of 1988.[24] "The Mexican government understood that many anti-PRI Mexicans, who live in California, return periodically to their communities and have influence there."[25] In other words, there emerged an interest within the Mexican government in deflecting criticism from the Chicano community toward Mexico and in avoiding a scenario in which Chicanos could turn out to be "Mexico's worst enemy" within the United States.[26]

A fourth goal of Mexican policy was increasing the participation of the Chicano community in certain aspects of greater U.S.-Mexican relations.[27] President Echeverría mentioned it briefly. His successor, President López Portillo, elaborated more extensively on this goal, stating that Chicanos

were critical allies of the Mexican government on one particular issue: immigration. He made his declaration during a time when the U.S. Congress
was debating various restrictive U.S. immigration bills that "could harm
both Mexican nationals and Chicanos."[28] President Miguel de la Madrid
went further in the delineation of the Chicano role in U.S.-Mexican relations, declaring that although the Chicano community had its own interests, it could function as a special "communicator" between Mexico and the
United States in certain situations. In his view, Chicanos were a potential
"bridge" between the Mexican and U.S. governments that could "solidify
and enrich a respectful and dignified friendship between Mexico and the
United States."[29] De la Madrid's successor, Carlos Salinas de Gortari,
praised the participation of the leaders and organizations of the Mexican-
origin community in another particular aspect of U.S-Mexican relations:
the debates on the North American Free Trade Agreement (NAFTA). Other
Mexican officials, including Secretario de Comercio, Jaime Serra Puche,
the major Mexican negotiator of NAFTA, followed Salinas's lead, articulating their position that Chicano organizations could be critical allies of the
Mexican government in such negotiations.[30]

A fifth goal of the Mexican government in the period 1970–1994 was
the promotion of business connections between Mexico and the Chicano
community. Luis Echeverría and José López Portillo initially stated this objective during their administrations.[31] Subsequently, Miguel de la Madrid's
regime supported this goal in the Proyecto de Acercamiento del Gobierno
y Pueblo de México con la Comunidad México-Norteamericana (Linkage
Program of the Government and People of Mexico toward the Mexican
American Community) in the late 1980s.[32] However, no further action was
taken on this issue until President Carlos Salinas's administration. Shortly
after his election, Salinas declared his commitment to the promotion of
business links with Chicanos.[33] His declaration was underscored by members of his administration such as Secretario de Relaciones Exteriores,
Fernando Solana, who remarked: "Today's Mexico is a propitious place to
create good businesses. In this endeavor, we want the participation of our
American friends, including, of course, those of Mexican origin."[34]

In a political system where the President has a key role in the entire decision-making process, Mexican presidents during the period 1970–1994 were in a decisive position to craft governmental policy toward the Mexican-origin community. They provided a mandate and the resources to various bureaus within the executive branch to pursue numerous efforts to reach out to the Chicano community. Individually, however, the administrations of Luis Echeverría, José López Portillo, Miguel de la Madrid, and Carlos Salinas designed such policy in different ways.

President Luis Echeverría was committed to a more active foreign policy at both bilateral and multilateral levels. His administration pursued new economic and political links with various countries, especially those of the Third World.[35] Moreover, Echeverría assumed a nationalistic and anti-imperialist political posture vis-à-vis the United States in the development of his foreign policy.[36] In this context, President Echeverría developed personal links with various Chicano leaders and adopted an ad hoc style to deal with Chicano issues.[37] He issued a directive to the Secretaría de Educación Pública (Ministry of Public Education, SEP) and the Secretaría de la Presidencia (Office of the Presidency), among other bureaus, stipulating that the ties with the Chicano community were a priority to be pursued.[38]

President José López Portillo developed his foreign policy in the context of the discovery and exploitation of additional oil fields in Mexico, developments that became linked to expressions of nationalism and that afforded a unique opportunity to design and implement new and more independent actions toward the United States.[39] As part of this new approach, soon thereafter, López Portillo implemented a more ambitious policy of reaching out to Chicanos in cultural and immigration matters. During his administration, various governmental agencies became further involved with Chicano issues. Thus, the Secretaría de Educación Pública continued its important role of promoting educational and cultural links. As a result, this agency developed new ties with a variety of Chicano cultural and educational institutions and became particularly instrumental in support of the provision of bilingual education programs in the United States.[40]

At the same time, José López Portillo sought to attract the new array of Chicano/Latino leadership that had emerged on the political scene in the late 1970s to a working relationship with his administration, especially on immigration matters. He created new mechanisms to achieve this task. For example, in the late 1970s the Secretaría de Trabajo y Previsión Social (Ministry of Labor), in charge of conducting a study of Mexican immigration to the United States, coordinated the work of the Comisión Mixta de Enlace (Binational Outreach Commission).[41] This was an ad hoc entity created to provide a forum where Mexican officials and Chicanos from various organizations held periodic meetings to coordinate positions on immigration matters.[42]

In an environment characterized by serious economic problems and political tensions in bilateral relations,[43] the administration of President Miguel de la Madrid set into motion new initiatives vis-à-vis the Chicano community, which initially focused on cultural and educational matters. As Professor Jorge Bustamante points out, President De la Madrid at first sought to "depoliticize the relationship with Chicanos to limit it to cultural and social contacts."[44] Thus, in the early 1980s the Programa Cultural de las Fronteras (Cultural Program for the Borders), established in 1986 within the Secretaría de Educación Pública, became one of the most active agencies.[45] In 1987 De la Madrid's administration inaugurated new and more ambitious efforts toward Chicanos. The Secretaría de Gobernación (Ministry of the Interior), through the Consejo Nacional de Población (National Council for Population, CONAPO),[46] issued the most comprehensive official memorandum regarding the relationship of the Mexican government with Chicanos. This document proposed an ambitious agenda that included economic and political links with Chicanos and involved the participation of numerous federal and state political agents under the coordination of CONAPO. However, before this ambitious project could be implemented the presidential administration of De la Madrid concluded.[47]

From the onset of his term, President Carlos Salinas, as indicated earlier, was committed to a closer relationship with the United States. As part of this agenda, Mexico clearly modified its positions in arenas previously characterized as conflicting with American foreign policy, such as with Central America, and international organizations.[48] The most impressive step toward this goal was the announcement of the negotiations on a free trade agreement with the United States and Canada that broke the nationalist tradition of "keeping a suspicious distance from the 'colossus of the north'."[49]

At the same time, President Salinas became personally involved in structuring various activities related to Chicano issues. On several occasions, he visited Midwestern and Southwestern cities on his trips to the United States to celebrate meetings with Chicano organizations and leaders.[50] Moreover, he issued directives to several agencies in order to promote an array of unprecedented actions vis-à-vis the Chicano community. To cite one key example, within the Secretaría de Relaciones Exteriores, the first permanent office in charge of Chicano affairs, the Dirección General del Programa Presidencial para la Atención de las Comunidades Mexicanas en el Exterior (Bureau of the Presidencial Program for Mexican Communities Abroad, hereafter referred to as the Programa Presidencial) was created in 1990. This bureau, also linked to the Office of the Presidency, served to institutionalize the connections between Mexico and the Chicano community. With Salinas's blessing, the Programa Presidencial enjoyed extensive resources, discretion in using them, and the political clout that matched its ambitious agenda on cultural and educational matters and for the promotion of business connections.[51] In addition, experienced politicians from the ruling Partido Revolucionario Institucional (Party of Institutionalized Revolution, PRI) were sent as consuls by the Secretaría de Relaciones Exteriores. Besides their traditional tasks, they had to oversee a "public-relations offensive and to improve relations with local Mexican Americans."[52]

As negotiations began on the North American Free Trade Agreement, various Mexican economic agencies became involved in Chicano issues. For instance, the Secretaría de Comercio (Ministry of Commerce) hired several Chicano/Latino public relations firms as well as three former Chicano politicians as lobbyists for the Mexican government.[53] Furthermore, the Banco Nacional de Comercio Exterior (National Bank of Foreign Trade) and Nacional Financiera (National Finance, NAFIN) created special programs to reach out to Chicano businesses. Other agencies, such as the Instituto Mexicano del Seguro Social (Mexican Institute for Social Security, IMSS), also developed new ties with Chicanos. In April 1990, the director of the IMSS and the leader of the United Farm Workers (UFW), César Chávez, signed a five-year agreement.[54]

President Salinas's administration also encouraged subnational agents to become involved in the policy toward Chicanos. As a result from 1990 to 1993, various governors from the states of significant migration to the United States—Guanajuato, Oaxaca, San Luis Potosí, and Zacatecas—

traveled to California, Illinois, and Pennsylvania to meet with their "constituency abroad." In addition, these governors also had "encounters" with Chicano organizations, especially private businesses, looking for new investments in their states.[55]

CHICANO ORGANIZATIONS AS TARGETS

The target populations are the subjects of governmental policies; at times, however, they can also be active participants in the policy making. In the case of Chicanos, as will be demonstrated, there exist several examples that show that Chicanos provided significant contributions that became essential to the formulation of specific Mexican policies.

During the period 1970–1994, the Mexican government targeted a variety of Chicanos regarded as leaders among the Mexican-origin population in the United States. President Luis Echeverría's administration cultivated links with the Chicano Movement leadership.[56] Among them, José Angel Gutiérrez and Reies López Tijerina had a particularly positive response.[57] Gutiérrez, founder and leader of La Raza Unida Party, advocated successfully for educational programs for Chicanos to be funded by the Mexican government. He suggested the creation of a pioneer program of scholarships for Chicanos to study in Mexico.[58] Reies López Tijerina, leader of the Alianza Federal de Mercedes, went further with his petitions. He requested the support of the Mexican government for his struggle to reclaim the land grants in New Mexico that had been taken from those Mexicans "left behind" in the United States after the 1846–1848 war.[59] Although President Echeverría stated his concern over the land-grant struggle in New Mexico, he finally admitted that he was unable to fully support this cause further.[60]

President José López Portillo adopted a different approach in the selection of targets within the Chicano community. He took advantage of the fact that a new crop of moderate Chicano leadership and organizations, such as the Congressional Hispanic Caucus, the Mexican American Legal Defense Fund (MALDEF), the National Council of La Raza (NCLR), as well as older organizations such as the League of Latin American Citizens (LULAC), had developed a deeper and broader interest in foreign policy, including economic matters and immigration. His interest in Chicanos coincided with a positive response from Chicano leadership sectors. During the 1980s, for example, Mario Obledo from LULAC and Representative Bill Richardson (D-New Mexico) from the Hispanic Caucus subscribed to the importance of a free trade zone on the border of Mexico and the United States.[61] In fact, Richardson, with the support of other members of the Hispanic Caucus, introduced to Congress the U.S.-Mexico Border Revitalization Act in 1985, which authorized the conversion of the U.S.-Mexico border into a tariff-free trade zone.[62] In addition, the Chicano/Latino leaders of ten organizations established an umbrella organization, the Hispanic Commission, which dealt with immigration issues.[63] Subsequently, this Commission accepted the invitation of the Mexican government to a dialogue on this matter within the framework of the Comisión Mixta de Enlace.[64]

In contrast to López Portillo, Miguel de la Madrid initiated a dialogue with Chicano intellectuals and artists; later, he targeted a variety of political and economic groups as well. However, he lacked enough time to implement this project. His efforts were also impeded by skepticism among some Chicano leaders. They doubted the possibilities of a meaningful political dialogue with a government that faced so many conflicts.[65]

De la Madrid's successor, Carlos Salinas, held meetings with numerous Chicano organizations from the early days of his campaign for the Mexican presidency; his agenda was very ambitious. In 1988, for example, he met with various Chicano leaders who had been invited by Dr. Armando Navarro, founder of Impacto 2000, and candidly discussed with them the potential for the creation of a "Chicano lobby" that would be active in U.S.-Mexican relations. The leaders included Congressman Albert Bustamante (D-Texas), who identified the conditions necessary for productive relationships as follows: "If the Mexican government would like to establish more fruitful relations with the U.S. Congress, it has to identify all members (of the Hispanic Caucus) who share a common interest with the economic and social progress of Mexico."[66]

President Carlos Salinas's initiatives paid dividends. He succeeded in developing distinctive ties with the Hispanic Chamber of Commerce and the National Council of La Raza as well as with individual members of the Hispanic Caucus; those ties proved useful during the North American Free Trade Agreement negotiations.[67] The National Council of La Raza and the U.S. Chamber of Commerce, although they took a cautious attitude at the beginning of the negotiations on NAFTA, ultimately endorsed the accord.[68] The chamber even became an active lobbyist in favor of the agreement.[69] The most explicit support came from the National Council of La Raza. It emerged as the strongest Chicano political ally of the Mexican government on NAFTA. At times, this organization even played the role of broker between the Mexican government and various Chicano/Latino organizations.[70]

Nonetheless, President Salinas did not find universal support from the targeted national Chicano leadership. For example, certain members of the Hispanic Caucus, on the basis of reasons linked to their constituencies, did not always endorse Mexico's stand on NAFTA.[71] Indeed, on 18 November 1993, the day when the House of Representatives passed this trade agreement, two Chicano members of the Hispanic Caucus voted against it.[72] NAFTA also generated the opposition of numerous Chicano unionists and a variety of grass-root organizations, although President Salinas and members of his administration attempted to persuade them to support the agreement. These groups were concerned that Chicano/Latino workers would experience job displacement because of the closure of U.S. plants and their relocation to Mexico; they also feared that wage depression would result from the agreement. To cite an example, Joaquín F. Otero from the AFL-CIO stated that "Hispanic workers in the U.S. will be more affected than anyone else, because we are the ones who are last hired, first fired. If we do not lose our jobs, then we will have to lower our standards in order to compete with the maquilas."[73]

President Salinas met with a positive response on the part of Chicano leaders on other issues besides NAFTA. As noted in the discussion of agents, Salinas also targeted the United Farm Workers (UFW). Salinas met with its leader, César Chávez, a longtime fighter for the rights of the Mexicans in the United States. They discussed the possibility that the Mexican government provide selected social welfare benefits in Mexico to Mexican nationals living in the United States.[74] According to the contract, Mexican-origin members of the UFW would be entitled to affiliate in the IMSS, assuring that their families would receive welfare benefits (health care and pensions) in Mexico.[75]

THE POLITICAL TOOLS

The tools are important pieces of Mexican policy design. They connect the governmental goals, its political agents, and its targets. Generally speaking, the tools in a policy design can prescribe orders, provide resources, create capacities, and appeal to ascribed values.[76]

Few tools that give orders can be found in use during the years 1970–1994. Certain regulations of the Programa Paisano (Program for Fellow Mexicans) are a case in point.[77] The specific restrictions—drafted by the Secretaría de Hacienda (Ministry of Finance)—on the time line for importation of cars into Mexico were very controversial.[78] On several occasions, U.S.-born Chicanos and Mexican nationals in the United States complained before federal authorities; however, such regulations are still in place.

Most of the tools that the Mexican government had used to implement its policy toward Chicanos provided new resources. Among them were the cultural and educational programs funded by Mexican administrations from that of Luis Echeverría to that of Carlos Salinas. As part of enhancing Mexican cultural activities, President Echeverría's regime sponsored numerous cultural events for Chicano audiences. Besides those that coincided with the *fiestas patrias* (the celebration of the Mexican Independence Day), numerous performances by traditional Mexican dancers and theater groups and exhibitions of Mexican art were supported.[79] In addition, Echeverría's administration even financed a full-length commercial film, *Raíces de sangre* (Roots of blood, 1978), that dealt with the relationship between Mexicans and Chicanos on the border. This movie was written and directed by Chicano film director Jesús Salvador Treviño.[80]

On educational matters, various pioneer projects were implemented during President Echeverría's term. Among them was a program of scholarships for Chicanos to study in Mexico. Almost 150 Chicano medical and social science students were funded to study in Mexico. Later, a formal scholarship program, Becas para Aztlán (Scholarships for Aztlán) was established by the Mexican government.[81]

José López Portillo continued with various cultural and educational programs for Chicanos. In 1980, the Mexican authorities established ties with selected school districts with large bilingual Chicano and adult education enrollments. The programs included the training of teachers in Mexico and the supplying of books and other educational materials in Spanish. In 1981, for instance, a pioneer group of 110 Mexican bilingual teachers was sent to Los Angeles to work closely with Chicano educators. Additionally, from 1983 to the present, the Secretaría de Educación Pública held several seminars and summer courses for more that 200 Chicano bilingual teachers and school administrators from California, Illinois, and Texas.[82]

During De la Madrid's administration, various cultural activities, which linked Mexico to the Chicano community, were also sponsored. The Programa Cultural de las Fronteras funded numerous artistic, cultural, and academic events that included Chicano themes. Moreover, this agency undertook the task of educating the Mexican public on Chicano issues, especially on cultural manifestations.[83] It also financed the publication of various manuscripts on Chicano history and culture, founded the journal *Cultura norte,* and produced a series of television and radio programs in Mexico on Chicanos.[84] Another prominent organization in this endeavor, CONAPO provided resources for seminars, publications, and art exhibitions related to Chicanos.[85]

Under President Salinas, new cultural programs were established. The numerous events included the Primera Feria del Libro Mexicano (First book fair of Mexican books) held in Los Angeles in 1990 and the Primera Semana de Cine y Videos Chicanos (First week of Chicano cinema and video) in Mexico.[86] Furthermore, the Secretaría de Relaciones Exteriores, through Mexican consulates in the United States, sponsored the creation of Institutos Culturales Mexicanos (Mexican cultural institutes) in twelve U.S. cities, including Chicago, Los Angeles, San Antonio, San Diego, and Tucson. Such institutos sponsored a variety of Mexican cultural activities in the United States, especially among Chicanos.[87]

In addition, in the early 1990s, President Salinas's administration funded new educational projects between Chicanos and Mexican agencies. Organizations such as the Hermandad Mexicana Nacional and One Stop Immigration in Los Angeles and the Consejo Hispano de Alfabetización in Chicago established ties with the Instituto Mexicano de Alfabetización para Adultos (Mexican literacy institute for adults). Moreover, Salinas's administration also developed new links with U.S. school districts in the area of the training of bilingual teachers. The Secretaría de Educación Pública provided books and other educational materials in Spanish for this purpose. The majority of the students to be served were of Mexican origin.

After 1990, the sponsorship of community organizations known as *clubes regionales* (regional clubs) in major cities such as Chicago and Los Angeles was also a new tool established to promote educational and cultural issues within the Chicano community. An example is the Federación de Clubes Zacatecanos Unidos (Federation of united clubs from Zacatecas) in Los Angeles, which included thirty-seven clubs within its domain.[88]

These initiatives were complemented by actions on the part of the Mexican ruling party, the Partido Revolucionario Institucional (PRI).[89] In the early 1990s, the PRI sponsored the Comités de Apoyo a los Mexicanos Residentes en el Exterior (Support committees for Mexican nationals residing abroad). The general purpose of these organizations was to disseminate a better image of Mexico, and, as noted earlier, gain support for the Mexican political system, particularly among Mexican nationals, in several Southwestern cities.[90]

Other tools established to provide new capacities were those directed at the Chicano (and Latino) business community. After 1990 the Programa Presidencial established contacts between members of the Hispanic Chamber of Commerce, mainly from Texas and California, and the Cámara Nacional de la Industria de la Transformación (Mexican Chamber of the Industry of Transformation) whose membership is composed of Mexican entrepreneurs of small and medium-sized enterprises.[91] Through this initiative, Salinas sought to establish new links of cooperation between Mexican businesses and their Chicano counterparts.

Under Salinas's regime, other economic bureaus developed new programs. The Secretaría de Comercio organized periodic meetings in sixteen U.S. cities for Hispanic (including Chicano) entrepreneurs regarding opportunities to do business in Mexico. The Banco Nacional de Comercio Exterior offered its assistance and facilities to Hispanic firms engaged in trade and investment in Mexico.[92]

The governmental resources for coinvestment projects between Chicano/Latino business people and Mexico also qualify as tools, because they provided new resources for Chicanos. Various Mexican agencies, including the Secretaría de Comercio and Nacional Financiera (NAFIN), signed an agreement to create the Reserva Hispana (Hispanic Reserve) with the Hispanic Chamber of Commerce and the National Council of La Raza. By the terms of this agreement, from 1992 on, NAFIN committed more than $35 million to the Hispanic capital fund to promote investment with Chicano/Latino entrepreneurs in Mexico.[93] So far, the projects submitted are diverse and their success rate has been mixed.[94]

The various capacity tools, although intended to serve the Mexican government primarily, also accrued benefits to Chicanos in the views of some Chicano leaders. They stressed that Chicanos gained political "experience and visibility" as a result of their dealings with Mexico. During the 1970s, for example, José Angel Gutiérrez and Vilma Martínez (of MALDEF) were two of the most active leaders who dealt with Mexico. As Vilma Martínez stated: "We all understand that Washington will finally have to listen to Chicanos because of Mexico."[95] Later, in the 1990s, Raúl Yzaguirre, the director of the NCLR, identified positive changes in the perceptions of Mexico and Latinos in the United States as a consequence of the Chicano involvement in negotiations on NAFTA. He stressed that "with NAFTA, the U.S. and Mexico have come to the table as equals; this newfound respect has got to help improve the image and prestige of Hispanic Americans."[96]

The Mexican government frequently utilized hortatory tools that refer to emphasizing shared common values with the purpose of "cementing" its relationship with Chicanos. For example, Luis Echeverría highlighted the "profound ethnic and cultural links" that exist between Chicanos and Mexico.[97] His successor, José López Portillo, mentioned that "the doors of this country [Mexico] are opened for all of you [Chicanos]."[98] Furthermore, Miguel de la Madrid stated that the links with Chicanos and Mexico will "solidify and enrich a respectful and dignified friendship between Mexico and the United States."[99] During Carlos Salinas's term, Secretario de Relaciones Exteriores, Fernando Solana, pointed out that as Mexico becomes a more respected country, the values that Mexican Americans exemplified within the pluralistic U.S. society will be more appreciated.[100] And Subsecretario Javier Barros Valero expressed that "important elements, such as language, beliefs, and values" identify Chicanos with Mexicans.[101] Even in the description of the objectives of the Reserva Hispana, it was stated that Chicano business has "the opportunity to contribute to Mexico's economic development." Such an assertion assumes that Chicano/Latino organizations are indeed concerned about this issue and are gratified by their own ability to contribute.[102]

Finally, another example of such hortatory tools alludes to the fact that for five consecutive years President Salinas's administration granted

Mexico's most prestigious award, the Aguila Azteca, to selected Chicanos. Until 1990 the award had not been given to a member of the Chicano community. Through this mechanism the Mexican government honored the leaders or prominent members of the Chicano community, and exalted the "common values" shared by Chicanos and Mexicans. Among the recipients of this award were: César Chávez, president of the United Farm Workers; Antonia Hernández from MALDEF; Luis Leal, academician; Gloria Molina, member of the County Supervisors of Los Angeles; Bill Richardson, Democratic congressman and member of the Hispanic Caucus; Raúl Yzaguirre from the NCLR; and Luis Valdez, film director.[103]

A FINAL NOTE

During the period 1970–1994, a variety of connections between the Chicano community and Mexico were established. This study focused on the characteristics of one particular aspect of these links, the political relations between the Mexican government and Chicanos. Several conclusions and lessons can be drawn. One conclusion is that Mexican policy toward Chicanos has been dynamic. It is characterized by change. Table 6.1 summarizes some of the most important elements of change that occurred in the period from 1970 to 1994.

Political developments in Mexico and the United States were critical to the evolution of Mexican policy. For example, as more Chicano/Latino organizations emerged onto the political scene with an agenda that included "intermestic" issues, such as immigration, or foreign policy issues, such as the promotion of business abroad, the Mexican government responded with an active policy. When the interests of Chicano leaders and organizations coincided with those of the Mexican administrations, a sort of "working relationship" was established.

Also, the emergence of a powerful presidential opposition candidate (Cuauhtémoc Cárdenas), who made substantial efforts to gain the support of Mexicans in the United States, made the Mexican government more conscious of the necessity of reinforcing its connections with new segments of the Mexican-origin community, especially with Mexican nationals. The record of Mexican policy suggests that future events in Mexican domestic policy, which might generate the interest of the Mexican-origin commu-

Table 6.1   Mexican Policy toward Chicanos

L. Echeverría (1970–1976)	J. López Portillo (1976–1982)	M. de la Madrid (1982–1988)	C. Salinas (1988–1994)
GOALS			
Defense of Civil Rights (U.S.-born Chicanos/Mex nationals)	Defense of Civil Rights (U.S.-born Chicanos/Mex nationals)	Defense of Civil Rights (Mex nationals)	Defense of Civil Rights (Mex nationals)
Enhancement of Mexican Culture	Enhancement of Mexican Culture	Enhancement of Mexican Culture	Enhancement of Mexican Culture
—	Participation in U.S./Mex Relations (immigration)	—	Participation in U.S./Mex Relations (NAFTA/ immigration)
AGENTS			
Presidency	Presidency	Presidency	Presidency
SEP	SEP	SEP	SEP
SRE	SRE	SRE	SRE
	Comisión Mixta		Programa Presidencial
			Secretaría de Comercio
			NAFIN
			IMSS
			Governors
TARGETS*			
La Raza Unida	Hispanic Commission	Intellectuals	Clubes Regionales
Alianza Federal de Mercedes		Certain School Districts	Comités de Apoyo a Mex. en el Exterior
			Hispanic Chamber of Commerce

Table 6.1 (*continued*)

L. Echeverría (1970–1976)	J. López Portillo (1976–1982)	M. de la Madrid (1982–1988)	C. Salinas (1988–1994)
			LULAC
			MALDEF
			NCLR
			One Stop Immigration
TOOLS			
—	—	—	Imposition of orders
Allocation of Resources	Allocation of Resources	Allocation of Resources	Allocation of Resources
New Political Capacities	New Political Capacities	—	New Political Capacities
Hortatory Tools	Hortatory Tools	Hortatory Tools	Hortatory Tools

*Mexican governmental discourse on the targets of its policy include Chicano population as a whole (U.S. born Chicanos and Mexican nationals). However, it has focused its attention on certain organizations during the period 1970–1994.

nity in the United States, will necessarily bring about governmental efforts to generate further support within the Mexican-origin community in the United States.

However, the evolution of Mexican domestic policy can set limits on the Mexican policy toward Chicanos. Specifically, the latest economic crisis will mean a reduction of resources for all governmental projects, including those that affect the Chicano community. There exists, for example, a concern that the Programa Presidencial will face the fate of previous efforts during the new administration of President Ernesto Zedillo (inaugurated in December 1994)—either elimination or great reduction in importance and resources.

The bilateral agenda can impose certain topics, such as immigration, upon the Mexican policy toward Chicanos. The passage of Proposition 187 in California and the rising tide of xenophobia and deep anti-immigrant feeling in the United States could possibly make the seeking of alliances with the Chicano community on immigration a major goal in future Chicano-Mexicano relations. In such an environment, new political tools could be implemented by Mexico, for instance, strengthening the role of Mexican consulates; granting Mexicans in the United States the possibility of keeping their nationality while applying for American citizenship (dual nationality); and the negotiation of a comprehensive bilateral agreement on Mexican labor.[104]

This one example does not mean, however, that the Mexican-origin community in the United States will support Mexico on every issue of the greater U.S.-Mexican agenda. A "partnership of mutual benefits" can be established with the Mexican government on certain themes—economic/ business issues or educational projects, for example—and even can have the blessings of the U.S. government, as in the case of NAFTA.[105] Concurrently, though, there will exist voices within the community, such as those of the Chicano unionists opposed to NAFTA, that can raise critical questions on Mexico's economic/business agenda. There are also complaints from certain voices (that of governor Pete Wilson, for example) regarding the U.S. government's condemnation of the efforts of Mexico to seek political allies on immigration.

In summation, the examination of Mexican policy toward Chicanos during the period 1970–1994 demonstrates that the construction of a "partnership" between the Mexican government and Chicanos seems highly possible in specific areas, such as the defense of the civil rights of undocumented workers, culture, education, and, increasingly, business. Certain organizations could be the most active in carrying out these tasks, although the effects of such interchanges can have repercussions in the community at large. However, the ideal of a unanimous advocacy of Chicano organizations in favor of all Mexican governmental goals that involve the Mexican-origin community in the United States seems totally unrealistic. The various goals of Mexican policy toward Chicanos will undoubtedly find different political allies (and critics) within the community, depending on the issue involved, as the case of NAFTA clearly exemplified. Yet one thing is certain: Chicano-Mexicano political relations have greatly evolved and matured in the recent era and now have taken center stage. Aztlán will remain a high priority for Mexico. Mexico, moreover, will likewise be at the forefront of Chicano political, cultural, and intellectual discourse for years to come.

NOTES

1. The terms "Chicano community," "Mexican-origin community," and "Chicanos" are used interchangeably in this chapter. They refer to the Mexican nationals who live permanently in the United States and to American citizens of Mexican descent.

2. Juan Gómez-Quiñones, *Chicano Politics: Reality and Promise 1940–1990* (Albuquerque: University of New Mexico Press, 1990), 202–05.

3. James Rothchild's book, *Ethnopolitics: A Conceptual Framework* (New York: Columbia University, 1981) is one of the few theoretical contributions to the study of the politics of ancestral countries toward ethnic groups.

4. Realism, the classic school of thought in this discipline, focuses only upon the interactions between nation-states, which are the key units of analysis. Neorealism takes into account non-governmental actors, although it seldom acknowledges the role of ethnic groups. Robert O. Keohane, "Realism, Neorealism and the Study of World Politics," in *Neorealism and Its Critics,* ed. Robert O. Keohane (New York: Columbia University Press, 1986), 7–11. Traditional approaches in contemporary politics and public policy focus upon domestic structures. They usually do not look beyond the borders of the nation-state.

5. The following works are among the exceptions: Denise Dresser, "La nueva política mexicana en Estados Unidos," *Estados Unidos, Informe Trimestral* 4 (1991): 15–21; Carlos González Gutiérrez, "The Mexican Diaspora," in *The California Mexico Connection,* eds. Abraham Lowenthal and Katrina Burgess (Stanford: Stanford University Press, 1993), 234; and Carlos H. Zazueta, "Mexican Political Actors in the United States and Mexico: Historical and Political Contexts of a Dialogue Renewed," in *Mexico-U.S. Relations, Conflict and Convergence,* eds. Carlos Vásquez and Manuel García y Griego (Los Angeles: University of California, 1983), 441–75.

6. See, for example, John García, *Mexicanos and Chicanos: Examining Political Involvement and Interface in the U.S. Political System* (Tucson: Mexican American Studies and Research Center, 1987); Rodolfo de la Garza, "Chicanos and the U.S. Foreign Policy: the Future of Chicano-Mexicano relations," *Western Political Quarterly* 4 (December 1980): 571–82; Juan Gómez-Quiñones, "Notes on the Interpretation of the Relationship between the Mexican Community in the United States and Mexico," in Vásquez and García y Griego, *Mexico-U.S. Relations,* 419–39; Tatcho Mindiola and Max Martínez, eds., *Chicano-Mexicano Relations* (Houston: University of Houston-University Park, 1986).

7. *Policy design* can be defined as "the logic through which policy intends to achieve its objectives." Anne Schneider and Helen Ingram, "Systematically Pinching Ideas: A Comparative Approach to Policy Design," *Journal of Public Policy* 8 (1991): 61.

8. The recent *goals* of Mexican policy design toward Chicanos can be defined as the "purposive statements" included in written documents, such as governmental programs or

statutes, or inferred from analysis of the policy examples or statements from high officials. Helen Ingram and Anne L. Schneider, "The Choice of Target Populations," *Administration and Society* 3 (1991): 336.

9. The *political agents* of a specific policy design are those agencies or individuals in charge of the implementation of the programs (or statutes) regarding certain issues. The level of the government in which such agents are located is considered important in terms of the fulfillment of the goals' policy design. The reason why they were selected for the implementation of the goals as well as the amount of discretion given to them in the program or statute are also worth noting. Schneider and Ingram, "Systematically Pinching Ideas," 68, 71.

10. The *target* populations are particularly important. They can be described as "the groups or individuals whose decision and behavior are related to policy goals directly or indirectly." Ingram and Schneider, "The Choice of Target Populations," 333–56.

11. The *tools* "are intended to motivate implementing agencies and target populations to make decisions and take actions consistent with policy objectives." Schneider and Ingram, "Systematically Pinching Ideas," 68. See also Anne Schneider and Helen Ingram, "Behavioral Assumptions of Policy Tools," *Journal of Politics* 52 (1990).

12. The elite status "depends not on their role in society but on their access to information that can help answer a given research question." A discussion on this method can be found in Jarol B. Manheim and Richard C. Rich, *Empirical Political Analysis: Research Methods in Political Science* (New York: Longman, 1991): 139–47.

13. Fausto Fernández Ponte, "Jubilosa recepción en Chicago: Chicanos y gobernador," *Excelsior,* 19 June 1972, p. 1; and Celeste Durant, "Officials Turn Out to Welcome Mexican President, Wife to L.A.," *Los Angeles Times,* 20 June 1972.

14. U.S. officials did not make any official comment about this point, although a source close to the event observed a cold response to the Mexican petition. Frank del Olmo, "Problem-Solving Lies with Chicanos, Echeverría Says," *Los Angeles Times,* 22 June 1972, p. 3.

15. José López Portillo, "Dignidad y confianza en México" (paper published by Comité del PRI en el D.F., 1 October 1979), 4, 5, cited in José Angel Gutiérrez, "The Chicano in Mexicano–Norte Americano Relations," in Mindiola and Martínez, *Chicano-Mexicano Relations,* 29–30.

16. One example derives from the meeting between President López Portillo and President Jimmy Carter in September 1979. According to some American sources, President Carter, "visibly annoyed" after some discussion of Chicano rights, replied to López Portillo, "Next time tell them [the Chicanos] to get in touch directly with me." Alan Riding, *Distant Neighbors* (New York: Vintage Books, 1985), 475.

17. David R. Maciel, "An Unwritten Alliance: Mexican Policy on Immigration to the United States," *The World and I: Chronicle of Our Changing Times* 7 (1986): 695–99.

18. "Palabras de Fernando Solana" (paper presented at the 15th meeting of MALDEF, Los Angeles, Calif., 30 November 1989), 3.

19. Barbara K. Strickland, "Simpson-Rodino, 1987–1988: bomba que no estalló," in *México-Estados Unidos, 1987,* eds. Gerardo Bueno and Lorenzo Meyer (México: El Colegio de México, 1989), 175–208; and Victor Cardoso, "SRE: darán consulados más protección a indocumentados," *La Jornada* 15 (1994): 23.

20. González Gutiérrez, "The Mexican Diaspora," 234.

21. "Texto completo del informe de LE," *Excelsior,* 2 September 1972, p. 15.

22. Armando Gutiérrez, "The Chicano Elite in Chicano-Mexicano Relations," in Vásquez and García y Griego, *Chicano-Mexicano Relations,* 16; and "Discurso pronunciado por el Lic. Miguel de la Madrid ante intelectuales chicanos, el 3 de Marzo de 1982," México, D.F., p. 4, cited in A. Gutiérrez, "The Chicano Elite," 59.

23. President Salinas won the presidency "with a bare 50.3 percent majority." Thomas E. Skidmore and Peter Smith, *Modern Latin America,* 3rd ed. (Oxford: Oxford University Press, 1992), 251.

24. Mexican official from the Secretaría de Comercio y Fomento Industrial, interview by author, Mexico City, 22 June 1994.

25. José Angel Gutiérrez, interview by Denise Dresser, Los Angeles, Calif., 19 June 1991, cited in Dresser, "La nueva política mexicana," 15–21.

26. Mexican official from the Secretariado Técnico del Gabinete de Política Exterior, Office of the Presidency, interview by author, Mexico City, 30 July 1991.

27. Before 1971, the idea to involve Chicanos in U.S.-Mexican relations was not openly discussed in the Mexican government. The only exception is President Adolfo López Mateos's speech in Los Angeles in February 1964. Carlos Denegri, "Mensaje a los mexicanos de E.U.," *Excelsior,* 23 February 1964, p. 1.

28. David Vidal, "Hispanic Americans Meet Mexico Leader," *New York Times,* 28 September 1979, p. 11.

29. "MMH: los Chicanos Puente para Afianzar la Amistad con EU," *La Jornada* 20 (June 1987): 1.

30. Jaime Serra Puche, "U.S. Hispanics Will Benefit," *Vista,* 4 (April) 1992: 6.

31. J. A. Gutiérrez, "Mexicano—Norte Americano Relations," 31.

32. Consejo Nacional de Población, *Proyecto de acercamiento del gobierno de México con la comunidad méxico-norteamericana* (México: Consejo Nacional de Población, 1987): 22–23.

33. Alfredo J. Estrada, "Interview with President Carlos Salinas de Gortari," *Hispanic* (1992): 22.

34. "Palabras de Fernando Solana," 3.

35. Mario Ojeda, *Alcances y límites de la política exterior de México* (México: El Colegio de México, 1984), 176–204.

36. "Mexican President Criticized U.S. in Tough Address to Congress," *Los Angeles Times,* 16 June 1972, p. 1.

37. Jorge Bustamante, as personal advisor of the president, also had a key role in setting the goals and direction of the policy toward Chicanos. A. Gutiérrez, "The Chicano Elite," 51.

38. J. A. Gutiérrez, "Mexicano–Norte Americano Relations," p. 24.

39. Rodolfo de la Garza, "Chicanos and U.S. Foreign Policy,'" in Vázque and García y Griego, *Mexico-U.S. Relations,* 571–82.

40. A. Gutiérrez, "The Chicano Elite," 52.

41. Centro Nacional de Información y Estadística de Trabajo, *Análisis de algunos resultados de la primera encuesta a trabajadores mexicanos no documentados devueltos de los Estados Unidos* (México: CENIET, 1979).

42. Marlise Simons, "U.S. Hispanics Petition Mexican Leader," *Los Angeles Times,* 27 September 1979.

43. The bilateral relations were characterized by their various points of conflict, such as Central America, voting in international organizations, and drugs. Bueno and Meyer, *Mexico-Estados Unidos 1987,* 9, 85–86.

44. Juan M. Vázquez, "Mexico-Chicano Political Dialogue Fades," *Los Angeles Times,* 12 August 1983.

45. Mexican officer from the Programa Cultural de las Fronteras, interview by author, Mexico City, 28 July 1989.

46. The Consejo Nacional de Población is in charge of demographic studies. During the period 1986–1988, it was the agency designated to deal with Chicano affairs.

47. Consejo Nacional de Población, *Proyecto de acercamiento,* 6.

48. Gustavo Ramírez Paredes, "Los políticos mexicanos miran hacia el norte," in *El sistema político mexicano visto por los mexicanos de afuera,* ed. Gustavo Ramírez Paredes (México: UNAM, 1991), 58.

49. Skidmore and Smith, *Modern Latin America,* 252.

50. Constanza Montana, "Salinas Won't Ignore Mexican Americans," *Chicago Tribune,* 10 April 1991, p. 17; and Constanza Montana and Melita Garza, "Chicago Greets Salinas," *Chicago Tribune,* 11 April 1991, p. 7.

51. Secretaría de Relaciones Exteriores, Dirección General de Información, *Entró en funciones el Programa Presidencial para la Atención de las Comunidades Mexicanas en el Exterior,* communiqué B-060 (Mexico City, 27 January 1990); Secretaría de Relaciones Exteriores, *Objetivos, políticas e ideas programáticas,* Dirección General del Programa Presidencial para la Atención de las Comunidades Mexicanas en el Exterior (Mexico City, 5 April 1990).

52. Tim Golden, "Mexico Is Trying Hard to Lift Its Political Profile in the U.S.," *New York Times,* 30 December 1991.

53. Dresser, "Nueva política mexicana," 22; Todd Eisenstadt, "Cabildeo y relaciones públicas en Estados Unidos," *Este País* (Mexico), 15 June 1992, p. 21; and Martha Frase-Blunt, "On the Fast Track to Free Trade," *Hispanic* (August 1991): 16.

54. "La solidaridad trasciende nuestas fronteras," *El Nacional* (Mexico City), Suplemento Especial, 3 June 1990, pp. 2–3.

55. Crónica de la Comunidad, *La Paloma. Organo de Difusión del Programa para las Comunidades en el Extranjero* (San Antonio), 16, September–December 1993, p. 4.

56. According to some sources, it was difficult for the Mexican government to select which Chicano organizations or leaders would be the targets of its policy. Celeste Durand, "Officials Turn Out to Welcome Mexican President, Wife to L.A.," *Los Angeles Times,* 20 June 1972.

57. The interest of Chicanos in support of the Mexican government had its critics. Certain Chicano leaders expressed opposition to the establishment of closer relations with the Mexican government. César Chávez, leader of the United Farm Workers union, and Rodolfo "Corky" González, leader of La Raza Unida Party, were among those who initially did not perceive any major advantages for the Chicano Movement in cultivating closer links with their homeland. J. A. Gutiérrez, "Mexicano–Norte Americano Rela-

tions," 30. In addition, in the early 1970s, some groups linked to La Raza Unida Party openly criticized specific authoritarian activities of the Mexican government, such as the repression of Mexican students in 1968 and 1971 and of the continued incarceration of "political prisoners" in Mexico. "No bastan carteles; hay que sostener tesis," *Excelsior,* 20 June 1972.

58. "Avance," *Ciencia y Desarrollo* 21 (July–August 1978), 73; de la Garza, "Chicanos and U.S. Foreign Policy," in Vásquez and García y Griego, *Mexico-U.S. Relations,* 571; and José Angel Gutiérrez, "Mexicanos y Chicanos" (paper presented at symposium, Encuentro Chicano, Palacio de Minería, México, 1986), 11.

59. Rodolfo de la Garza and Karl Schmitt, "Texas Landgrants and Chicano-Mexican Relations," *Latin America Research Review* 1 (1986): 133–34.

60. Reies López Tijerina, *Mi lucha por la tierra* (México: Fondo de Cultura Económica, 1978), 544, 548, 549.

61. Mario Obledo, "U.S.-Mexico Border, A Common Market," *Nuestro* 2 (1981): 44–47.

62. "Free Trade Zone Bill Introduced," *Hispanic Link Weekly Report,* 12 August 1985, p. 2.

63. Christine Sierra, "The Political Transformation of a Minority Organization, the Council of la Raza 1965–1980" (Ph.D. diss., Stanford University, 1983), 258.

64. In September 1979, President Jose López Portillo established the Comisión Mixta de Enlace, an ad hoc task force oriented to institutionalize the links of the Mexican government with Chicanos. Marlise Simons, "U.S. Hispanics Petition Mexican Leader," *Los Angeles Times,* 27 September 1979, p. 12.

65. In 1988, Antonia Hernández from MALDEF stated that she was disenchanted with the state of the economy and the political system in Mexico. Specifically, she said: "They [Mexicans] have to get their house in order [before they] get in touch with Chicanos." Diana Solis and Alfredo Corchado, "Mexico Looks for Friends among the Family," *Wall Street Journal,* 4 January 1988, p. 14.

66. Congressman Albert Bustamante, "La formación de una relación más amigable y de mayor cooperación entre Estados Unidos y México" (paper presented at symposium, Encuentro del Lic. Carlos Salinas de Gortari, candidato a la Presidencia de la República con los representantes de la comunidad mexicano-norteamericana, Tijuana, B.C. [México], 8 April 1988), 5.

67. Mexican official from the Secretaría de Comercio y Fomento Industrial, 22 June 1994. See also, "Programa para las comunidades mexicanas en el extranjero," *Estados Unidos Informe Trimestral* (Mexico City) 4 (October–December 1991): 59.

68. The National Council of la Raza, along with other organizations and individual leaders, became part of the Latino Consensus on NAFTA. This association was dedicated to lobby in favor of the agreement. Latino Consensus on NAFTA, *There Are 20 Billion Reasons to Support President Clinton's* NAFTA (Montebello, CA: Latino Consensus on NAFTA, 1993), 3.

69. Rick Mendosa, "Taking the Fast Track to Mexico," *Hispanic Business* (July 1990): 10. See also, "México podría aumentar exportaciones en 100% con el TCL, prevé John Ciaccia," *Uno más uno* (Mexico City), 27 February 1991.

70. Mexican official from the Dirección General de América del Norte, interview by author, Mexico City, 29 July 1989.

71. Héctor Cantú, "New Muscle in Washington," *Hispanic Business* (February 1993): 16; Rodolfo Medina, "TLC y el hueso latino," *Uno más uno,* March 26, 1993.

72. They were Luis V. Gutiérrez (D-Illinois) and Matthew Martínez (D-California). "How They Voted," *Los Angeles Times,* 18 November 1993.

73. Frase-Blunt, "On the Fast Track," 20.

74. "Es importante saber cómo vamos a actuar, aseguró el líder chicano" *El Universal,* 5 April 1988; "No podemos responder con la cabeza baja o con tibieza a los golpes y ofensas que hacen los estadounidenses en perjuicio de la nación mexicana," *El Universal,* 5 April 1988.

75. A major criticism of the program was raised by Cuauhtémoc Cárdenas who said that it can only cover 15,000 of the 2 million undocumented workers. "Mexican President Blasts Abduction of Drug Suspect," *Los Angeles Times,* 24 April 1990.

76. Schneider and Ingram, "Behavioral Assumptions," 514–22; and Anne L. Schneider and Helen Ingram, "Electoral Dynamics, The Cultural Construction of Target Populations, And Citizen Participation" (paper prepared for the Public Policy Conference on Policy Design and Citizen Capacity, University of Arizona, March 1991).

77. "Exhorta Salinas a compatriotas residentes en EU a visitar 'la nueva mexicana,'" *Uno más uno,* 18 December 1989.

78. Secretaría de Hacienda y Crédito Público, "Resolución que establece para 1990 reglas fiscales de carácter general relacionadas con el comercio exterior," Administración General de Aduanas, June 1994, 25–27.

79. J. A. Gutiérrez, "Mexicanos y Chicanos," 14.

80. Jesús Treviño, "*Raíces de sangre.* First Feature Film Directed by a Chicano," *SOMOS* (1978): 16–19.

81. J. A. Gutiérrez, "Mexicano–Norte Americano Relations," 32–33; and J. A. Gutiérrez, "Mexicanos y Chicanos," 11.

82. Mexican official from the Dirección General de Relaciones Internacionales, Secretaría de Educación Pública, interview by the author, Mexico City, 28 August 1989; "Cinco años del Programa para las Comunidades Mexicanas," *La Paloma,* 22 January–February 1995, p. 1.

83. Mexican officer from the Programa Cultural de las Fronteras, interview by author, Mexico City, 28 July 1989; and "Encuentro chicano-México 1987," *Cultura Norte* 4 (1988): 6.

84. "Televisión para chicanos," *Cultura Norte* 5 (1988): 18.

85. Mexican official from the Programa Cultural de las Fronteras, interview by author, Mexico City, 28 July 1990. Regarding CONAPO, see David Maciel and José Guillermo Saavedra, eds., *Al norte de la frontera: el pueblo chicano* (México: Consejo Nacional de Población, 1988).

86. For a detailed account of the cultural activities, see *La Paloma,* January 1991–December 1994.

87. Mexican official from the Dirección General del Programa Presidential para la Atención de las Comunidades Mexicanas en el Exterior, interview by author.

88. Mexican official from the Dirección General del Programa Presidencial para la Atención de las Comunidades Mexicanas en el Exterior, interview by author, Mexico City, 28 June 1994. See also, González Gutiérrez, "The Mexican Diaspora," 228–99.

89. A classic study that explores the links between the PRI and the Mexican government

is Frank Bradenburg, *The Making of Modern Mexico* (Englewood Cliffs: Prentice Hall, 1964), 19.

90. Created by 1990, one of the few reports about the characteristics of these organizations refers to the meeting between the governor of the state of Sonora, Manlio Fabio Beltrones, and the members of the comités in Tucson and Phoenix. Olga Magallanes, "El gobernador de Sonora se reúne con los Comités de Apoyo a los Mexicanos Residentes en el Exterior," *Ave Fénix de Arizona* (Phoenix), 11 November 1991, p. 9.

91. Mexican official from the Dirección General del Programa Presidencial para la Atención de las Comunidades Mexicanas en el Exterior, interview by author, Mexico City, 25 June 1991.

92. Secretaría de Relaciones Exteriores, Dirección General del Programa Presidencial para la Atención de las Comunidades Mexicanas en el Exterior, *Objetivos, políticas e ideas programáticas,* 7–8; Serra Puche, "Hispanics Will Benefit," 8.

93. Nacional Financiera, *Reserva Hispana* (México, 1994), 10; Rick Mendosa, "Natural Bridges of Opportunity," *Hispanic Business* (January 1993): 22.

94. As an example, Manuel Rosales, president of the California Hispanic Chamber of Commerce, submitted a project related to helicopter transportation and drinking-water distribution in Mexico City. Sandra Márquez, "Closing the Deal," *Hispanic* (April 1993): 40, 42–43.

95. Cited in de la Garza, "Chicanos and U.S. Foreign Policy," in Vásquez and García y Griego, *Mexico-U.S. Relations,* 408. See also J. A. Gutiérrez, "Mexicano Norte-Americano Relations," 23.

96. Latino Consensus on NAFTA, *20 Billion Reasons,* 1.

97. "Echeverría en Los Angeles," *Excelsior,* 2 September 1972, p. 1.

98. "Unidad con México, meta de los chicanos. JLP nos abrió las puertas del país." *Excelsior,* 26 January 1978, p. 1.

99. "MMH: los chicanos, puente para afianzar la amistad con EU," *La Jornada,* 20 June 1987, p. 1.

100. "Palabras de Fernando Solana," 3.

101. "Palabras de Javier Barros Valero, Subsecretaría de Relaciones Exteriores" (paper presented at the annual meeting of the National Council of La Raza, Washington, D.C., 19 January 1990), 5.

102. Nacional Financiera, *Reserva Hispana,* 8.

103. "Mexico Promotes Ties with the Mexican American Community," *La Paloma,* September 1992, p. 2.

104. In late 1994, a congressional commission in Mexico held hearings on these matters. Sandra Dibble, "Stronger Role Pushed for Mexican Consulates," *San Diego Union Tribune,* December 18, 1994.

105. The U.S. Department of Commerce even sponsored several business seminars between Chicanos and their business counterparts in Mexico. "Frequently Asked Questions about the Free Trade Agreement," *Business America* 8 (1990): 5–6.

PART THREE. CHICANA/O EDUCATIONAL

STRUGGLES: DIMENSIONS,

ACCOMPLISHMENTS, & CHALLENGES

Historically, public education has been the only legitimate hope for escape from poverty for the majority of Chicano/as and other people of color. Consequently, Chicanas/os have invested extensive time and energy and other resources to reform educational institutions at all levels. In so doing, they have created a rich and extensive record of struggle that serves as a testament to the importance of education in Chicano society. During the 1980s, however, the record was ignored. During the Reagan administration, for example, Secretary of Education Lauro Cavazos alleged that Chicanos and other Latinos did not value education. Nevertheless, Chicanas/os labored to extend the tradition of educational struggle.

Historian Guadalupe San Miguel examines Chicano education-reform activism since 1980 in the context of scholarly treatments of the Chicano Movement and the history of educational activism by Chicanos since the 1960s in order to fathom the continuity and change in this activism. According to San Miguel, the activism underwent transformation in the context of the political environment of the decade. Moreover, it was also influenced by developments such as the emergence of a new crop of activists who differed significantly from the Chicano generation of activists in terms of identity, goal, and strategic choices. As a result, the effort to reform the schools on the part of the Mexican-descent population became a contradictory process. To date the results of this struggle have been mixed. Thus the struggle continues.

Ignacio García examines the evolution of Chicano Studies. After examining its roots and original goals, García explores the fate of Chicano Studies during the 1980s and into the 1990s. He argues that during the 1980s Chicano Studies faced difficult times, suffering in the face of budget cuts, among other things. Moreover, Chicano Studies scholars experienced isolation, difficulty in achieving tenure, and heavier workloads. As the 1980s evolved, Chicano Studies underwent a transformation and confronted several challenges; whether and how Chicano Studies will be able to meet these challenges remains uncertain. In García's view, Chicano Studies is approaching a critical juncture in its development. The discipline faces the task of choosing from several options that will determine its place in the academy and its relationship and ultimate significance to Chicanas/os.

ACTORS NOT VICTIMS:

CHICANAS/OS AND THE STRUGGLE

FOR EDUCATIONAL EQUALITY

Guadalupe San Miguel

In the last several years, Chicano scholars have begun to assess the Chicano Movement, i.e., that important period of increased political and cultural activity that began in the early to mid-1960s. The general interpretation that has emerged about the Chicano Movement suggests that it was comprised primarily of individuals from local communities seeking change on behalf of working-class interests. The vast majority of these individuals were working-class youth, and particularly students. The latter, especially those at the university level, were central to the development of this movement, scholars argue. (The decline in the student movement in the early or mid-1970s in turn led to the decline of the Chicano Movement in general.) The Chicano Movement was viewed as a qualitatively different type of political and cultural mobilization in the Mexican-origin community. "The Chicano Movement, unlike earlier reform movements by Mexican Americans," notes Mario García, "was characterized by its direct challenge and rejection of the U.S. system."[1] In challenging or rejecting aspects of the American social order, it dramatically broke with the identity and politics of the members of the Mexican American Generation.[2]

The existing interpretation of the Chicano Movement embodied in the views just delineated needs to be reassessed in light of evidence pertaining to activists involved in school reform. The "Movimiento" in general was not confined to one major social class with one set of interests. It was comprised of a diverse group of individuals from various classes who shared contrasting ideologies and perspectives. Middle-class groups, grass-roots organizations, and youth of all ages were involved. Youth, and especially students, were not the only or primary actors in this political and cultural movement; however, they were an integral and important component.

The Movimiento did not die out during the 1970s despite governmental repression, an increasingly conservative political environment, and bitter internal conflicts. It continued, in various forms, into the recent more conservative era.

The following remarks provide a brief and tentative history of the Movimiento during the period of increasing conservatism in American life that covered the years largely from 1977 to 1990. The emphasis is on activism associated with public school reform. Historically, the Mexican-origin community, similar to most Americans, has placed great faith in public education as an instrument of social mobility. This faith in education was strengthened during the Chicano Movement era, as illustrated by the widespread efforts made to change the schools so that they would be more responsive to the linguistic, cultural, academic, and political needs of the Mexican-origin population.

The intention of this brief history, then, is to provide a greater appreciation of the continuities and discontinuities in ethnic-identity and social-change strategies in the educational aspect of the Chicano Movement during the late 1970s and 1980s. In the following comments I argue that the effort to change the schools was a continuous but contradictory and multifaceted process involving large numbers of individuals of varied ages, political persuasions, and gender.

THE CHICANO MOVEMENT:
THE FIRST DOZEN YEARS, 1965–1977

During the 1960s an increasing number of Mexican-origin individuals began to involve themselves in this nation's political life. The emphasis of their involvement was on eliminating inequality, especially institutional discrimination, and on gaining recognition of their Mexican identity.[3] Although the burst of political activity was directed at all forms of institutional life, much of it was centered on the public schools because of their importance for the community's socioeconomic development.

The movement for equality and cultural diversity in the schools, similar to the parent Chicano Movement, was affected by the same forces and included many of the same actors.[4] This school movement was comprised of a diverse group of individuals and organizations with multiple ideologies and perspectives. Men and women from different classes and of different ages and outlooks worked independently or cooperatively to change the schools so that they could better serve the Mexican American population.

Many of these individuals and groups initially followed in the footsteps of the Mexican American Generation.[5] But by the late 1960s, a significant number, especially the youth, broke from this tradition and collectively challenged the cultural, ideological, and political hegemony of this older generation. (In fact, many of the younger group accepted the new term "Chicano" to distinguish themselves from the earlier generation.)[6] The break, however, did not occur all at once, nor was it as dramatic as several authors have stated. It was a gradual and uneven process. Some Chicano activists broke with the past completely, but others did so only partially.

Chicano Movement activists used a variety of strategies to bring about reform. First, they sought to influence federal agencies and to develop policies aimed at improving the schools and at gaining recognition of the Mexican-origin population's cultural and linguistic needs. Middle-class groups such as the American GI Forum (AGIF), the League of United Latin American Citizens (LULAC), and others focused on lobbying as a strategy of reform. They pressured the federal government for inclusion of their political interests in federal programs[7] and for recognition of their linguistic, cultural, and academic needs.[8] They also sought federal assistance in overcoming both the problem of discrimination and of cultural degradation and linguistic exclusion in the schools.[9]

Other middle-class leaders and groups pursued litigation as a strategy for reforming the schools. Most of these legal challenges to assimilationism and discrimination in education were based on the Chicano population's emerging status as an ethnic-minority group. During the late 1960s and into the 1970s, Chicano and Chicana activists filed a variety of lawsuits that challenged segregated schools, the testing and placement of culturally distinct children in classes designated for the "educationally mentally retarded" (EMR), and unequal funding of public education.[10]

Working-class youth and groups, unlike middle-class leaders, focused their efforts on changing the schools at the local level through the use of mass mobilization, community organization, and political protest. They expanded and strengthened the campaign against inequality by launching an ideological assault against cultural assimilation, a political attack against

Anglo control of education, and an onslaught against discriminatory treatment in the schools. They also utilized unorthodox methods such as protest and confrontation tactics to achieve their goal of school change.[11]

Mexican American youth, especially high school students, voiced their opposition to discrimination and their support for significant changes in the schools by conducting school boycotts. College students protested the lack of minority recruitment by universities and supported the establishment of Chicano Studies programs.[12] Militant strikes and protest actions at times were the primary means for bringing about change in higher education. During the late 1960s and early 1970s, institutions of higher learning, at times grudgingly, began to establish Chicano Studies programs in those areas where significant pressure was applied by students and their allies.[13]

During the 1970s, Mexican-origin activists continued to lobby, litigate, and mobilize for changes in the structures, policies, and content of public education, even as the national political climate became more conservative and as the level of radical activism among some youth and working-class groups decreased. From 1970 to 1977, radical activism precipitously declined due to state repression and differences of opinion among the activists themselves. The federal government sought to disrupt the Chicano Movement through surveillance, use of provocateurs, and a campaign of misinformation. Within the movement, there were differences over organizing strategies,[14] clashes over personalities, and tensions between different groups subscribing to varied political ideologies such as conservatism, liberalism, nationalism, and marxism.[15] As a result, the groups were unable to reach consensus on strategy or tactics. The community was also divided along gender lines, as males failed to seriously heed the charges of sexism raised by Chicanas.[16] The result was disunity in purpose and loss of some of the gains made by the Chicano Movement. There was also a loss of commitment to collective struggles on behalf of workers and either withdrawal, cooptation, or pursuit of narrow self-interests.

The decrease in radical activism did not signal the collapse of the movement for educational equality and cultural recognition, merely its transformation. During this entire period, activism in general increased as a result of the growing participation of educators, parents, feminists, and a new generation of youth in the universities.

At the federal level, middle-class Mexican Americans sought several major types of changes. They expanded and strengthened educational policies that were in their interests, pressured the federal government, especially the Department of Justice, to file lawsuits against segregation in local school districts with large numbers of Mexican-origin children,[17] coaxed federal agencies such as the Office for Civil Rights and the Congress to investigate and issue public reports on the extent of discrimination against Mexican Americans in the schools, and lobbied for appointments to important policy-making agencies such as the Office of Bilingual Education, the Department of Education, Office of Economic Opportunity, and the White House. Through these efforts, middle-class activists increased federal involvement in the promotion of change on state and local levels.

Their efforts were modestly successful as indicated by the expansion of education programs that benefitted Mexican American children, the larger numbers of Mexican Americans in important policy-making positions in a few federal agencies, and the publication of various reports on the status of culturally distinct children in the schools.[18] Their modest success in increasing federal involvement in school reform is best illustrated in the case of bilingual education. In the early 1970s, bilingual-education policy was a minor piece of legislation that few districts took seriously. This policy was transformed into a significant instrument of school reform by the end of the decade.[19]

Those involved in legal struggles also continued their efforts. Although there were many groups involved in litigation, the Mexican American Legal Defense and Education Fund (MALDEF) led these efforts in the 1970s. During this decade, for instance, it monitored desegregation and language cases. It also extended its legal challenges to include exclusion and discrimination in the area of school-board elections,[20] employment hiring practices, and school access for undocumented children.[21]

By the latter part of the decade legal activists had won several important cases in the courts. They gained official recognition of their legal status as an ethnic-minority group and were successful in declaring segregation, testing, language exclusion, and at-large elections to be unconstitutional.[22] Thus, the more blatant discriminatory practices of administrators and teachers, such as the use of biased testing for the placement of Mexican-origin children in slow tracks and the "no Spanish-speaking" rules, were eliminated.[23]

At the local level, Mexican American activism became increasingly diverse but also more selective. The participation of students in reforming public education at the local level decreased, while that of parents and a school-based professional middle-class group of Mexican Americans increased. Mexican American parents and professionals continued the struggle initiated by students against school discrimination and for cultural recognition, but they reverted to the politics of accommodation in order to realize their social change goals. They led the efforts to diversify the professional staff and to introduce language and culture into the schools.[24] They also led the efforts to improve school-community relations and to increase the number of Mexican Americans in important policy-making positions throughout the local school districts. The push for changes in the local schools, as well as added federal pressures and reforms in school governance structures, led to a gradual but steady increase in the number of bilingual and ethnic studies classes offered, as well as in the number of Mexican Americans who were hired as teachers and administrators or elected to school board positions.[25]

Student involvement at the college level, unlike that at the secondary grades, continued during the 1970s. It did not die, collapse, or fade away as most historians have argued.[26] University students continued to struggle for equality and cultural recognition after 1973, but they abandoned their militant tactics. These students, at times with the support of the faculty or opposed by them, led the efforts to increase Mexican American access to higher education, to strengthen Chicano Studies programs, to expand Chicano Studies classes to include gender issues, and to develop a critical and conscientious Mexican American literary and intellectual tradition in American higher education.[27]

Students were relatively successful given the context of and opposition to their efforts.[28] This is reflected in the increased access of college-age students to the post-secondary grades, the institutionalization of Chicano Studies programs throughout the country, and the continued development of the field of Chicana and Chicano Studies.[29]

CONTINUATION OF MOVIMIENTO STRUGGLES IN THE ''HISPANIC ERA''

During the latter part of the 1970s and into the 1980s, the struggle against assimilation and inequality in the schools continued despite the trend towards conservatism and moderation in American political life. Although a small number of progressive activists, comprised of civil rights lawyers, students, Chicana feminists, and vocal members of the emerging gay and lesbian community, continued to promote radicalism, the dominant trend in the 1980s was toward moderation.

These new moderate activists within the Mexican-origin community sought to restore their hegemony over the community's political, cultural, and ideological development. Led by members of LULAC in the community and a variety of apolitical groups in the public and private schools, this new set of leaders replaced the Chicano ideology with an all-encompassing Hispanic model. More specifically, the identity of Chicanismo, or cultural nationalism, was discredited and replaced by a new identity based not on *mestizaje,* or the indigenous past, but on the Hispanic or white-European heritage of Spain. The goal of radical social change, and its implicit call for a critical view of American institutions and ideals, was replaced by one of moderate social change based on the lack of a critical perspective toward governmental authority. Street politics was also frowned upon and replaced by the politics of persuasion and negotiation. The "Hispanic generation" had arrived.[30]

Activists also had to contend with an increasing conservative political climate during the 1980s. This was reflected in the election of Ronald Reagan to the White House in 1980, the loss of the Senate to the Republicans, the emergence of the New Right, the loss of nerve by liberal politicians to fight for their own ideals, the restlessness of the lay public over minority rights, domestic and international economic conditions, immigration, especially from non-European countries, and the fragmentation of the left and of progressive organizations into groups with specific, single-issue concerns.[31]

The new political environment, as well as the emergence of the Hispanic generation, had a significant impact on the struggle against discrimination and assimilation in education. It either slowed, redirected, or diluted this struggle and its programs, but it did not halt the Movimiento, as several scholars argue. More specifically, due to the hostility of the federal government and the presence of moderate or conservative forces within the community, the cultural aspect of the movement was de-emphasized by some of the new leaders, and the tactics became less confrontational; but the efforts to eliminate various forms of discrimination continued. In other words, during the "Hispanic era" Chicana and Chicano activists continued their efforts to oppose, at all levels of government, the structural exclusion of Chicano culture and community from the schools.

During the period from 1978 to the early 1990s, middle-class activists continued to pressure the federal government for assistance in their struggle for equality. They sought additional legislation for meeting the needs of the new immigrants, fought to maintain existing funding levels for special educational programs, and pressured federal agencies to be more responsive to Mexican American interests.

These activists were only minimally successful in their efforts. The number of Mexican-origin individuals appointed to federal positions, for instance, increased although they were still underrepresented in important policy-making positions.[32] Some of these individuals, such as Lauro Cavazos who in 1987 was the first Chicano appointed to the position of secretary of education, were blatantly used by the administration to further the conservative political interests of the Republican party, not those of the community.[33] Chicano and Chicana activists were also able to preserve existing school programs that served the poor and to enact new ones aimed at meeting the needs of immigrant children.[34]

Middle-class activists likewise developed private, nonprofit organizations in order to influence the development of positive public policy as it affected the education and employment of Mexican-origin students. Groups such as the Inter-University Program for Latino Research and the Hispanic Policy Development Project (HPDP) were founded to conduct research on the Mexican-origin population, to publish demographic studies on its growth and impact on the schools, to conduct surveys and polls, to issue position papers on important issues such as education, and to promote structural changes that would improve Chicano and Chicana performance in the schools.[35] One study that had a significant impact on increasing awareness about the failure of schools to meet the needs of Mexican-origin children and the need to promote reform, especially at the secondary level, was the report, *Make Something Happen,* issued by HPDP in 1984. The report argued that a shocking proportion of the "Hispanic" youth was being wasted "because their educational needs are neither understood nor met, their high aspirations unrecognized, their promising potential stunted."[36] It issued the report as a means of encouraging changes in the schools. "Curriculum prescriptions are designed to provide Hispanics with skills they will use throughout their lives, and with an education that will challenge and fulfill their intellectual and cultural potential," it argued.[37]

Most of the activists at the federal level, however, were on the defensive, as the federal government sought to dismantle many of the gains made during the 1960s and 1970s. This was especially the case during the 1980s, when the federal executive branch of government was controlled by Republicans.[38] In 1980 President Ronald Reagan initiated the most recent effort to reverse the trend toward federal involvement in social policy, especially education, and his policy was continued throughout the decade. During that period, programs fought for by the Chicana and Chicano activists were consolidated, reduced, weakened, or eliminated.

An example of the area in which the community activists lost ground was bilingual-education policy. In the 1970s bilingual education had been strengthened and expanded to accommodate the increasing needs of language-minority-group children. During the decade from 1978 to 1988, bilingual-education policy was transformed from a major piece of legislation, allowing the promotion of bilingualism and multiculturalism, to a minor one aimed at teaching monolingualism and monoculturalism. The reforms of bilingual-education policy were led by individuals who were part of a national conservative movement opposed to cultural and linguistic pluralism in American life and to the use of the schools as instruments of minority empowerment. They opposed bilingual education in order to disfranchise recently empowered ethnic-minority groups such as Mexican Americans and to assert the dominance of Anglo-American cultural and linguistic forms. By the mid-1980s they succeeded in halting the growth of bilingualism in public life, in shifting the politics of debate away from language maintenance towards assimilation, and in increasing divisiveness over language-based policies.[39] Not only was the goal of bilingual education changed, but under the Reagan and Bush administrations, the budget was significantly cut and the enforcement mechanisms eliminated. The Reagan administration also made systematic efforts to undermine the demographic, philosophical, and research basis for bilingual education in this country.[40] Despite these great odds, Mexican-origin activists and other committed educators continued to struggle against the attempts to undermine bilingual education and continued to reaffirm the need for its further development.[41]

Chicana and Chicano activists, especially civil rights lawyers and professional educators, also continued their legal struggles for equality during the late 1970s and 1980s, despite the increasingly conservative political climate. Unlike what had occurred in earlier years, the number of groups involved in litigation probably decreased due to the dismantling of federal programs. For this reason MALDEF became the most important group leading these efforts during this period. In order to carry out its activities MALDEF sought funding from a variety of sources, including foundations, corporations, labor unions, and individuals.[42] With these funds they were able to file lawsuits against some school districts for obviously discriminatory practices such as segregation. (As late as 1986, MALDEF filed a desegregation case against the San Jose, California, schools.)[43]

MALDEF also challenged the inadequate enforcement of laws requiring provision of bilingual education to Hispanic students. In 1981 it won an important case reaffirming the civil rights of language-minority children such as Mexican Americans. Under the Reagan administration, the Office for Civil Rights (OCR) had been cut to such an extent that it was no longer involved in enforcing legal mandates for bilingual instruction. MALDEF filed suit to enforce the provision for bilingual education as required by an earlier 1974 law, the Equal Educational Opportunities Act (EEOA).[44] In the *Castañeda v. Pickard* case, the appeals court ruled that districts failing to provide language-minority children with special language assistance violated their civil rights, whether or not they were victims of deliberate discrimination. The decision added that vaguely defined "good faith efforts" did not discharge school officials of their responsibilities to provide these children with language instruction. The court also noted that because Congress had failed to define "appropriate action," the court was obligated to define its own criteria for a program serving limited-English-proficiency (LEP) students. (The court's three criteria were that the program had to be based on "a sound educational theory," it had to be "implemented effectively" with adequate resources and personnel, and, after a trial period, it had to be evaluated as effective in overcoming language problems.)[45]

Gómez v. Illinois State Board of Education was another important case in which MALDEF challenged a local school district's inadequate response to the language needs of Mexican Americans. On 30 January 1987 the U.S. Circuit Court of Appeals ruled that the state of Illinois was required by law to implement the Transitional Bilingual Education Act in a way that assured that Spanish-speaking children were not deprived of equal educational opportunity.[46]

Not only did MALDEF tackle existing practices, it extended the discrimination struggle to new areas. For example, it challenged the schools' blatant exclusion of undocumented children and filed lawsuits against inequities in public school finance and in public school resource allocation.[47] In the case on immigrant children, known as *Plyer v. Doe,* MALDEF won a landmark ruling from the U.S. Supreme Court. In this case, MALDEF's attorneys, Vilma Martínez and Peter Roos, argued that the Texas code, which allowed school districts to exclude immigrant children, violated the Fourteenth Amendment. The Supreme Court agreed with MALDEF and held that the children of undocumented aliens were protected by the equal protection clause of the Constitution. This case provided MALDEF with its "best victory" during the early 1980s.[48]

The inequitable funding of public education was also expanded to institutions of higher education in the late 1980s. In late 1987, for instance, three Chicano organizations—MALDEF, LULAC, and the American GI Forum—filed a wide-ranging lawsuit against the state university system in Texas, charging that it discriminated against the state's growing Mexican American population. The suit alleged that the state had failed to provide equal educational opportunities to "Hispanic" residents by failing to adequately recruit and admit Mexican Americans to public universities and by failing to offer necessary programs, particularly at graduate and professional schools in predominantly Mexican American areas.[49] Chicano organizations were successful at the local district level when in 1992 the court decided in their favor.[50]

The lawsuits against discrimination in public education policies and practices at all levels of instruction were indicative of the continuity in the middle-class struggle for equality and against assimilation. In some cases, MALDEF joined with additional groups to challenge the existence of other discriminatory policies or practices that impacted education. In the late 1970s, for instance, MALDEF joined with LULAC to file charges of employment discrimination against the school district in Houston, Texas.[51] During the latter part of the 1970s and throughout the 1980s, it also joined forces with the Southwest Voter Registration and Education Project and the Texas Rural Legal Aid to file hundreds of lawsuits against at-large elections in Texas, New Mexico, and California.[52] These legal challenges, among other things, served to increase Mexican American involvement in school-board politics and to elect Chicanos and Chicanas to these policy-making positions.[53]

At the same time that individuals and groups persisted in their legal struggles, activists at the local level continued to fight for school reform. Unlike what happened in earlier years, the number of Chicano students and parents involved in the promotion of change in the schools decreased. Much of this decline in activism during the late 1970s and 1980s was probably due to the increasing conservatism among students and to the dismantling of federal and state educational programs. Individuals and students from the community continued to complain about unequal resources, discriminatory treatment, and the continued pattern of poor school performance, but little was done about their complaints. In cities throughout the country, community activists sought to have Chicanos or Chicanas appointed to important administrative and policy-making positions within their districts as a means for increasing change in the schools.[54] In some cases, students took to the streets and protested inferior school conditions.[55] Although student and parent activism in the local schools decreased, it did not die out totally. A new group of activists comprised primarily of middle-class reformers, such as school administrators, counselors, and teachers, emerged to take the place of parents and students.[56]

Middle-class activists at the school level, in a way similar to what students and parents had done, struggled to increase their presence in the schools and to bring about changes in the method of instruction, in the curriculum, and in the manner in which the school related to the community. However, by the late 1980s many of these middle-class reformers lessened their commitment to change. The absence of strong parent and student involvement, as well as the strength of the conservative political climate, encouraged these developments. A significant proportion of middle-class professionals assumed roles in the schools that reinforced the exclusionary, discriminatory, and assimilationist policies of American education. Some of them even came to believe in the presumed inferiority of Mexican-origin children and in the need to quickly replace an individual's linguistic and cultural heritage with the English language and American customs.[57]

During the conservative 1980s, a few discriminatory policies and practices, prohibited by law, either continued to exist or else re-emerged in the schools. Access to the curriculum for limited-English-proficient children, for instance, decreased as a result of the dismantling of federal and state programs. Biased testing and the discriminatory placement of Mexican Americans in EMR and slow-learning classes, as well as the degree of segregation and of unequal funding of these schools, also increased.[58]

The dropout issue likewise continued to be a problem. The proportion of Mexican-origin children that dropped out declined from 50 to 32 percent between 1980 and 1986, but these rates were still more than twice as high as the rates for whites. The community thus continued to be disproportionately affected by the economic and social costs of dropping out.[59]

On university campuses, a similar phenomenon of determined activism and mixed results was apparent during the conservative 1980s and early 1990s. Among students and faculty, there was an increasing professionalization and fragmentation of groups that impacted activism on and off campus. Some evidence indicates that activism increased among students, but it was primarily social or apolitical in nature. During the 1980s, for instance, many Chicano and Chicana students established groups geared toward advancing their own narrow professional self-interests. Countless numbers of new interest groups such as pre-law, pre-medicine, and pre-engineering were established during this period. Other Chicanos and Chicanas established Greek societies and engaged in activities that did not directly benefit the working-class community on or off campus.[60]

Not all student groups were social or apolitical. Some of these organizations, such as those established by Marxist groups, Chicana feminists, or lesbian and gay groups, continued to struggle against inequality on campus.[61] These groups, either working in conjunction with or, at times, in opposition to established organizations such as the Movimiento Estudiantil Chicano de Aztlán (MECHA), challenged the varied systems of exploitation and domination that faced the Mexican-origin community in the university. In the late 1980s and early 1990s, for instance, students in California helped organize rallies and marches in Sacramento to oppose budget cuts in higher education. Students at a variety of universities throughout the country, e.g., Stanford University, the University of California system, and the University of Wisconsin at Madison, likewise mobilized against the continuing racist, sexist, and assimilationist forces on campus. Chicana feminists on and off campus challenged sexism within the movement and within the discipline of Chicano Studies and developed a more comprehensive analysis of the history and contemporary status of the Mexican-origin population.[62]

Muñoz has argued that while these student groups were ideologically diverse, the majority of them were assimilationist, reformist, and conventionalist; that is, they tended to reject self-designated terms based on an indigenous or mestizo identity, revolutionary change, and nonconventional strategies and tactics. In the place of the Chicano ideology, they substituted a Hispanic model, i.e., a government-imposed European white-ethnic identity, a demand for moderate reforms, and use of conventional social change strategies.[63] I would argue that, while reformist in nature, the most politically involved were not Hispanic in identity and did not resort primarily to conventional social change strategies. They had a distinct Chicano or Chicana identity, believed in radical social change, especially in eliminating the racist, classist, and patriarchical systems of domination, and were willing to use all types of strategies in their efforts. They utilized marches, rallies, and demonstrations as well as litigation, education, and lobbying. The activists of the 1980s were much more ideologically and politically committed to equality and ethnicity than what contemporary scholars have said about them.

Chicano and Chicana faculty also continued to be involved, but mostly in the hiring and promotion of minority faculty, in their own research and teaching concerns, and in the development of a new intellectual tradition in academia. In the process of this involvement, they accepted the university's norms for survival and advancement and began either to isolate themselves from student-oriented campus struggles or to exclude students and community from governing Chicano Studies departments. Many, if not most, struggled against discrimination in the university and in the intellectual community, but did so independent of the students.[64] Despite the tensions caused between the faculty and students, they were able to institutionalize Chicano Studies in certain places and contribute especially to the growth of a Chicano and Chicana Studies intellectual tradition in higher education.[65]

In addition to the struggles around specific issues pertaining to their status as either students or faculty, there were also much broader types of political encounters. During the second part of the decade, for instance, students, faculty, and staff, especially administrators, played increasingly vital roles in challenging the intellectual and political hegemony of Anglos in the university.[66] Several key actions were taken beginning in 1986. First,

Chicano and Chicana activists, at times in cooperation with other students of color, protested racial and sexual harassment on campus and demanded the development of racial awareness classes for the campus community and demanded procedures and policies against this type of treatment. In other words, they demanded a more hospitable environment in the universities. Second, they protested the low enrollment and low retention of minority students and faculty on campus and demanded the development of increased commitment to affirmative action.[67] Third, they protested the omission or distortion of the Chicana and Chicano experience in the core curriculum. In other words, the activists on campus, students as well as faculty and staff, demanded the extension of the Chicana and Chicano curriculum to mainstream students. This was part of a larger effort aimed at incorporating minority perspectives and frameworks into the mainstream or Eurocentric curriculum. Chicana and Chicano Studies thus was no longer simply for Chicana and Chicano students, but for all students. The strategies the new activists utilized ranged all the way from rallies, to persuasion, to mandating course requirements and pressuring faculty into accepting them.

The extension of Chicano Studies into the mainstream curriculum, as well as the continued pressure for increased access to universities, led to a strong backlash among whites and contributed to the resurgence of a campaign against diversity in American life. This new campaign against diversity and for conformity was visible in the emergence of the Politically Correct Movement (PCM), a systematic effort aimed at eliminating or reducing cultural and linguistic diversity in the schools. More specifically, it was a campaign against cultural diversity in education in general and non-white minority cultures in particular.

These developments, as I noted above, did not go unanswered. Mexican-origin organizations, as well as other groups, vigorously opposed these assimilationist, racist, and sexist efforts and vociferously defended diversity in the schools. A major result of these pressures and counterpressures was conflict and controversy in the politics of curricular reform. The struggle thus continues to this day.

CONCLUSION

The above remarks have provided a brief overview of Mexican-origin activism in education during the latter part of the 1970s and the 1980s. The effort to eliminate discrimination and to promote ethnicity in the schools was a continuous process that did not die out. The struggle against assimilation and discrimination continued, despite a changing environment and internal conflicts. This struggle also was also carried on by a multiplicity of groups that included the middle class, grass-roots organizations, and youth. Youth, and especially students, were not the only or primary actors in this historical movement for equality and against assimilation. They were, however, an integral component of a larger effort to improve the schools.

The struggle for educational equality was also a contradictory process that led to mixed results. At one level, the struggle against discrimination in the contemporary period challenged the dominant ideology of assimilationism, but was unable to replace it with a more pluralistic model. At another level, the quest for education, in most cases, successfully challenged discriminatory structures and processes, but did not eliminate the practice of discrimination. Much of this failure was due to governmental opposition and to the contradictions and tensions within the Mexican American activist population. At still another level, the exclusion of the Chicano community and its heritage was corrected, but only partially. These individuals and their experiences were incorporated into the structure and content of public education, but they were still vastly underrepresented in important decision-making positions within the schools or were inaccurately portrayed in the schools.[68]

In summary, then, this study has shown how Mexican-origin people during the 1980s were not passive victims of an oppressive and racist public school system, but active participants in the historical process of change. This population group constantly contested, challenged, adapted, rejected, or struggled against policies and practices viewed as contrary to their political and cultural interests. The Chicano Movement, in other words, was still very much alive during the period of increasing conservatism and moderation. It underwent transformations but it never collapsed, not even under the weight of the "Hispanic generation."

NOTES

1. Mario T. García, "John Chávez, The Lost Land," in *Chicano Discourse,* eds. Tatcho Mindiola, Jr., and Emilio Zamora, (Houston: Mexican American Studies Program, 1992), 164.

2. Juan Gómez-Quiñones, *Chicano Politics: Reality and Promise, 1940–1960* (Albuquerque: University of New Mexico Press, 1990), 103; Mario T. García, *Mexican Americans* (New Haven: Yale University Press, 1989); Carlos Muñoz, Jr., *Youth, Identity, Power: The Chicano Movement* (New York: Verso, 1989).

3. Muñoz argues that the Chicano Movement was a quest for identity and power. I would argue that, for some, it was a quest for identity, but for others, it was a quest for public recognition of their Mexican heritage. I would also argue that social change, not power, was the goal of the Chicano Movement. Power, in my view, was merely a means to an end, not an end in itself. See Muñoz, *Youth, Identity, Power.*

4. Gómez-Quiñones (*Chicano Politics,* 103) refers to this process as "a variegated burst of activity."

5. Members of the Mexican American Generation were born or reared in the United States in the early part of the twentieth century and became involved in civil rights and labor-organizing activities during the years from the 1930s to the early 1960s. They believed in acculturation, in reforming the existing social order, and in using conventional means to realize social reform. For an excellent history of this generation, see M. García, *Mexican Americans.*

6. For a brief history of this school movement, see Rudolfo Acuña, *Occupied America: A History of Chicanos,* 3rd ed. (New York: Harper Collins, 1988), 324.

7. The American GI Forum, for instance, in April 1965 protested the exclusion of Mexican Americans from the drawing up of federal guidelines for implementing War-on-Poverty programs in the Southwest. See American GI Forum, "Testimony on the Office of Economic Opportunity Submitted by Rudy Ramos, Director of the Washington, D.C., Office of the American G.I. Forum," 26 April 1965, Héctor P. García Archives, Corpus Christi, Texas; see also, AGIF, Washington, D.C., Report, "Anatomy of a Presidential Statement on Equal Employment Opportunity and Civil Rights for Mexican Americans, 1966" (Washington, D.C.: AGIF, 1966), Héctor P. García Archives, Corpus Christi, Texas. For a brief narrative of these events, see Carl Allsup, *The American G.I. Forum: Origins and Evolution* (Austin: University of Texas, 1982), 134–37.

8. For an example of the role of Mexican Americans in federal-policy development in the mid-1960s, see Gilbert Sánchez, "An Analysis of the Bilingual Education Act, 1967–1968" (Ph.D. diss., University of Massachusetts, 1973).

9. Some activists wanted the Department of Health, Education, and Welfare (D/HEW) to conduct an investigation of school discrimination against Mexican Americans in the Southwest. See, for instance, James De Anda, "Civil Rights—Need for Executive Branch to Take Positive Steps to Rectify Discrimination in Jury Selection, Voting Eligibility, and School Enrollment," in *The Mexican American: A New Focus on Opportunity* (Washington DC: Inter-Agency Committee on Mexican American Affairs, 1968), 217–21.

10. For a brief history of these efforts, see Thomas P. Carter and Roberto Segura, *Mexican*

Americans in the Schools: A Decade of Change (Princeton: College Entrance Examination Board, 1979).

11. Muñoz, *Youth, Identity, Power;* Guadalupe San Miguel, Jr., "The Community Is Beginning to Rumble," *Houston Review: History and Culture of the Gulf Coast* 13, no. 3 (1991): 127–48.

12. Acuña, *Occupied America,* 323.

13. Alfred I. Zúñiga and Barbara Rigley-Acosta, "A Study of the Nature of Chicano Studies Written between 1968 and 1974: A Tentative Description," in *Perspectives on Chicano Education,* eds. Tobias and Sandra González (Stanford: Chicano Fellows Program, 1975), 103–23.

14. The farm worker movement, for instance, was divided over organizing strategies. César Chávez, in California, did not support the organizing of farm workers in south Texas, and those in south Texas were divided over whether they should be independent of Chávez or part of his farm worker group. See Acuña, *Occupied America,* 324–30.

15. Richard García, "The Chicano Movement and the Mexican American Community, 1972–1978: An Interpretative Essay," *Socialist Review,* 40/41 (1978): 117–36.

16. See Sonia A. López, "The Role of the Chicana within the Student Movement," in *Essays on la Mujer,* Anthology 1, eds. Rosaura Sánchez and Rosa Martínez Cruz (Los Angeles: Chicano Studies Center Publications, 1977), 16–29.

17. The Nixon administration had opposed the Mexican American community's efforts to be declared an identifiable minority group for desegregation purposes in the Austin Independent School District case. See *United States v. Austin Independent School District,* docketed, No. A-70-CA-89 (W.D. Tex., 28 June 1971), appeal docketed, No. 71-2508 (5th Cir., 7 Aug. 1971).

18. These reports were not limited to schooling. Other areas and institutions such as politics, law enforcement agencies, and federal employment were also investigated. Some of the most important reports issued in the early 1970s were those pertaining to the findings of the Mexican American Education Study conducted by the U.S. Commission on Civil Rights between 1969 and 1974. These reports dealt with the education of Mexican Americans in the five Southwestern states of Arizona, California, Colorado, New Mexico, and Texas, where about 85 percent of all Chicanos lived in the early 1970s. For a list of these reports, published 1971–1974, see *Para los niños—For the Children: Improving Education for Mexican Americans* (Washington, D.C.: U.S. Commission on Civil Rights, October 1974), 27.

19. For two different interpretations of the history of bilingual education, see Guadalupe San Miguel, Jr., *"Let All of Them Take Heed": Mexican Americans and the Campaign for Educational Equality in Texas, 1910–1981* (Austin: University of Texas Press, 1987); and Diane Ravitch, *The Troubled Crusade: American Education, 1945–1980* (New York: Basic Books, 1983).

20. MALDEF initially met success in 1973 in the White case, which involved the constitutionality of at-large election districts. See *White v. Regester,* 412 U.S. 755 (1973). A focal point of later challenges was aimed at other at-large elections and at enforcing the provisions of the Voting Rights Act of 1965, which were extended to Mexican Americans in 1976. The Voting Rights Act covered a wide range of electoral practices and in certain ways offered greater protection than reapportionment lawsuits. It was explicitly intended to

remove structural barriers that limited access of minorities such as Mexican Americans to the political process.

21. For a history of MALDEF's efforts, see Karen O'Connor and Lee Epstein, "A Legal Voice for the Chicano Community: The Activities of the Mexican American Legal Defense and Educational Fund, 1968–1982," *Social Science Quarterly* 65 (1984): 245–57.

22. O'Connor and Epstein, "Legal Voice"; Carter and Segura, *Mexican Americans in Schools.*

23. They were less successful in the area of school finance. For the successful litigation in California, see *Serrano et al. v. Ivy Baker Priest,* 96 *California Reporter,* 487 P. 2d 1241 (1971). For the major defeat in school finance at the U.S. Supreme Court level, see *San Antonio Independent School District v. Rodríguez,* 411 U.S. 1 (1973).

24. See, for instance, the letter from Alicia Alvarez, a parent activist, demanding the hiring of Mexican American teachers and the implementation of bilingual-education classes in one local district in Michigan, cited in Alfredo H. Benavides, "A Midwestern Community and Its Schools: An Analysis of Mutual Images and Interactions," in *Bilingual Education and Public Policy in the United States,* ed. Raymond V. Padilla (Ypsilanti: Department of Foreign Languages and Bilingual Studies, Eastern Michigan University, 1979), 212–28.

25. Increased parental involvement was also apparent, especially in the establishment of bilingual-education programs and in a variety of compensatory education programs such as migrant education. Despite the participation of parents in these programs, however, the professionals, such as program directors, teachers, and curriculum specialists, dominated the type of curricular, instructional, and administrative changes promoted at the local level. For a study of parental and professional involvement in the local schools during the 1970s, see Rodolfo Rodríguez, "Citizen Participation in ESEA Title VII Programs: An Inquiry into the Impact of a Federal Mandate," in Padilla, *Bilingual Education,* 260–80.

26. Muñoz, *Youth, Identity, Power;* Gómez Quiñones, *Chicano Politics.*

27. Muñoz, *Youth, Identity, Power,* 127–70.

28. Opposition came from various sources, including federal and state governments, traditionalist administrators and professors, and Chicano males. For one of the earliest published accounts of the barriers to Chicana concerns within the student movement during the early 1970s, see López, "Role of the Chicana," 16–29.

29. Muñoz, *Youth, Identity, Power.*

30. For an overview of this generation, see Gómez-Quiñones, *Chicano Politics,* 155–87; Acuña, *Occupied America,* 363–451; and Muñoz, *Youth, Identity, Power.* 171–89.

31. Ira Shor, *Culture Wars: School and Society in the Conservative Restoration, 1969–1984* (New York: Routledge and Kegan Paul, 1986). For a contemporary account of the significance of Reagan's election on educational policy during the early 1980s, see J. Shuster, "Out of the Frying Pan: The Politics of Education in a New Era," *Phi Delta Kappan* 10 (1982): 583–91.

32. For an overview of the growing presence of Chicanos in important policy-making positions in the federal bureaucracy during the late 1970s and early 1980s, see Harry Pachon, "Hispanic Underrepresentation in the Federal Bureaucracy: The Missing Link in the Policy Process," in *The State of Chicano Research on Family, Labor, and Migration,* eds. Armando Valdez, Albert Camarillo and Tomás Almaguer (Stanford: Stanford Center for Chicano Research, 1983), 209–18.

33. Gómez-Quiñones (*Chicano Politics,* 172) notes that the appointment of prominent Chicanos such as Cavazos or Manuel Luján of New Mexico as secretary of the interior were made "to dilute protest or to facilitate negative change in a particular program." See also Pachon, "Hispanic Underrepresentation"; and Acuña, *Occupied America.*

34. During this period, middle-class groups such as the National Association for Bilingual Education and others also supported the formulation and implementation of new programs aimed at meeting the needs of local school districts with large numbers of immigrant children. For a review of the variety of services provided for limited-English-proficient and immigrant children, see Terrell H. Bell, *The Condition of Bilingual Education in the Nation, 1984: A Report from the Secretary of Education to the President and the Congress* (Washington, D.C., 1984), 51–56.

35. Acuña, *Occupied America,* 381.

36. Hispanic Policy Development Project, *Make Something Happen: Hispanics and Urban High School Reform,* vol. 1 (Washington, D.C.: Hispanic Policy Development Project, 1984), 3.

37. This study was based on a series of hearings held in some of the largest metropolitan areas containing significant numbers of Mexican, Puerto Rican, and Cuban school age children. For a list of these cities as well as a list of the individuals who appeared before the commission, see Hispanic Policy Development Project, *Make Something Happen,* vol. 1, 50–52.

38. Shor (*Culture Wars*) notes that the "big chill" in education generally began in the late 1960s with the election of Richard M. Nixon as president. Conservatism, however, gained significant support in the decade 1977–1988.

39. The arguments on behalf of English and against bilingualism are outlined in S. I. Hayakawa, *The English Language Amendment: One Nation . . . Indivisible?* (Washington, D.C.: Washington Institute for Values in Public Policy, 1985). See also Gerda Bikales and Gary Imhoff, *A Kind of Discordant Harmony: Issues in Assimilation,* Discussion Series, no. 2 (Washington, D.C.: U.S. English, 1985).

40. For a history of these efforts, see Guadalupe San Miguel, Jr., "Bilingual Education Policy Development: The Reagan Years, 1980–1987," *NABE Journal* 12 (1988): 97–113.

41. Some of the early pioneers of bilingual education such as Blandina Cárdenas Ramírez, José A. Cárdenas, Josué González, Joe Bernal, Albar Peña, Gloria Zamora, and Carlos Truan are still very much in the forefront of the struggle for equality and against assimilation in the 1990s. For a list of these and several other pioneers in bilingual education, see the brochure published by the National Association for Bilingual Education (NABE) for its annual conference, NABE, 22nd annual International Bilingual/Multicultural Education Conference, Houston, Tex., 24–27 February 1993, 38–39.

42. Maurilio E. Vigil, "MALDEF: Chicano Advocate for Educational, Economic and Political Reform," in *Community Empowerment and Chicano Scholarship,* eds. Mary Romero and Cordelia Candelaria (Berkeley: National Association for Chicano Studies, 1992), 233.

43. The case was known as *Vásquez v. San Jose Unified School District.* For a summary of this case, see Mexican American Legal Defense and Education Fund, *Annual Report,* 1986, 8. See also Vigil, "MALDEF," 231–44 for a good summary of MALDEF's litigation strategies during the 1980s.

44. Section 1703 (F) of the EEOA required that each school district take "appropriate action to

overcome language barriers that impede equal participation by its students in its instructional programs."

45. See *Castañeda v. Pickard,* 648 F. 2d 989 (1981), especially pp. 1009–10.

46. MALDEF, *Annual Report* (1986–1987), 8; Vigil, "MALDEF," 236.

47. *Plyer v. Doe,* 457 U.S. 202 (1982); *Edgewood v. Kirby,* 777 S.W. 2d 391 (Tex. 1989). The challenge to the allocation of resources within the district occurred in Los Angeles and was called *Rodríguez v. Los Angeles Unified School District.* For a review of this as well as the other cases, see Vigil, "MALDEF," 235.

48. *Plyer v. Doe.* For MALDEF's comment, see MALDEF, *Annual Report* (1982), 4.

49. Peter Applebome, "Texas Hispanics Sue Colleges, Claim Bias," *Santa Barbara News-Press,* 4 December 1987.

50. *Richards v. LULAC,* no. 12-87-5242-A (Texas, 31 July 1992).

51. *Houston Post,* 18 December 1977; 18 June 1978; and 4 February 1979. See also Arnoldo De León, *Ethnicity in the Sunbelt: A History of Mexican Americans in Houston* (Houston: Mexican American Studies, University of Houston, 1989), 203–19, for a summary of these types of actions in Houston, Texas; the actions taken by the local school district in the *Castañeda v. Pickard* case.

52. In New Mexico it helped to end at-large elections in 1982. See William V. Flores, "Chicano Empowerment and the Politics of At-Large Elections in California: A Tale of Two Cities," in Romero and Candelaria, *Community Empowerment,* 186.

53. For an overview of the legal strategies to eliminate at-large elections during the 1980s, see Flores, "Chicano Empowerment," 188–200.

54. For an example of community activists pushing for added changes in the local district in Houston, Texas, during the 1980s, see De León, *Ethnicity in the Sunbelt,* 208–9.

55. The walkout at Burbank Middle School, a predominantly Mexican American school in Houston is an exmple. See William Pack and Daren Roebuck, "One Hundred Students Protest at HISD Middle School," *Houston Post,* 23 February 1991. See also Javier Rodríguez, "Blackboard Bungle: What Has HISD Learned from the Walkout at Austin High School?," *Houston Press,* 26 April 1990.

56. The dominance of middle-class individuals in local reform was evident in the multitude of workshops offered at the 1993 NABE conference. Even the "Parent Institutes" offered at NABE were dominated, not by parents, but by professionals involved in encouraging selective involvement of parents in the education of their children.

57. This generalization is based on the author's personal participation in school improvement plans as a parent representative in two different school districts—Santa Barbara, California, and Houston, Texas—between 1988 and 1992.

58. Gary Orfield, *Public School Segregation in the United States, 1968–1980* (Washington, D.C.: Joint Center for Political Studies, 1983).

59. For an overview of the social and economic costs of dropping out of school, see Russell Rumberger, "Chicano Dropouts: A Review of Research and Policy Issues," in *Chicano School Failure and Success,* ed. Richard Valencia (New York: Falmer Press, 1991), 64–89.

60. Acuña, *Occupied America.*

61. For a brief look at the events leading to the formation of Chicana feminists within the

National Association for Chicano Studies between 1982 and 1984, see Teresa Córdova, preface to *Chicana Voices: Intersections of Class, Race, and Gender,* eds. Teresa Córdova et al. (Austin: Center for Mexican American Studies, 1986), ix–xi. During the 1990s the lesbian and gay students organized on campus and within the community. Two such groups that have emerged as powerful and vocal advocates for change within the National Association of Chicano Studies (NACS) have been the Lesbian Caucus and the National Association of Lesbian and Gay Activists (NALGA). Personal notes taken from the NACS 21st annual conference, San Jose State University, 25–27 March 1993.

62. For a brief look at the efforts made by Chicanas to impact the field of Chicano Studies, see Alma García, "Chicana Studies and 'La Chicana' Courses: Curriculum Options and Reforms," in Romero and Candelaria, *Community Empowerment,* 53–62. See also Cynthia Orozco, "Sexism in Chicano Studies and the Community," in Córdova, *Chicana Voices,* 11–18.

63. The diversity of ideological perspectives was very much apparent at the seventh annual National Chicano Student Conference held at the University of California, Berkeley, in the spring of 1986. Muñoz, *Youth, Identity, Power,* 185–86.

64. For an analysis of Chicano/Latino perceptions of their academic pursuits in the university during the late 1980s, see Hisauro Garza, "Academic Power, Discourse and Legitimacy: Minority Scholars in U.S. Universities," in Romero and Candelaria, *Community Empowerment,* 35–52.

65. Muñoz, *Youth, Identity, Power,* 127–80; Alma García, "Chicana Studies," 53–62. For a more critical view of Chicano Studies in the early 1990s, see René Núñez and Raúl Contreras, "Principles and Foundations of Chicano Studies: Chicano Organization on University Campuses in California," in Mindiola and Zamora, *Chicano Discourse,* 32–39. For a critical view of NACS in the 1990s, see Hisauro Garza, "Origins and Evolution of an Alternative Scholarship and Scholarly Organization," in Mindiola and Zamora, *Chicano Discourse,* 40–51.

66. See "A Report on the Status of Chicanos/Latinos at the University of California," presented by the University of California Chicano/Latino Consortium, June 1988. See also *Final Report* (or *The Holly Report*) (Madison: Steering Committee on Minority Affairs, Nov. 1987).

67. These activists demanded increased access of Mexican Americans to undergraduate programs as well as to professional and graduate programs. They also demanded increased resources, especially financial aid, to ensure their survival and advancement in the universities. Gradually, and largely as a response to the pressure by Chicanas/os, the numbers of Mexican American college students increased in the 1980s.

68. Linda Salvucci, "Completing America's Self-Image: Mexican Americans and the Politics of Textbook Adoption for U.S. History (1986–1992)." (paper presented at the 7th annual Martín de León Symposium on the Humanities, The History of Mexican American Education, University of Houston, Victoria, Texas, 24 April 1993).

JUNCTURE IN THE ROAD: CHICANO STUDIES

SINCE "EL PLAN DE SANTA BÁRBARA"

Ignacio M. García

Chicano Studies as a field of inquiry and a stimulus for social and political change is nearing a critical juncture, which will determine both its direction as an academic discipline and its contribution to the struggle for civil rights in the Mexican American community. Within the next ten years Chicano Studies will either retake its place as an agent of change or simply become another stepchild of the academic ivory tower. This juncture is approached as the field completes its twenty-sixth year, and as it continues to receive into its ranks a growing number of scholars who have no ideological connection with the original premises of Chicano Studies. It also comes at a time of renewed interest in Chicano Studies on college campuses nationwide.

The juncture seems to provide two major options and an added option that will become possible only through much negotiation and academic militancy.[1] The first option, and one which most non-Chicano faculty members and administrators favor, is that the Chicano Studies programs become integrated into larger ethnic studies programs, limit their courses to those cross-listed with core departments, or become diffused through having Chicano scholars and professional staff receive joint appointments within mainstream departments. The end result of this option is that Chicano Studies would be taught as a supplement to "legitimate" studies and that "bright" scholars would be attracted to programs other than Chicano Studies, for fear of not getting tenure. The second option is for Chicano Studies programs and centers to remain as they are, usually underfunded, understaffed, and considered only peripheral or marginal in importance as an academic field. This status will eventually lead to the loss of, or the inability to attract, good scholars and to an eventual decline in quality, leading these programs to the first option or an eventual phase-out.[2]

The third option, and the one most Chicano Studies adherents would rather see, is that these programs receive adequate funding, gain departmental status, have approved degree programs, and that their courses be part of the general education requirement of all students at the university level. This would allow for a large client population and a subsequent increase in the number of faculty members. This option would provide autonomy from other departments, whose faculty members are often hostile to Chicano Studies, yet allow the program to compete on an equal footing for university resources. It would also represent legitimacy, something that Chicano and Chicana scholars have been seeking since the decline of student activism and the rise of an academic backlash. More important, a stable base would allow Chicano Studies scholars to reach out toward the community to assist in resolving the problems that *la raza* faces daily. That was, in essence, the reason why Chicano Studies was founded. At the moment, many Chicano Studies programs remain stepchildren in the academy, with few resources, a limited staff, and often, a marginal reputation. This situation minimizes the programs' ability to do community service.

To understand why Chicano Studies as an academic pursuit approaches the twenty-first century in a precarious condition, it is important to summarize its history, some of its accomplishments and failures, and the issues which have continually arisen in the field. Chicano Studies has its roots in the work of the scholars who belonged to what Mario T. García calls the "Mexican American Generation": scholars such as Américo Paredes, Jovita González, George I. Sánchez, Carlos Castañeda, Arthur Campa, and others who first published works on Mexican Americans in the late 1940s, 1950s, and early 1960s.[3] These scholars had, in turn, been influenced by the folklorists who wrote numerous works on Chicanos during the 1940s, oftentimes under the auspices of the various writers' projects developed during the Great Depression.[4] These pre-1960s scholars usually gained their academic appointments the conventional way. While their works focused on Mexican Americans and were often critical of Anglo academic racism, these scholars stayed within the mainstream of their departments and their field. Though they published important introductory works during the beginnings of what is now Chicano Studies, they provided no Chicano paradigm,[5] nor did they stimulate a large number of Chicanos or Chicanas to pursue an academic career. (The fact is that there were few *raza* students at the university level.) It was not until the advent of the Chicano Movement that the idea of Chicano Studies began, first in California in the aftermath of the Los Angeles school blowouts of 1967–1968. From these school protests came the demand for Chicano courses and the rise in the interest in studying the Chicano experience. In 1968 California State College in Los Angeles became the first postsecondary institution to establish a department of Mexican American studies.[6] Several other California campuses followed suit with an assortment of centers and programs by the following year. By the early 1970s, there were programs in several other states, particularly Texas.

The main stimulus for Chicano Studies came from a conference at the University of California, Santa Barbara, sponsored by the Chicano Coordinating Committee on Higher Education. The committee, composed of students, faculty, and administrators, gathered together over 100 representatives from 29 California institutions of higher education to develop a master plan for Chicanos in higher education. The plan would also provide a guide for recruiting students to the university, map a strategy to hire and retain more Chicano faculty, and help in the development of support programs for students. Also from the conference came the idea of forming the student group Movimiento Estudiantil Chicano de Aztlán (MECHA) and the creation of Chicano Studies as an academic pursuit. The basis for the organization of both was the "Plan de Santa Bárbara," an educational blueprint that called for institutional reform within the "context of politics for change."[7] This meant that Chicano Studies had a responsibility beyond instructing students about their history and culture and helping them to meet their degree requirements. Carlos Muñoz, in writing about Chicano Studies, stated the purpose of the plan: "Clearly [the plan] was written to direct the development of Chicanos Studies toward the goals established by the [Chicano] student movement. Key to that movement were pride in Mexican identity and Mexican cultural traditions and in the working class legacy of Mexican Americans, and active involvement in struggles for social and political change. The student movement thus reflected an unequivocal break from the assimilationist, middle class ideology of the Mexican American Generation."[8]

Much like the rest of the movement, the Chicano Studies movement did not define its terms in a constrictive manner. Each student group with its faculty and administrative mentors was to identify its particular "context for change." Notwithstanding the nebulous foundations, the Plan de Santa Bárbara identified the educational needs of Chicanos as being unique and prescribed an autonomous approach to meeting those needs. Chicanos, and a small number of Chicanas, demanded the space and the authority to redirect the university's resources to the educating and empowering of the Mexican American community. "Chicanismo," as the Chicano Movement ideology came to be known, would serve as the fundamental ideology of the Chicano Studies educational policy. Because Chicanismo meant different things to different people, el Plan de Santa Bárbara created a stimulus for the creation of Chicano Studies programs throughout the Southwest, each with a different mission and oftentimes a unique curriculum.[9] On some campuses, junior faculty led the struggle for Chicano Studies, while on others the students spearheaded the move. Some groups sought academic degree programs, others just general "concienciación," and still others saw the centers as stimulus for political action within the universities and the community they served. The battles to establish these programs brought many students into the Chicano Movement. Even where centers were no more than a director and a part-time secretary, they attracted students into study groups, cultural activities, and university politics. Some also facilitated the students' linkage with community organizations.[10]

With the idea of a Chicano field of study blossoming, Chicano scholars and intellectuals sought a Chicano paradigm to answer the question of why Chicanos were where they were. Influenced by African American writings and those of Latin American scholars, Chicano scholars such as Juan Gómez-Quiñones, Carlos Muñoz, Mario Barrera, Charles Ornelas, Tomás Almaguer, and others developed the concept of Chicanos as an "internal colony." In an article entitled "The Barrio as an Internal Colony," Barrera, Ornelas, and Muñoz wrote that "internal colonialism means that Chicanos as a cultural, racial group exist in an exploited condition which is maintained by a number of mechanisms [and] the lack of control over those institutions which affect their lives. [It] results in the community finding its culture and social organization under constant attack from a racist society."[11]

With time, a Marxist framework was applied to the internal-colony analysis. This framework sought to connect monopoly capitalism and the development of internal colonialism in the Southwest. It also recognized the working-class legacy of the Mexican population in the United States. The internal-colony paradigm revolutionized the intellectual discussion of the Mexican American experience. It broke the ideological hold that assimilation and pluralism had on the intellectual development of those Mexicans born in this country and of those who had accepted the fact that their future lay in their activities north of the Río Grande. It destroyed the myth of the passive Chicano and the even more passive Chicana and relieved the burden that self-victimization brought to many Mexican Americans. The internal-colony model became, and still serves somewhat today as, a theoretical model for studying Chicanos. By the early 1970s, however, the internal-colony model had come under fire from Marxist scholars, and even from its original proponents, because it lacked the rigidity of a true ideology and particularly because its class analysis was weak. Still others attacked the theoretical model because its "rigidity" posed the danger of redirecting Chicano research into a "respectable" and "legitimate" direction acceptable to the university, but not necessarily conducive to the struggle for Chicano liberation.[12]

On 18 May 1973, thirty-six individuals, of whom eight were women, met to establish what came to be known as the National Association of Chicano Studies (NACS). The delegates condemned traditional scholarship dealing with Chicanos and called for social science research that was "problem-oriented, interdisciplinary, was critical of American institutions, and emphasized the relationship between class, race, and culture in determining the Chicano historical experience."[13] The association grew quickly in the 1970s, and by the end of the decade several major centers of Chicano Studies existed nationally. In the mid-1980s, the membership hovered around one thousand members.

The 1980s proved to be the beginning of difficult times for the programs that had been established the decade before. By the end of the 1970s, the Chicano student movement had waned significantly. Few campuses had active MECHA groups, and even fewer had militant faculties. The decade of the 1980s brought a conservative backlash, and with it the election of Ronald Reagan and George Bush, which translated into an attack on concepts like Chicano studies, bilingual education, and affirmative action. Most university and college administrations had been forced to accept Chicano Studies because of student unrest and because, for a short period of time, some communities had joined the students in demanding access to higher education. However, as student activism decreased, the administrative accommodation ceased. Budgets became tighter, and some programs faced cutbacks. In their study of Chicano Studies programs in 1985, José Rivera and Luis Ramón Burrola found that humanities and social science divisions, in which Chicano Studies is usually located, received a disproportionate percentage of budget cuts. They concluded that "financial crisis would mean that only essential courses will be offered . . . ending opportunities to experiment with new curricula and interdisciplinary courses."[14] Because Chicano Studies has rarely been seen as essential, it gets very low priority for funding and top consideration for cuts. The few Chicano faculty members in the 1980s found themselves alone in their battles with administrators. They also faced a mainstream faculty that had little regard for Chicano Studies, considering the field to be marginally academic at best.[15] By the time of the backlash, a number of former student activists were going through their own tenure process and faced criticism for their activism and their publications in a marginal field. For those who had published in Chicano journals, or had self-published because of the refusal of mainstream journals to publish works on Chicanos, the tenure process became a nightmare. It became a common occurrence to have Chicano scholars failing to get tenure, especially at major universities.[16]

For those who received tenure, the work expectations were often tougher than those for other similar-level scholars. Aside from teaching their normal loads, they had to mentor Chicano students and be on most committees dealing with Chicano issues. They had to work extra hard on being published by mainstream journals and presses and often had to socialize and become integrated into the university community without a mentor. Many of them became, in the words of Arturo Madrid, "onlies," the lone individuals in their departments to be involved in the field of Chicano Studies. By the early 1980s, there also began a steady decline in the number of students taking Chicano Studies courses. The heightened activism of the late 1960s and 1970s had generated a great interest in these courses, but growing conservatism and a more narcissistic attitude on the part of students led to a steady decline in enrollment. Finding a job and getting a "useful" degree became of greater importance than becoming culturally aware for most students.[17] In addition, many Chicano Studies programs began to move away from activist scholarship, which decreased their attractiveness. In these particular programs, it also meant the disfranchising of students: fewer and fewer students participated in decision making, in evaluating programs, or in the hiring process. The "militant" or "radical chic" faculty saw no need for student input as they felt they represented Chicano intellectualism, and conservative Chicano faculty and Anglo administrators saw the students as a threat to order and discipline in the academy.

In the 1980s, the field itself went through a metamorphosis that in some areas has changed the programs so much that they hardly resemble what the authors of el Plan de Santa Bárbara had in mind. Rather than teach a militant identity and a history of struggle, these programs emphasize degree requirements and deal with diversity in the United States. Much of the change came as a reaction to the attacks on the field as well as a result of a lack of Chicano influence in the training of new scholars. The fact remains that Chicano scholars have had little success in implementing the ideals of the Plan de Santa Bárbara as it relates to control of these programs. Few Chicano Studies programs ever became departments, with the exception of the ones at Northridge and San Diego. Last year a battle was waged to make one of the oldest programs—that at UCLA—a department, but resistance by the administration and faculty proved strong. After weeks of protests and a two-week fast, the students won a partial victory by getting the university to establish the César Chávez Center for Interdisciplinary Instruction in Chicana and Chicano Studies, a quasi-department that hires its own faculty and develops its own curriculum. However, it remains a center, not a department.[18] As programs, and even departments, most of the Chicano Studies units do not offer doctoral degrees. This means that most students seeking to enter the field may not receive much assistance or mentoring beyond the master's level. One example is the University of Arizona, which offers a master's program in Mexican American Studies through the Mexican American Studies and Research Center. However, the center itself offers only three courses—two at the entry level—and has no real mechanism for influencing the content of courses offered by other departments. Most of the other departments offer one to two courses on the subject area, meaning that a student wishing to emphasize Chicano Studies within his or her particular program, will receive only a very general view of the field. Few scholars in other departments have any understanding of Chicano Studies paradigms or theoretical models; thus instead of teaching Chicano Studies, they end up teaching a subject area in which the studied population happens to be Mexican American.

Another challenge to Chicano Studies is the influx into the field of Chicano scholars who were trained in the aforementioned manner. Their dissertations have been on a myriad of Chicano topics, but few have been trained in the historiography of the field. Their doctoral committees have often been composed of faculty members from departments in which Chicano Studies are marginalized. When they arrive at their first Chicano Studies position, many of them receive joint appointments in Chicano Studies and a mainstream department, which immediately places Chicano scholars in a dilemma—which department do they please? Joint appointments were meant to be advantageous to minority scholars by giving them status in a "legitimate" department.[19] Both Chicano Studies programs and the particular department are to monitor the tenure process and provide mentorship. Unfortunately, it becomes very clear early on that survival or tenure depends heavily on the core department. Those who choose to emphasize Chicano Studies agendas usually end up on the short end of the tenure process. A significant number of entry-level Chicano scholars who have already been intimidated by the "publish-or-perish" threat choose to concentrate on the demands of the core departments. Even that, however, does not guarantee tenure. What it does do, however, is to make a number of these scholars peripheral to the field of Chicano Studies.

Another group of scholars who have become peripheral to the field since the early 1980s consists of many of the older, tenured scholars who taught in the field from its beginning. Their absence from the leadership of NACS and the numerous Chicano Studies centers has created a vacuum that has not been adequately filled. Most have chosen to go on with their promotion odyssey or have concentrated on teaching and publishing. Some have played the "negotiations game," applying to different institutions to enhance their salary and research support in their own universities. A group of Chicano males appears in almost every major candidate search conducted. They have become obstacles to junior and entry-level scholars in gaining upward mobility.[20] But more unfortunate, some of the older scholars' productivity has diminished. Without the nationalist paradigm and with Marxism partialy disgraced by political events in the former Soviet Union, these scholars find themselves with other interests. For those who are still active researchers and instructors, the idea of being in administrative positions within Chicano Studies where they would constantly have to fight budget cuts, hiring freezes, institutional racism, and critical colleagues is not attractive. Many of these older scholars fought for Chicano Studies in its first decade or two and now find many of the same battles being waged, but without the benefit of a large number of student sympathizers. Some of these older scholars also see some of the new battles as much more divisive and unwinnable. Their absence from administrative roles has created a vacuum filled by academic bureaucrats who understand university politics but have little commitment to serious research or to the spirit of el Plan de Santa Bárbara. Their programs consequently lack vision and often find themselves floating toward "soft money" grants, which may increase staff, but usually move the programs away from activist scholarship.

Post-modern sectarianism—lesbian-feminism, neo-Marxism, and a militant form of Latinoism—is another challenge to the field since the 1980s. Many centers find themselves challenged by non-Chicano Latino scholars who want to promote their scholarly interests. They argue that all Latino groups have a common experience with racism and poverty in American society. Also, programs which emphasize the inclusive Hispanic approach are more likely to gain research and support funds more easily. Because immigration has been a major area of study for Chicano Studies and because the immigrant groups are now more diverse among numerous Latino groups, there is an intellectual challenge to Chicano Studies to become inclusive or else to be seen as shallow and exclusionary.[21] Neo-Marxist scholarship has also been a challenge to Chicano Studies, as it remains critical of the nationalist vestiges of the field and threatens to destroy the cultural relevance of the Chicano experience. Most neo-Marxists, however, offer little in terms of workable paradigms, even as they seek to critique a nationalist slant to Chicano scholarship. Their contribution lacks even the scholarly analysis of the "class-struggle Marxists" of the early years of the Chicano Studies movement.

Chicana Studies, as an extension or at times a competitor of Chicano Studies, has become possibly the major challenge to the field. Women scholars are searching for new paradigms, and in the process have debunked or critically assailed much of the early Chicano scholarship.[22] Much of this debunking has occurred in conference presentations, lectures, and new anthologies. Better trained in theory and using an interdisciplinary approach, Chicanas have opened new avenues of research and scholarship.

They have helped define the community to be inclusive of women and children. Their research on the role of women in unions, resistance leagues, journalism and the arts, and in the economic life of the barrio has provided a clearer picture of the community's survival. Their discussion of patriarchy in the Chicano family has also exposed some of the self-inflicted ills that hurt Chicanos.

At the moment, Chicana scholars seem to have a greater fervency for *raza* scholarship than do many of their male colleagues. However, a small but influential number of Chicana scholars have taken on an adversarial role in their relations to Chicano Studies, and they are influencing the direction of Chicana scholarship. These gender nationalists find the lurking "macho" in every Chicano scholarly work. Because they are critical of the ideological premises of the Chicano Movement, they reject much of what came out of it. They believe that the concepts of community and family much extolled by early Chicano intellectuals are sexist and seek to limit Chicanas' intellectual and nondomestic growth. At the same time, these Chicana feminists attempt to distance themselves from white feminists, who, they believe, do not speak for the Chicana experience.[23] At the University of California, Davis, there is a move to establish a Chicana Studies program, exclusive of Chicano Studies, and at variance with traditional Women Studies programs nationally.

Some Chicana feminists have, however, not limited themselves to attacking Chicanos, but have been extremely critical of Chicanas who do not follow their brand of feminism. Their adversarial approach has created divisions in a number of institutions, particularly those in California.[24] While they see themselves as victims, they are in fact quite influential in their programs and in NACS. The lesbian Chicana scholars have even gone as far as promoting the idea that homosexuality is an integral part of Chicano culture.[25] Over the last three years, their influence or presence has increased substantially at the NACS conferences. Already two different student groups, one in Arizona and one in Texas, have sought to distance themselves from the association.[26] It is even more likely that these scholars will further alienate themselves with their gender politics, which, unlike the politics of the Chicano Movement, are not based on what the predominantly working-class community thinks. The academy has become the only world for some of these scholars, because they have redefined the concept of community.[27] These scholars have much to offer Chicano

Studies, but their approach must include integration and accommodation, not just confrontation. The fact is that neither traditional Chicano Studies nor the individual Chicana scholars have a sure footing in higher education. They are both stepchildren who face an even greater opponent in the insensitive, still predominantly white, male-oriented, Eurocentric university community. Chicano scholars must facilitate the entrance of Chicanas into the field and allow them elbow room to debate and to create new paradigms. Chicanas must also be willing to help Chicano scholars move toward a progressive scholarship. To engage in conflict without a serious attempt to accommodate is to repeat the schism that brought down much of the social movement in the barrios in the first place.

Radical Chicana and lesbian scholars should not be singled out as the only ones moving away from the community. After all, most Chicana scholars retain a strong sense of community, and many participate in community activities beyond the university. Many of them have also done more work on the working-class nature of their community, while most male scholars of late have shifted their focus toward the Mexican American middle class.[28] It has become clear that Chicano Studies—including Chicana Studies—has failed to live up to its impressive credo. With regard to the community, the Plan de Santa Bárbara authors wrote that "research should not be abstracted or disembodied from pressing social concerns. . . . Scholarship cannot be justified for its own sake: It must be committed scholarship that can contribute to Chicano liberation. . . . In order to bridge the gap between theory and practice, Chicano social scientists must develop close ties with community action groups."[29] Since the end of the major Chicano activism of the 1960s and the 1970s, scholarly ties to the community have declined as scholars concentrate on gaining tenure and promotion, or on building networks with politicians and educational lobby groups who are politically correct and who offer opportunities for professional enhancement. The former propensity by Chicano Studies faculty to invite people from the community to the university, or to take students to the barrio to get them involved in issues affecting Mexican Americans, has been almost forgotten. Chicano scholarship, and to some extent Chicana scholarship, has simply failed to become the liberating force envisioned by its founders, despite some admirable successes. There are three probable reasons for this. First, most of the scholars who first attempted to interact with the community are now administrators or full professors with less time to do so, or are in universities with less identifiable Chicano communities. The fact that many do not teach in the community in which they grew ideologically and politically makes it harder to become integrated into the new setting.

A second reason for less contact with the community is that nowadays more non-Chicano students take these courses because of diversity requirements. When primarily Chicano students took the courses, there were unlimited possibilities for activities in which a Chicano Studies program could engage in in the barrio. When large numbers of non-Chicanos take a course, it becomes more difficult to engage in controversial activities. The third reason, touched on before, is that a different kind of scholar is entering the field. These are scholars with little connection to the activism of past years; they are often middle class, or lower middle class, and were not weaned politically or intellectually in a Chicano working-class environment. Many of these new Chicano scholars have been removed from their community because of their class status or because they have spent five to ten years at a university away from home or at a university devoid of community networks. Removed by class or physical distance, these scholars are also removed intellectually. A few, lucky enough to have mentors with a knowledge of the field, understand the historiography of the movement, but many do not. Some do not understand or even know the ideological foundations of the Plan de Santa Bárbara, and they teach Chicano Studies without the "context of change." [30]

While some of these scholars are simply ignorant of the field, others are disciples of a self-serving professionalism. They focus their research on the Chicano population and teach the courses because they know the population group better, or seem to think they do. Their interest in Chicano Studies is much like that of a historian fascinated by maritime activities during the Civil War. It is a topic of interest, not a lifelong passion for progressive scholarship. These scholars rarely become involved in Chicano Studies program activities, in mentoring Chicano students, or in lobbying for a greater offering of Chicano Studies courses in their departments. Yet they enjoy their status as the Chicano "experts" in their departments. These scholars remain within the periphery of the field, taking advantage of opportunities that become available to well-connected scholars within the field. Oftentimes these scholars become reviewers of Chicano Studies programs and scholars and become an obstacle rather than a help.

The National Association for Chicano Studies has not played a major role in combatting opportunism or Hispanic revisionism. Nor has it attempted to find a common ground between those who favor Chicano Studies as an intellectual pursuit and those who only see it as a stimulus for activism. The organization has failed to continue the debate on a Chicano paradigm and to attempt to set standards for the field. In trying to provide a forum for every Chicano or Chicana scholar or student to develop academic presentation skills, it promotes mediocrity and opportunism. A number of the longtime members, both male and female, do not present papers at NACS conferences and avoid the sectarian politics. The militant organizational resolutions issued after every conference seem to have little relation to a large number of the presentations. NACS has become everything to everyone; but it has failed to maintain a clear-cut direction, and it has failed to an even greater degree to gain a legitimate reputation within both the academic and Mexican American communities. Both the "professionals" and the "radicals" lack the zeal to provide a clear focus. NACS seems, at times, in Rodolfo "Corky" González's words, "like a monster with two heads eating out of the same trough."

This ambivalence, as well as the opportunism that prevails in some programs, discourages and can destroy any real intellectual development within the field of Chicano Studies. The scholarship coming from this particular group of scholars is both academically and socially insignificant and provides little to the debate on the Chicano/a experience. Many Chicano and Chicana scholars, educated in the old system or the new sectarianism, contribute little to the field of Chicano Studies or to the struggle for civil rights in the Chicano community at large. Chicanos, even scholars and intellectuals or maybe especially these, have not been able to escape the individualistic and often narcissistic approach to personal and professional fulfillment that is common in American society. The "lure" of tenure, promotion, and success in academia has sullied the aspirations of the Plan de Santa Bárbara authors. The fact that the authors relied on the fervency of the movement as a substitute for details on how to accomplish their task did not help those caught up in emotional turmoil over choosing between activism and professional growth.

What, then, is the future of Chicano Studies? To answer that question, it is necessary to review the strengths of the field—as I have dwelled mostly on the challenges—and see how they match up to its weaknesses. The strengths are very much individual strengths. In this sense, Chicano Studies has not changed. It is still dependent on the individual efforts of scholars, students, and people in the community. Chicano Studies emerged out of a need to legitimize the Chicano experience and to provide the people in the barrio with a collective identity. Having been treated as an ahistorical community, Chicanos suffered not only exploitation and poverty, but also an identity crisis that divided the community. Those who sought economic stability, upward mobility, and acceptance often found themselves moving toward assimilation and away from the community. Those who rejected the kind of assimilation that threatened Chicanos with cultural genocide often found themselves unable to attain the aforementioned goals and became segregated from the community at large.

Those who became involved in Chicano Studies activities and classes acquired a strong sense of self-esteem as Chicanos. They learned they had a history, heroes, heroines; that they had not succumbed passively to the conquest of the Southwest; and that their literature, art, theater, and culture were rich in diversity and quality. Because the field was slanted toward activism, many of the students became active participants in history, which changed the way they related to society in general. The militancy of Chicano Studies helped overcome years of collective insecurity for many students.

Chicano Studies attracted many toward the academy and toward other intellectual pursuits. Although the number of courses offered remained small, and initially little material existed on Chicanos, Chicano Studies excited many students to do research on their own and stimulated constant discussions, debates, and arguments on the status of the Mexican American community. In Chicano Studies everyone became a philosopher, a political scientist, and a reformer, and those roles were often taken beyond the classroom. The number of students interested in academic careers, the arts, and government service increased dramatically. The cultural renaissance in the Chicano community found a source of strength in reading clubs, art exhibits, lecture series, and fiestas sponsored by Chicano groups at the university. This function of Chicano Studies continues today in a number of universities with Chicano Studies programs.

The field of Chicano Studies has created new avenues of research, and Chicano scholars have produced a substantial number of works on the Chicano experience. This scholarship has forced mainstream scholars to recognize the presence of Mexican Americans in the development of the Southwest and the West. The research has also provided data for policy decisions and political agendas.

The most important function of Chicano Studies, however, has been to provide Chicano students and faculty with an environment where they can develop intellectually and where they can find refuge from the often insensitive mainstream. There are still students "discovering" their history and seeing their cultural experiences in a new light. There are others becoming motivated to work in their communities after receiving a degree or even before. The Chicano Studies programs, or at least the proponents of Chicano Studies, have led many students to youthful activism, a necessary experience in the development of character and personal identity. While collectively the field of Chicano Studies has been unsuccessful in becoming a unified and powerful educational reform movement, it has nonetheless been a stimulus for individual and small-group development within the postsecondary level. Where tenure battles have been won, they have been individual or local community victories. Where programs have been expanded and new faculty hired, the victors have been either an individual or small group. It has been the tenacity of small student groups, faculty members, and community organizations that has helped Chicano Studies grow nationally. Chicano Studies seem to reflect a reality of the Chicano experience in that individual success has always been tempered by group stratification.

Chicano Studies adherents are to be admired for their tenacious will for survival. Most institutions have paid lip service to the field and have tolerated its existence for political reasons. Without dedicated Chicano and Chicana scholars, a number of whom have retarded their own professional growth, the field would not have prospered in the areas in which it has. The outstanding scholarship, especially of late, has also provided legitimacy in numerous academic circles. In fact, European scholars and institutions have often recognized the value of Chicano scholarship before the American academy has.[31]

The future of Chicano Studies may well rest on the ability of proponents to regain the perspective of the Plan de Santa Bárbara, or in the development of a new perspective that will facilitate the enhancement of Chicano Studies, while not destroying its heart. First, let us consider what a return to the plan would mean for Chicano Studies. Initially, it would mean a return to the debate on a Chicano paradigm, or paradigms, that would provide scholarly direction to the field. This would not mean a rigid theoretical model such as the "internal-colony" model, but rather a series of scholarly signposts to guide young scholars and graduate students toward those issues applicable to the Chicano experience. This new quest for a paradigm would include works and paradigms developed by Chicana scholars and nonacademic Chicano intellectuals. This new intellectual debate would bring a new sense of vibrancy to the field and lead to the development of Chicano think tanks, which have been almost impossible to establish because of the lack of political and scholarly consensus among any sizeable group of scholars.

Next, the return to the plan would mean another effort to develop a master plan for educating Mexican American students. Currently, much of the discussion on recruitment and retention of Chicanos in college occurs among individual scholars and not within a collective. Individual scholars suggest different approaches but little discussion occurs. Curriculum and research are other areas about which there is little discussion or agreement. Many Chicano scholars have returned to what activist scholar Mario Compean calls the "Lone Wolf" approach.[32] The master plan must recognize that the education of Chicanos begins in a culturally strong and economically viable community. This, of course, would mean more political involvement by faculty and students in the host community and the revival of student groups that would agitate not only university officials, but also politicians and bureaucrats, for changes in the barrio. The Chicano/a scholars would have to regain the status that they once held during the Chicano Movement, when few rallies or protests took place without an academician or student there to provide a historical and intellectual focus on the struggle.

It is quite evident that a return to the plan requires the kind of commitment often lacking in times of political passivity. The fact is that Chicano Studies are a result of the Chicano Movement and not the other way around. Consequently, it may be unrealistic to assume that Chicano scholars can turn back the clock and put into practice the passionate tenets of the plan. Also, the community has changed significantly in the last twenty-five years. There is now a large cadre of politicians, bureaucrats, social workers, and educators who have learned to survive and even prosper in the current environment. Also, a large percentage of the Chicano Ph.D.'s entering the academic workforce see themselves as scholars and not activists. Their large educational debts and academic goals become a detriment to political activism. And finally, for many students and people in the community, there is no longer the extreme level of alienation that many Chicanos felt toward American society during the 1960s and 1970s.

The Plan de Santa Bárbara, much like the Chicano Movement, had definite separatist tendencies and sought to distance Chicano Studies from the Anglo-American academic mainstream. Most Chicano students attending universities today, while still only a small group and not completely integrated into campus life, have more fellow students with whom to interact and have access to minority student services to assist them in their odyssey through higher education. Chicano faculty members are less likely to face blatant discrimination or racism, even as many struggle to gain tenure. However, the sophistication of academic discrimination makes it hard to pinpoint and gives the impression that it does not exist. Without the fervency of the movement, Chicano Studies faculty members often become just another scholarly group seeking academic legitimacy.

If, then, a return to the Plan de Santa Bárbara does not seem a viable option currently, what is the alternative, at least until activism rises again among Chicanos? I would argue that the alternative is to develop small-scale parallel institutions and associations and to sponsor conferences with the aim of solidifying the standards of the field. Rather than seeking to change NACS, Chicano and Chicana scholars should form regional or statewide associations that require fewer resources to maintain them and are more manageable in size. These organizations would be inclusive but would not see the need to become mass-membership groups. NACS currently has a "foco" (chapter) system, but the regional focos are composed of scholars from several states, and they have been for the most part rather passive in setting academic agendas or standards. They are simply smaller versions of NACS.

The regional associations that I envision would provide guidelines and assistance in defining the needs of the field of Chicano Studies in their region. They would sponsor regional conferences and demand a higher standard of scholarship, while providing younger scholars and graduate students with what NACS has failed to provide: mentoring and training in the various aspects of the field, such as research techniques, writing for publication, mentoring students, and strong teaching skills. The smaller settings would also allow a discussion of Chicano paradigms and an interpretation of the Chicano experience regionally. Rather than factionalize Chicano Studies, it would allow scholars to feel that their regions have much to contribute to a national debate on the Chicano experience. It would also bring them face to face with the critical issues in their community, thus linking them to those who most need the scholarship. The debate over whether to establish a Chicano Studies or a Latino Studies center would be resolved at the local or regional level. It might mean a slight redefinition of the word Chicano, but not a major shift in scholarly direction. The fact is that there are not enough Salvadorans, Guatemalans, and others to overwhelm the Mexican-origin population of the Southwest, Midwest, and West. The Puerto Rican and Dominican population, who have a very strong historical deviance from Chicanos, should retain their own study centers.

NACS, as a scholarly organization, would remain as it is, a forum for everyone, but it would also provide a place where all these regional groups could congregate and share their work. The opportunity to experiment with new research, to meet new scholars, and to establish institutional links makes the NACS conferences important. It is also a good place to recruit scholars and to survey the graduate students soon to receive their doctorates.

The regional associations would also lobby for the establishment of strong programs in selected areas. These programs would be earmarked for the largest amount of resources, so that they could become strong teaching and research units. They would then be able to attract the more committed students to receive a thorough training in Chicano Studies. Rather than leading to elitism within the field, it would allow better-trained, committed scholars to assume academic appointments throughout the country. The consolidation of resources would lead to the founding of high-quality refereed journals and one or two legitimate Chicano scholarly presses. These programs would also offer fellowships and residencies to both junior and senior scholars, as well as short-term seminars for graduate students. As programs strengthened, new programs would be established.

These regional associations, in conjunction with centralized Chicano Studies programs, could develop a strong community-service component in which faculty and students use their research and teaching skills to assist the Chicano community in its liberation from the social ills it faces. Students and junior faculty would be encouraged to complete internships with community organizations. Senior scholars would be encouraged to use part of their sabbatical leave to work within the Chicano community. In essence, these scholars would be on loan from their centers to community organizations. Chicano Studies tenure and promotion committees would then truly evaluate community service, unlike the lip service it gets now in most tenure evaluations.

Student groups would be more likely to become involved with regional scholarly associations because of their proximity, and they could interact with faculty members who are working within the Chicano community and thus become linked to the Chicano community at large. One of the problems in attracting Chicano students into the field is that many of them perceive Chicano Studies as a subfield without academic legitimacy or without economic benefits. Having strong programs, active scholarly associations, and a strong community component would make Chicano Studies an attractive field of study for many students now in college, and for those nearing graduation from high school. When the time came for these scholars to join the academic ranks, it is more likely that they would have a better understanding of and greater commitment to the field.

In the long run, this type of approach would move Chicano Studies closer to the spirit of el Plan de Santa Bárbara than it is at present because it would accomplish some of the plan's major goals. It would lead to sound Chicano Studies programs with a strong link to the community; and it would mean the expectation higher standards from scholars better trained to meet those standards. Better scholars might well lead to the kind of scholarship necessary to free the community from its social and political dilemmas. It is imperative that Chicano Studies regain its relevance to the Mexican American community. For too many years, a number of Chicano scholars have been involved in an intellectual voyeurism that sounds progressive but has little relationship to the everyday problems of poverty, unemployment, poor health, lack of a cultural identity, political powerlessness, historical myopia, and delinquency.

The approach would require the commitment of both new and established scholars. It would also demand unselfishness, as the programs would need to work closer together, and some of them would have to be deemphasized as others would be targeted for growth. This, however, is nothing less than what el Plan de Santa Bárbara required of its adherents and the minimum that Chicano scholars must do to keep the field viable.

The recent struggle of Chicano students and scholars at UCLA only re-emphasizes the challenges that still face Chicano Studies as a field of inquiry. While scholars and students nationally empathized with the efforts at UCLA, there was neither the mechanism nor the collective mindset to provide assistance to the struggle. The UCLA compromise was a minor victory for the field, but if the most established Chicano Studies program in the country can win only half a victory from a supposedly liberal administration, what is the future of Chicano Studies in less fertile areas?

The case of Rudy Acuña at the University of California, Santa Barbara, is another example of Chicano Studies not having the academic muscle to win a major conflict. Acuña's reputation in the field notwithstanding, his scholarship was assailed as not being legitimate enough and he was unable to become director of the Chicano center there.[33] How many other scholars with that type of standing in their disciplines would have been treated as Acuña was in 1992 at Santa Barbara—ironically, the birthplace of Chicano Studies? In the same vein, how many institutions would have interviewed top candidates in a discipline and rejected them all as not being strong enough? The University of Arizona did so when it interviewed four of the top Chicano historians in the country and made no offer to any of them.[34] Chicano scholarship itself is unlikely to become extinct. After all, Chicano scholarship has played a role in the community's struggle for liberation since the early days. However, Chicano Studies as an academic pursuit may never be a strong presence in the academy, and consequently in the community, if Chicano students and scholars do not reevaluate the present situation and seek solutions.

It may well be that another conference is needed to provide a master plan for the future of Chicano Studies. The experience gained over the last twenty-five years should provide a basis for new ideas and a reinitiation of old ones. The options are clear: be manipulated by the academy, slowly decay because of lack of resources and commitment, or take command of our destiny as Chicano scholars. There is a clear choice as to what option Chicanos must pursue. They cannot get lost within the academic mainstream because that will mean a loss of purpose. And Chicano Studies cannot continue to be an academically anemic child of higher education. Chicano Studies began as a vibrant educational and cultural reform movement with little financial means and even less administrative support. What has been accomplished is nothing less than admirable, but the future requires a recommitment to scholarship that will empower Chicanos and Chicanas in their struggle to liberate their community from poverty, political powerlessness, and a collective identity crisis.

NOTES

1. Liberal scholars have always sought to convert Chicano Studies into an assimilationist civil rights educational movement. Conservatives have never considered the field legitimate.
2. See "Strengthening Chicano Studies Programs," *La Red/The Net* 1 (1975): 11–30.
3. See Mario T. García's *Mexican Americans: Leadership, Ideology and Identity, 1930–1960* (New Haven: Yale University Press, 1989) for a discussion of this generation, and specifically of Carlos Castañeda and Arthur Campa.
4. José R. Reyna, introduction to "Readings in Southwestern Folklore," in *Perspectives in Mexican American Studies,* eds. Juan R. García and José Reyna, 1 (Tucson: Mexican American Research Center, 1988), v–x.
5. Here I refer to a set of theoretical guidelines that would attempt to put into perspective the Chicano experience and provide new scholars an intellectual roadmap to pursue, or at least be aware of, in their research agendas. See Carlos Muñoz, Jr., *Youth, Identity, Power* (London: Verso, 1989), 127–30, for a short discussion on the Mexican American Generation's academic views.
6. Ibid., 130.
7. Ibid., 134–38.
8. Ibid., 138–39.
9. A notable characteristic of Chicano Studies would be its diversity. Most programs reflected the unique political and cultural environment of the home community.
10. See Rodolfo "Corky" González's discussion of student/community links in Christine Marín, *A Spokesman of the Mexican American Movement: Rodolfo "Corky" González and the Fight for Chicano Liberation. 1966–1972* (San Francisco: R & E Research Associates, 1977); see also "El Plan de Santa Bárbara," in Muñoz, *Youth, Identity, Power,* 201–2.
11. See "The Barrio as Internal Colony," in *People and Politics in Urban Society,* ed., Harlan Hahn (Beverly Hills: Sage Publications, 1972), 465–98.
12. See Muñoz, *Youth, Identity, Power,* 148–49; see also Gilbert González, "The Internal Colony Model: A Critique," *Latin American Perspectives* 1 (1974): 154–61.
13. Muñoz, *Youth, Identity, Power,* 150–51.
14. José Rivera and Luis Ramón Burrola, "Chicano Studies Programs in Higher Education: Scenarios for Further Research," *Aztlán* 15 (1985): 277–94.
15. See Refugio I. Rochín, "The Current Status and Future of Chicano Studies Programs: Are They Academically Sound?" (paper presented at the 14th annual conference of the National Association for Chicano Studies, El Paso, 10–12 April 1986).
16. In 1986, I personally counted eleven Chicano scholars, most of them acquaintances, who did not receive tenure. See Ignacio García, "Chicano vs Academia: It's Same War, Different Battle," *The Forum* 1 (1986): 13.

17. See Rochín's article, "Current Status of Chicano Studies," for a discussion on student apathy.

18. See "UCLA Hunger Strike Ends; Chicano Studies Solidified," in *Hispanic Link Weekly Report* (14 June 1993): 1.

19. For a few years in the 1980s, and in some places still, a joint appointment is seen as the best of all situations. It provides "legitimacy" as well as an opportunity to work in Chicano Studies.

20. Some of these established scholars are referred to as "flagship Chicanos" because they are recruited by every university that wants a Chicano on board but is not willing to recruit and support new scholars.

21. This challenge has prompted a reaction by some Chicano groups toward a stronger nationalism. At the national MECHA conference in spring 1993, the students voted to refer to themselves as Chicanos and not admit anyone to the national organization who did not use that term.

22. See Adela de la Torre and Beatriz Pesquera, eds., *Building with our Own Hands* (Berkeley: University of California Press, 1993); and Margarita Melville, ed. *Twice a Minority: Mexican American Women* (St. Louis: Mosby, 1980).

23. See Chela Sandoval, "U.S. Third World Feminism: The Theory and Method of Oppositional Consciousness in the Postmodern World," *Gender* 10 (1991).

24. Institutions such as the Claremont Colleges; University of California, Santa Barbara; University of California, Berkeley; and the University of California, Los Angeles, have been recent hotbeds of feminist discourse.

25. When the Chicana Lesbian Caucus attempted to get official status in NACS during the national conference in Albuquerque in spring 1990, that supposition was one of their arguments.

26. The MECHA group at the University of Arizona and the Amigos Club from Texas A&M University, Corpus Christi, were both surprised and bothered by the high profile of lesbian politics. Neither group is homophobic but they felt—naively—that the NACS conference was a forum for discussing scholary research, making networks, and basking in nationalist *ondas* (vibes). They were also very clear that that kind of politics would not go over well in their communities, so the Corpus Christi group, which had thought of hosting the conference, decided against it.

27. These new definitions reduce the community to single females, or single-parent families led by females, who are poor and abused. There is very little vibrancy in that community beyond the mother-daughter relationship. Their definition of community stands in stark contrast with the community most Chicano/a scholars know.

28. The current works of historians Richard García, Mario T. García, and Guadalupe San Miguel, and political scientists Benjamín Márquez, Rodolfo de la Garza, and others are examples of such scholarly activity.

29. Muñoz, *Youth, Identity, Power,* 150.

30. Lorena Oropeza, conversation with the author, Tucson, May 1993. Oropeza, a doctoral student at Cornell University, is interested in a joint appointment in Chicano Studies and history. She expressed concern that she would be expected to be an activist, when in

reality what she wanted to be was a scholar. She also expressed the fact that she had no real sense of community because she, like many other students in her circumstances, did not come from a traditional working-class environment.

31. Several European universities have small Chicano Studies programs and sponsor conferences or scholarly meetings on Chicanos almost every year.

32. This means an attempt to get things done by the sheer strength of character, which ends up usually promoting the ideals of an individual or group that claims to have most, if not all, of the answers.

33. See "Ethnic Bias Alleged by Chicano Scholar in Hiring Dispute," *Chronicle of Higher Education,* 20 November 1991, A18; see also "New Clash in Legal War," *Chronicle of Higher Education,* 23 February 1994, A18.

34. Interviewed over a period of two to three years (1987–89) for an American historian position were Mario T. García, Alberto Camarillo, Richard Griswold del Castillo, and Ramón Gutiérrez. Oscar J. Martínez was eventually hired. Although he is an outstanding borderlands scholar, Martínez is not specifically a Chicano historian.

PART FOUR. GENDER, FEMINISM, AND CHICANAS/OS: DEVELOPMENTS AND PERSPECTIVES

Although the "Movimiento" addressed various critical issues, one that remained unfulfilled, particularly in the early stages, was women's struggles. However, by the onset of the 1980s, Chicanas began assuming more prominent and diverse roles in the political arena, as well as in academia and art. Chicanas developed their own distinct organizations to advance their particular agenda, which includes representation and gender issues, empowerment equality issues, alternative lifestyles, health, and others. The two essays in this section offer insights into the changing gender relationships associated with certain political and social developments and Chicana ideological diversity.

The complexity of gender relations among Mexicans and Chicanos is the focus of the chapter by anthropologist Adelaida R. Del Castillo. Drawing upon the findings of social science studies conducted during the 1970s and 1980s and personal field research, Del Castillo discusses cultural discrepancies in Mexican and Chicano gendered relations. She conceptualizes these discrepancies as representing discontinuities in patriarchal hierarchies and traditional gender roles. She argues that the discontinuities reveal localized concepts of gendered behavior and represent cultural alternatives to traditional practice. Lastly, she finds a cultural flexibility in gendered behavior among Mexicans that has not been acknowledged nor understood.

In contrast to Del Castillo, Beatriz Pesquera and Denise Segura offer insight into the position of Chicana concerns vis-à-vis the feminist movement and its theories and institutional programs. They examine the perspectives of a select group of Chicanas, the membership of the Mujeres Activas en Letras y Cambio Social (MALCS), an organization dedicated to the documentation, analysis, and interpretation of the experiences of Chicanas and Latinas in American society. Their analysis illustrates that Chicanas continue to interpret reality through a triple-oppression lens rooted in their experiences as Chicanas in the United States. It reveals that while significant change occurred in other areas of their experiences, the position of Chicanas has not undergone substantial change. Chicanas are no longer omitted from the feminist movement, scholarship, or programs, in the view of the Chicana feminists in MALCS. According to Pesquera and Segura, however, Chicana concerns remain subordinated within the American women's movement and feminist theories. Moreover, Chicanas perceive that Women's Studies programs and centers are not meeting the needs of Chicanas. In short, Chicanas remain marginal in American feminism.

GENDER AND ITS DISCONTINUITIES IN

MALE/FEMALE DOMESTIC RELATIONS:

MEXICANS IN CROSS-CULTURAL CONTEXT

Adelaida R. Del Castillo

Gender is a kind of persistent impersonation that passes as the real.
—Judith Butler, *Gender Trouble*

The affinity between things Mexican and Mexican American/Chicano has a basis in a common history, border space, culture, and language long renewed by migration and immigration, which more recently has come to signify the mexicanization of the United States. This continuity of Mexican-ness between Chicanos and Mexicans is graphically underscored by the spatial distance between them—by the fact that 80 percent of all persons of Mexican origin in the United States live less than two hundred miles from the U.S.-Mexico border. Still, the differences within and between Chicano and Mexican communities are considerable and cannot be ignored.

In studying Mexico's gendered cultural norms, I have found that lower-income Mexicans appear to be undergoing radical changes in male/female domestic arrangements not yet reported for Mexican Americans. In part, the Mexican situation is due to long periods of unemployment and under-employment for unskilled males and to female access to traditionally sex-typed employment strategies. The resulting disparity between the earning power of Mexican men and women has had a subversive effect on the domestic relations of men and women.[1] Though no direct cultural correlation between Mexicans and Chicanos is intended here, nor is a cause-effect relationship suggested between changes in their domestic relations, I do believe that domestic role changes taking place in lower-income neighborhoods in Mexico City serve to indicate what lower-income groups in the United States, including Chicanos, may eventually undergo due to similar socioeconomic periods of duress. Nor is this to suggest that traditional gendered behaviors are ever consistent and credible cultural norms, unruptured and uncontested from generation to generation, for, as we shall see, gendered discontinuities on both sides of the border take on (and have taken on in the past) unique forms in specific contexts among distinct Mexican and Mexican American groups. These discontinuities of patriarchal hierarchies and traditional gender roles, in turn, disclose local notions of gendered behavior suggestive of cultural alternatives to tradition. Gender thus conceived is no longer just an attribute associated with a particular sex, but a cultural phenomenon to be assumed, contested, and transacted, to be performed, played with, and collaborated in.[2]

The discussion begins with a review of the American literature on the family and domestic relations from the 1970s to the present, emphasizing the contributions of feminist theory as well as Latina scholarship on Mexican American families and domestic decision making. This section is then followed by a consideration of Mexican male/female gender-appropriate norms and gender identity. Finally, I discuss ways in which gendered phenomena have been understood, invoked, and displaced in specific Mexican and Chicano contexts. Much of the discussion on Mexican gendered behavior is illustrated by ethnographic material I collected among lower-income groups in Mexico City between 1986 and 1988. Although the American and Mexican areas of research are not precisely comparable in scope, theme, or disciplinary approach, because much of the American literature is influenced by a sociological approach privileging quantitative data, and the Mexican literature is framed as ethnography privileging qualitative data, a truly comparative approach between the two literatures remains a challenge. Consequently, this cross-cultural discussion is, at best, suggestive.

ANTECEDENTS

The twentieth century has seen an exponential growth in published research on the family, and in the latter half of the century there has been an emphasis on interactional and transactional behavior within the family.[3] Marital quality in the family literature of the 1970s ranked among the most widely studied topic of the decade, a trend already firmly established in the preceding decade.[4] In comparison to the dearth of material on sex roles in the 1960s, the 1970s saw a plethora of studies on sex roles in the family establishing the importance of this variable in family literature.[5] In addition, the research on quality of marriage has emphasized patterns of dominance and submission creating a subtopic of major importance, which highlights sex roles, power relationships, and decision making.[6]

The 1970s and 1980s were decades of revision for family studies from both feminist and racial/ethnic perspectives. During this period feminist scholarship made unprecedented theoretical contributions to family studies through the use and eventual critique of the notion of sex roles, with its emphasis on the binary construction of ideal gender types implicitly suggesting complementarity and equality.[7] By the 1980s sex-role use was increasingly replaced by gender theory and the analysis of gender as a process of categorization and stratification inviting the deconstruction of gendered phenomena.[8] This approach acknowledged the importance of the family as a locus for sustaining gendered behavior through work-family relations that have different implications for men and women. Because both men and women participate together in the construction of gender meaning,[9] men became far more significant and visible in family studies as gendered family members.[10] Moreover, unlike the research of the previous decade, in which the family was approached by researchers as if it were a cohesive nonconflictive domain, feminist scholarship in the 1980s grappled with the myth of the homogeneous, consensual family model.[11] This model overlooked differences in class, standard of living, goals, and interest, just as sex roles had assumed behavior to be "clear, consistent, and uniform" without attention to conflict and contradiction.[12]

During the 1980s feminist scholarship reconceptualized the examination of marital and family relations by embedding these in broader ideological, socioeconomic, and political structures and, subsequently, undermining the public/private domain dichotomy popular in the 1970s.[13] Feminists viewed the family as one of several environments for creating and sustaining gendered relations through gendered labor, such as housework, that overbenefits husbands.[14] This perspective brought to the forefront three family issues thought to be trivial to the mainstream investigation of families: waged work, housework, and control over household income, crucial to understanding the construction of gender within the context of the family.[15]

The 1970s contributed to the increased investigation into alternative family forms by incorporating the variables of race and class as well as expanding the scope of studies to encompass cross-cultural studies.[16] The decade saw the presentation of ethnic families in a more positive light; studies in previous decades had, without an empirical base, deprecated families of color.[17] Insiders had found, for example, that the Mexicans and Chicanos depicted in early studies were "somewhat unreal."[18] The 1970s witnessed a growth in the number of descriptive and empirical studies on Chicano families by insider family researchers who contested the literature of their predecessors, having found its methodology and objectivity to be flawed and biased.[19] In the 1980s studies of Latino families became even more diversified due to greater attention to population growth resulting from immigration, internal migration, and high fertility rates.[20] Research on Latino families also stressed gender-role flexibility, which was encouraged by the entry of women into the labor force.[21] Indeed, gender relations and issues comprised a primary area of concern and research by Latina scholars in the field.

In the 1970s Latina family scholarship acknowledged the conflict and contradictions within Chicano families and attributed these to broader socioeconomic structural constraints,[22] saw them as a source of gender and political strength,[23] or saw these contradictions as indicative of a universal trend in domestic relations toward greater gender-role egalitarianism.[24] There was also concern over the public-policy implications of the economic needs and resources of Chicana lower-income female-headed households.[25] This research underscored the economic precariousness of female-headed households among Chicanos as well as substantiated the diversity of family formations among Chicanos. Research on Mexican American domestic groups generated data calling into question the homogeneity and patriarchal structure of the family.[26] For the period 1850–1880, for example, Griswold del Castillo found that 21 percent of all Chicano families living in Los Angeles were female headed and were twice as likely to be so when compared to the families of foreign-born groups in other parts of the country. Such data raise questions about the universality of the nuclear family among Chicanos as well as undermine the common misconception that female-headed households are the modern outcome of social dysfunctionality. Griswold del Castillo speculates that Chicano female-headed households for the period 1850–1880 may have been the outcome of several factors including statistical error resulting from the count of highly mobile populations, higher death rates for Chicano males due to conflict between Anglos and Mexicans, and male abandonment of the home.[27] He also shows that gender-role flexibility among Mexican-origin families of the Southwest is not a recent phenomenon, but one that dates back, at least, to the nineteenth century.[28]

During the 1980s Latina scholars studied various aspects of family life: Denise Segura examined the impact of women's work on family networks; Rosario Torres Raines, women's work attitudes and family roles; Alicia Chavira and Julia Curry Rodríguez, the impact of immigrant women's agricultural work on the family; Maxine Baca-Zinn, the effect of women's work on conjugal decision making. Magdalena Mora and Vicki Ruiz studied the impact of women's work and union organizing on the family; Baca-Zinn and Patricia Hernández, the influence of Chicana activism on the family; Margarita Melville and Lourdes Argüelles, the coping strategies of recent immigrant women; Baca-Zinn, theoretical dimensions of familism; and Baca-Zinn, Segura, Adaljiza Sosa Riddell, and Lea Ybarra, machismo and patriarchy. Indeed, Zavella's ethnographic study of female cannery workers in northern California questions the power of machismo and familism (exaggerated family loyalty) among Mexican Americans.[29] In the 1990s Latina scholars have continued descriptive and empirical studies: for example, Argüelles addressed the life-organizing principles of immigrant women; Adela de la Torre, the impact of immigrant women's agricultural work on conjugal decision making; Alicia Chavira-Prado, the effect of women's agricultural work on health and the family; Pesquera, the consequences of women's waged work on the household division of labor; Del Castillo, women's use of contested gendered behavior in domestic relations; and Baca-Zinn, family theory building.[30]

MEXICAN GENDER IDEOLOGY

Traditionally, gender in culture has been assessed through a sex/gender dichotomy in which the former is a biological given and the latter a cultural construction. As such, gender in culture is expressed through individuals who are bearers of prescribed male/female social roles. In the past, gender roles have been identified, described, and explained by anthropologists through the observation of the patterned, recurrent, and typical contributing to the reification of predictable and fixed gender roles. This approach offers a binary frame of reference, which posits the oppositional (he's strong, she's weak, etc.) as universal in male/female gender-based norms and relegates all other gendered possibilities to the realm of the exceptional, the unexplainable, or the deviant. For although tradition may express expected practices, beliefs, and cultural ideals, it cannot account for cultural flexibility, contradiction, and indeterminacy.

According to gender-based norms, the family in Mexico is hierarchical in structure, asymmetrical in social and gender relations, genealogical in patterns of residence, and loyal to the family in its moral economy.[31] According to the traditional ideal, men have authority over women, the husband has authority over his wife as does the brother over his sister; and while the older have authority over the younger, the father remains the ultimate authority over the household and family matters.

It is significant that Mexico's most distinguished authors and pundits (mostly males) have also had something to say about the character, status, and gender-based norms of the Mexican male and female, thus contributing to the social construction of sex/gender ideology in Mexican society.[32] Their conceptualizations cannot go unnoticed because they are probably more widely read internationally than any other literature of social scientific significance. The most notable of these authors is Nobel Prize laureate, Octavio Paz. Through the use of various forms of literary license, Paz offers insights into the character and motives of the *macho* by positing a dialectical relationship between men and women whose relational duality is as 'closed' is to 'open.' "The ideal of manliness is never to 'crack,' never to back down. Those who 'open themselves up' are cowards. . . . Women are inferior beings because, in submitting, they open themselves up. This inferiority is constitutional and resides in their sex, their submissiveness, which is a wound that never heals."[33] For Paz, the sexual encounter itself speaks to a socio-moral asymmetry between the sexes, reified in physiology: "The *macho,* the male . . . rips open . . . the female, who is pure passivity, defenseless against the exterior world."[34] Thus, a woman who transcends passivity is a cultural anomaly representative of gender chaos. Here, also, Paz offers a portrayal of the bad woman, *la mala mujer,* which serves logocentric propositions of unchaste female behavior in a Mexican context. The *mala mujer,* he tells us, is a woman who does not conform to the traditional female ideal and assumes male attributes such as the independence of the macho. Mexican gender ideology, its observations and portrayals, expresses cultural ideals of gender-appropriate behavior which may or may not have correlations in actual behavior.

GENDER DISCONTINUITIES

Half a century ago, in an anthropological study of the Mexican village of Tepoztlán, Oscar Lewis found that Mexican women exhibited behavior that raised questions over "authority and the respective roles of the spouses," for it was the women in the village who were in greater conflict with traditional ways than were males. This discovery led Lewis to suspect that ideal gender-role behavior expected of Mexican husbands and wives was for the most part "a social fiction."[35] A decade later, Fromm and Maccoby followed with a psychological study of a village in the same area; having found that nearly half of the families in the village were female dominated, they asked: "Why are so many men dominated by women in a society with patriarchal values?"[36] More recently, Mexican studies refer to "the existence . . . [in Mexico City] of a 'subproletarian' group, where women, as the more certain breadwinners, choose and discard their menfolks, in a kind of matriarchy, a curious reversal for macho Mexico."[37] My own research reveals that economically empowered women in lower-income settlements in Mexico City use their power to displace ideal notions of gender-appropriate behavior and patriarchal dominance in the family.[38] Surprisingly, these discrepancies may go unnoticed, may be dismissed as exceptional, or be misunderstood by researchers in the field. Little wonder that Fromm and Maccoby were perplexed by and qualified the prevalence of female dominance in the Mexican village they studied as deviant, because their cultural paradigms for Mexico insist that gender is uncomplicated in this context.[39] This closure prematurely dismisses gender flexibility, conflict, and ambiguity exemplified, for example, in a mother's control of the macho.

THE FEMALE CONSTRUCTION OF MACHISMO

"Ladies, watch your chickens well for my rooster is on the loose."[40] This Mexican folk saying expressing a mother's pride in her son is indicative of but one of the many attitudes of Mexican women concerning men.

In their psychological profile of the Mexican, Fromm and Maccoby provocatively attribute sadistic machismo and unproductive male behavior to mother-centeredness and dependence on women.[41] Mexican women themselves describe machismo as an expression of male weakness and immaturity; most strikingly, Fromm and Maccoby found it to be an indication of male fear of women.[42] The macho need to control women is associated with feelings of inferiority, rejection, and powerlessness, which are compensated for by the male use of extreme gender-based behavior.[43] Ironically, Fromm and Maccoby state: "We assume that a large percentage of wives of the *macho*-type man pretend that he dominates the family because they know that he needs this conviction in order to function well . . ." then finally conclude, "but [women] privately dominate or even sabotage their husbands."[44]

Again from a psychological perspective, it has been suggested that Mexican women not only dominate the macho, but they also assist in his cultural perception of the female sex. Romanucci-Ross's work among the Mexican villagers studied by Fromm and Maccoby found that the mother plays a pivotal role in her son's perception of women: "The mother is . . . far more influential than the father in giving the son his image of the opposite sex. . . . All women are whores, Jezebels, and betrayers; the mother alone will not betray. . . . The man is therefore strongly attached to his mother emotionally and strangely bound by her authority. He is certain to distrust women, whom he thinks will betray him or disgrace his manliness by making him a cuckold (*pendejo*)."[45]

This maternal control over the son is partially explained as the outcome of the uterine family. The literature speaks of the uterine family as one in which women divide and dominate domestic units to undermine the authority and power of the patriarch.[46] Women accomplish this by strengthening the mother-child bond and instilling in male offspring a fierce loyalty and devotion to them. As the sons mature, the mother is able to exert greater influence on her husband due to the support of grown sons. Thus, in compensating for her isolation from her husband, the mother forms a 'subfamily' unit with her children, to the exclusion of the husband who represents "the enemy."[47] Eventually, the enemy may assume the female form when the mother's close relationship with her son(s) is threatened by his marriage to another woman, if the daughter-in-law is perceived as an outsider intent on alienating the son's loyalty to his mother. Thus the mother will portray women (except herself) as untrustworthy and may even encourage her son's use of extreme macho behavior, whether in the form of adultery or wife-abuse.

Here the female construction of machismo represents the reformulation of a gender hierarchy based on the supremacy of the maternal progenitor, as practiced by a select group of women who benefit from the patriarchal division of society. Thus women support male dominance of other women as long as an elite group of elder women (mothers) have control over men (sons). This gender hierarchy, however, is a fictive construction of the culture's gender hierarchy because women ultimately underrate and undermine males as competent power brokers, yet these very women invoke the culture's gender-based norms to sustain their power. In this sense, a mother's gendered behavior strategically violates the binary male/female opposition by creating a third agency which identifies with neither sex (the ideal Mexican mother is, after all, asexual), but which in the guise of the maternal dissimulates as gender-appropriate behavior.

With respect to Chicanos, the pioneering literature of the 1970s defined machismo in a more positive light and found commendable attributes in its practice.[48] This literature was in sharp contrast to the descriptive and subjective accounts by Chicana feminists of machismo and sexism in the Chicano Movement of the late 1960s and 1970s.[49] The literature of the 1980s, much of it by Latina scholars, approached this behavior in a more sober light by looking at both positive and negative aspects of machismo. The notion of Chicano patriarchy in the family was not verified by empirical studies.[50] However, given the dearth of studies on the topic, it may be too soon to say anything conclusive about machismo among Chicanos, although I would venture to say that it is alive and well among us, that both men and women assist in its construction, and that there are regional and generational variations of this complex social phenomenon.

INVOKING GENDER-BASED NORMS

In the context of domestic space, where the tension between traditional male/female gender roles (gender-based norms) and gender discontinuities is played out, contested daily, or negotiated, the invocation of traditional gender roles need not be calculated nor false, but may actually be spontaneous or unconscious. For some women involved in the daily contestation of gender, there remain traces of loyalty to traditional gender-based norms, even though these women may actually undermine and contradict these very norms through their behavior. Traces of traditional gender inflexibility are detected in women's invocation of what they believe to be proper male/female gender roles to which they allegedly subscribe. Take, for example, the female informants of Benería and Roldán's study of Mexico City working-class housewives. When asked to describe how they treated their husbands, the women responded with the prescribed gender-appropriate answer: husbands are treated with respect. The women then recited a list of the "dos and don'ts" of respectful behavior toward their mates. However, when pressed, the women (especially older women) did admit to violating the gender-appropriate behavior they professed to practice. Benería and Roldán explain this discrepancy by noting that wives make a distinction between being disrespectful in public or "before his [the husband's] very eyes," which they avoid, and being disrespectful privately or behind their husbands' backs, which some women consider permissible.[51] Writes Lewis in his study of a Mexican village: "Women's standards of behavior for their husbands and themselves are influenced by their own needs and experiences and are not always consistent with the ideal roles."[52] Hence, the invocation of prescribed gender-appropriate norms by these women turns out to be a recitation of normative cultural ideals contradicted in actual practice.

A similar discrepancy seems to be reported in the literature on conjugal decision making among Mexican American (Chicano) families.[53] Both Ybarra-Soriano and Baca-Zinn found that egalitarian decision making between husbands and wives coexists with patriarchal beliefs among Chicano families. An ironic twist on this is indicated by Mexican couples who report greater patriarchal decision making than Chicano couples, when actually egalitarian decision making was most common for both Mexicans and Mexican Americans.[54] Baca-Zinn has observed that a patriarchal ideology is strongly invoked by practitioners of both egalitarian and male-dominant family structures.[55] Perhaps this ready reflex of verbal affirmation of cultural ideals gives voice to the moral precedence of traditional ways even when these are no longer practical or practiced.

Hawkes and Taylor suggest three possible explanations for the occurrence of discrepancies in ideal (patriarchal) and real (more egalitarian) decision-making patterns among migrant Mexican American families in California.[56] The researchers question whether male-dominant and female-submissive gender roles were ever really a cultural ideal. If so, the researchers question whether they were ever real gender roles, and if this is the case, Hawkes and Taylor can only speculate that ideal gender roles have been undergoing a radical change. This change may not be entirely disruptive for Mexican American couples. Bean, Curtis, and Marcum found, for example, that Mexican American husbands and wives expressed greater satisfaction with an egalitarian decision-making domestic structure.[57]

GENDER AS RELATIONAL

The meaning and use of gender in culture has a relational dimension specifically sensitive to context. It is this relational aspect of gender which has been more seriously examined by feminist anthropologists calling into question anthropology's traditional treatment of gender and gendered relations. Gender here is approached as a negotiated relation to be contested and questioned, never to be taken for granted as a rigid social role.[58] In this sense, gendered relations are more like strategies which are culturally sensitive to sexed meaning and context, and as such are read, utilized, and negotiated according to changing circumstances and objectives.

It can, for example, be argued that the *mujer sola* (single woman) in Mexican society is under the cultural compulsion to become a mated woman (when not already monitored, controlled, regulated, and protected by an adult male) in order to become a socially acceptable woman. Because Mexican society is based on the conjugal couple, the status of the single woman is socially subversive for it is as wife and mother that the woman fulfills her primary social role. What is more, because the *mujer sola* is deprecatingly thought of as "a woman with a past" *(una mujer con un pasado),* her virtue is suspect and easily maligned by gossip. In lower-income communities the single woman is particularly vulnerable to abuse by neighbors and strangers alike. One woman, mother of a small child, told me of the television repairman who chased her around the living room until she was forced to beat him off with a broom. Asked what might possibly explain his behavior, the woman responded: "Knowing I was a single woman *(sabiendo que era mujer sola)* he felt at liberty to take advantage of me." Another single mother candidly told me: "A woman without a man is alone and damned, she pays with blood." Separation from her companion resulted in this woman's alienation from an entire social network of friends. Lastly, Benería and Roldán note the opinion of an older working-class woman who compares the respect associated with being a wife (if only in free union) with the vulnerability of living single: "It's preferable to be married, or to live in free union if you can't get married . . . for the respect . . . one gets. . . . People think . . . you fool around if you [live] alone."[59]

Though a woman's status is measured and morally evaluated by the absence or presence of an adult male in the household, there are women who cannot or will not marry. These women may try to discourage sexual harassment by mating through an informal variation of the conjugal relation known as free or consensual union. By virtue of his physical presence, the adult male warns other males (all potential transgressors of a woman's honor) to keep their distance. Women also use free-union relations to stave off the stigma and social alienation of being a mujer sola. By incorporating an adult male into the household, economically empowered women in lower-income neighborhoods gain access to the social standing and status of a wife without relinquishing juridical control of their families to men they may eventually want to replace.[60] In return for their role as the "man of the house," men who enter into free-union relations with economically empowered women may expect economic support. Conceptually, women use consensual unions as a strategic defense of their moral, social, and physical person without having to engage in ideal marriage practices. They do so by reading the cultural meaning of the conjugal relation as inclusive of consensual unions.

GENDER AS PRETENSE

In her study of Mexico's Zapotec women, Chiñas found that women utilize "covert nonformalized roles" to propitiate male dominance. These roles need not be illicit, because according to Chiñas most Zapotec women use covert nonformalized roles for "benevolent manipulative purposes," as in preventing male resentment, envy, or violence.[61] Díaz also finds the power of women in the Mexican village of Tonalá to be "implicit and hidden," resulting in informal and manipulative power. Women, Díaz argues, must manipulate "accepted roles of behavior and role expectations" to get their way or cause conflict because they have "little overt authority," because a woman's status in this society is one filled with responsibilities without power.[62]

As a cultural artifice, gendered behavior may be used by both men and women to affect gender-appropriate roles even when these have lost much of their practical use in daily life. Still, these roles are performed in order to comply with the culture's gender expectations.[63] One must then distinguish between the cultural compulsion to act according to traditional gender-based norms and the expression of gendered behavior as cultural pretension.[64]

The discrepancy between the real and the ideal has long been of interest to anthropologists, because it does sometimes happen that they are told one thing, but observe another. Social scientists have observed that women who do not subscribe to gender-based norms bridge the chasm between what is culturally expected of them and their actual behavior through pretense.[65] Fromm and Maccoby, for example, found that rural women in female-dominated families pretend their husbands are in command.[66] Similarly, in her study of gender in a French rural village, Rogers found that women pretended to defer to their husbands even though these women were in control of the family and in control of many of the economic transactions of the village.[67] Rogers explains that these women enact subordinate gendered behavior in the presence of males due to an understanding that perceives the public sphere, though controlled by men and considered prestigious, as relatively small compared to the private sphere controlled by women. I found that economically empowered women in Mexico City defer to their male companions as a negotiated understanding between women who earn a wage income and men who depend on this income for their livelihood. In this sense, there is a public and performative aspect to gendered behavior in which both men and women collaborate as performers, each enacting prescribed gender-based roles publicly before others, but knowing privately that things are otherwise.[68]

THE ECONOMIC EMPOWERMENT OF GENDER

The single most important variable empowering Mexican American women in joint decision making is a wife's employment outside the home.[69] For example, in a study in which acculturation was held constant, Baca-Zinn found that "in all families where women were not employed, tasks and decision-making were typically sex-segregated. However, in all families with employed wives, tasks and decision-making were shared."[70]

220   *Adelaida R. Del Castillo*

Other research suggests that working-class status is related to shared decision-making patterns for Mexican Americans, Mexicans, and Anglos.[71]

However, in her ethnography of cannery workers in northern California, Zavella cautions that research that finds a correlation between women's waged income and greater egalitarian decision making must distinguish between women's full-time, part-time, and seasonal work loads.[72] Most of the women in Zavella's study were part-time seasonal workers whose husbands worked full-time jobs and who were not always supportive of their wives' work strategies. Though Zavella found that working women gained greater control over decision making and family expenditures, she also noted that it is women's parity with men's wages that enables them to better enforce change in their domestic relations, even to the extent of terminating troubled relationships.[73] Zavella argued that as long as women's wage-earning opportunities remain inferior to those of men, domestic egalitarianism in decision making and in the performance of household duties is unlikely. Regarding the domestic relations of seasonal cannery workers, Zavella concluded: "I came across no families with an equal division of household labor and virtually no informants who characterized marriage in terms of equally shared responsibility for home duties."[74] Thus, women who work at seasonal, low-income jobs are not in a position to resolve conflict with their spouses over work strategies, nor are they able to negotiate an equal division of domestic duties between husband and wife once the woman begins working. Subsequently, Zavella was careful about necessarily associating a more egalitarian family structure with Mexican American working couples.[75]

My own research among working housewives in Mexico City supports Zavella's contention that there is a relationship between women's earning power and greater decision making in the family. Domestic conflict between spouses in my study arose not over whether women worked outside the home, but rather over where women worked and, more importantly, over the moral implications of their work: the women worked as bar girls in nightclubs throughout the city.

Working in clubs has advantages because it allows women with little or no education or skills to earn an income three times the minimum-wage income of the unskilled Mexican male laborer. Bar girls may also augment their income through tips and extravagant gratuities provided by clients, the selling of drugs, and by engaging in prostitution. Some women increase their earnings by placing their income in various savings accounts, purchasing life insurance, and investing capital in real estate and retailing strategies. Ultimately, these women have an economic advantage over their male domestic partners who, at best, earn a minimum-wage income and, at worst, are unemployed or underemployed.

Women's economic empowerment decidedly gives them the upper hand in the resolution of conflict with their mates over their decision to work as bar girls, and results in a more egalitarian division of household work. Because bar girls must often sleep during the day, unemployed male companions were responsible for cleaning the house, feeding and caring for children, doing the laundry, buying groceries, and making dinner.

Nonetheless, economic dependency on woman represents a serious social, cultural, and moral dilemma for men. First, their dependency on women violates cultural manhood codes, and their subsequent loss of power undermines the cultural norm that gives the adult male in the family ultimate control of decisionmaking power in domestic affairs. Second, having a female companion who earns a living by using her sensuality/ sexuality to entertain and service other men presents the moral dilemma of having a "prostitute" for a wife. And, third, having a "bad" woman for a wife places the husband in the socially undesirable category of cuckold and pimp. Together these cultural and moral violations undermine the self-confidenceof the male as a man and as a family provider and foster resentment against women.

To get even, men commit petty crimes and engage in substance abuse; once intoxicated they may physically abuse their wives. Women respond to this violence by fleeing their homes, moving out temporarily, calling the police, or locking themselves up until their husbands sober up or are placated by others. Most importantly, women attempt to address this conflict through the negotiation of gender roles and the use of pretense to feign male control and dominance of domestic relations. In this context, women pretend their men are in command of domestic affairs, as gender-based norms would have it, so long as men do not interfere with women's work strategies nor publicly denigrate their reputation for working in morally suspect professions associated with the commercial sex industry.[76]

CONCLUSION

The 1970s and 1980s were decades of growth for both feminist and Latina scholarship on the family. Feminist scholarship called attention to the importance of waged work, housework, and control over household income in domestic relations; through the use of gender theory, this scholarship displaced the notion of ideal gender types. Since then, the domestic unit and domestic relations remain an important locus for the expression of gendered power relations, its displacement and deconstruction.

Traditionally, gender has been given expression as either male or female role patterning; however, behavior at the local level suggests a broader, more creative range of gender in both a Mexican and an American social context. In particular, contemporary studies of Chicano families have stressed conjugal decision making, indicating a growing egalitarianism associated with the entry of women into the labor force. Similarly, Mexican family studies have sought to articulate male/female gendered behavior, and though traditional patterns have been advocated, social scientists have observed and documented female dominant patterns for more than half a century. In part, this gender flexibility is the outcome of women's resolve to address the immediate needs of daily survival, which may render patriarchal absolutes impractical. However, though both Mexican and Chicano literatures suggest the domestic empowerment of women, the invocation of patriarchal gendered norms continues to be given expression by Mexican and Chicana women who no longer subscribe to or practice these norms. In part, the Mexican case may be explained by a cultural phenomenon that monitors the status of women as wife, mother, or woman of virtue as contingent on the presence of a male companion or patriarch. Subsequently, conjugal couples which violate traditional norms, such as those dependent on the earnings of economically empowered women, may find themselves having to publicly pretend that they subscribe to traditional cultural roles. Though it is not clear why Chicanas invoke traditional norms when these are no longer practiced, it is possible these women may be recent Mexican immigrants and/or may not want to overtly contest the power of the male; this raises additional questions about overt and covert strategies of influence and power in domestic arrangements.[77]

Together the studies discussed suggest that Mexican and Chicano families should not be constructed, even generally, as male dominated, nor should they be characterized as based on rigid gender roles which privilege patriarchal domestic arrangements typically characterized as traditional. Failure to understand that Mexican and Chicano gendered behavior is far more variable and complex than traditionally conceived tends to attribute the expression of alternative gendered behavior to necessarily modern influences. On the contrary, that there has been recurrent contestation of rigid gender roles by Mexican women suggests a past tradition of cultural flexibility (which has yet to be acknowledged and understood by scholars and writers) in Mexican gendered behavior.

NOTES

1. Adelaida R. Del Castillo, Displacing Gender Identity: The Negotiation of Gendered Behavior in Mexico City's Domestic Space (Albuquerque: University of New Mexico Press, forthcoming).

2. In a radically subversive analysis utilizing the genealogy of sexuality as a conceptual approach, Judith Butler has argued that the distinction between sex and gender is a false one by showing sex to be as culturally constructed as gender, and because both are fabrications, though tools of cultural formation, "gender does not necessarily follow from sex." This disaggregation of sex and gender acknowledges gender discontinuities and allows the impersonation of any gender by any sexed body. See Judith Butler, *Gender Trouble: Feminism and the Subversion of Identity* (New York: Routledge, 1990): 128–41.

3. Reuben Hill, "Whither Family Research in the 1980s: Continuities, Emergents, Constraints, and New Horizons," *Journal of Marriage and the Family* 43 (1981): 255–57.

4. Graham B. Spanier and Robert A. Lewis, "Marital Quality: A Review of the Seventies," *Journal of Marriage and the Family* 42 (1980): 825.

5. Marie W. Osmond, "Cross-Societal Family Research: A Macrosociological Overview of the Seventies," *Journal of Marriage and the Family* 42 (1980): 995–1016; and John Scanzoni and Greer L. Fox, "Sex Roles, Family and Society: The Seventies and Beyond," *Journal of Marriage and the Family* 42 (1980): 743–56.

6. Gerald W. McDonald, "Family Power: The Assessment of a Decade of Theory and Research, 1970–1979," *Journal of Marriage and the Family* 42 (1980): 841–54.

7. Helena Z. Lopata and Barrie Thorne, "On the Term 'Sex Roles'," *Signs* 3 (1978): 718–21; and Myra Marx Ferree, "Beyond Separate Spheres: Feminism and Family Research," *Journal of Marriage and the Family* 52 (1990): 866–84.

8. Ferree, "Beyond Separate Spheres," 866–69; and Linda Thompson and Alexis J. Walker, "Gender in Families: Women and Men in Marriage, Work and Parenthood," *Journal of Marriage and the Family* 51 (1989): 845–71.

9. Linda Thompson, "Feminist Methodology for Family Studies," *Journal of Marriage and the Family* 54 (1992): 3–18; and Candace West and Don H. Zimmerman, "Doing Gender," *Gender & Society* 1 (1987): 125–51.

10. Harry Brod, ed., *The Making of Masculinities* (Boston: Allen and Urwin, 1987); Ferree,

"Beyond Separate Spheres," 870–74; and Joseph Pleck, "The Theory of Male Sex Role Identity: Its Rise and Fall, 1936 to the Present," in Brod, *The Making of Masculinities,* 21–38.

11. Though feminist scholarship makes greater use of the distinction between family and household than is common in conventional family studies, the literature continues to confuse the referents of the family and those of the household to the extent of treating them as interchangeable entities. Bender offers conceptual clarity on the difference between domestic groups by showing that families, households, and domestic functions are conceptually distinct and not inherent attributes of one another. He argues that these domestic phenomena are comprised of three logically discrete categories: kinship, coresidence, and the performance of domestic activities which may or may not group together. Not all families form households, not all households are comprised of families, nor does the membership of these necessarily perform domestic functions together (such as eating or sleeping together). Because the referent of the family is kinship and the referent of the household is coresidence, the family and the household are distinct and empirically different categories. Food production, provision, and consumption, as well as the social reproduction of human life and its care, are the social referents of domestic functions. Bender believes that families and households are often confused because they both perform domestic functions the execution of which is actually independent of them. See Donald R. Bender, "A Refinement of the Concept of Household: Families, Co-Residence, and Domestic Functions," *American Anthropologist* 69 (1967): 493–504; cf. Sylvia J. Yanagisako, "Family and Household: The Analysis of Domestic Groups," *Annual Review of Anthropology* 8 (1979): 161–205.

12. Ferree, "Beyond Separate Spheres," 867.

13. Ferree, "Beyond Separate Spheres," 866–84; Barrie Thorne and Marilyn Yalom, eds., *Rethinking the Family: Some Feminist Questions* (New York: Longman, 1982); Michelle Zimbalist Rosaldo, "The Use and Abuse of Anthropology: Reflections on Feminism and Cross-Cultural Understanding," *Signs* 3 (1980): 389–417. For the anthropological thesis on the public/private domain, see Michelle Zimbalist Rosaldo, "Women, Culture, and Society: A Theoretical Overview," in *Women, Culture and Society,* eds. Michelle Zimbalist Rosaldo and Louise Lamphere (Stanford, CA: Stanford University Press, 1974), 17–24.

14. Ferree, "Beyond Separate Spheres," 868–71; Heidi I. Hartmann, "The Family as the Locus of Gender, Class, and Political Struggle: The Example of Housework," *Signs* 6 (1981): 366–94; Beatriz Pesquera, " 'In the Beginning He Wouldn't Lift Even a Spoon': The Division of Household Labor," in *Building with Our Hands: New Directions of Chicana Studies,* eds. Adela de la Torre and Beatriz Pesquera (Berkeley: University of California Press, 1993), 181–95; Thompson and Walker, "Gender in Families"; and Patricia Zavella, *Women's Work and Chicano Families: Cannery Workers of the Santa Clara Valley* (Ithaca: Cornell University Press, 1987).

15. Ferree, "Beyond Separate Spheres," 870–79; Hartmann, "Family as the Locus."

16. Osmond, "Cross-Societal Family Research," 995.

17. Robert Staples and Alfredo Mirandé, "Racial and Cultural Variations among American

Families: A Decennial Review of the Literature on Minority Families," *Journal of Marriage and the Family* 42 (1980): 887–903.

18. For a critique of the early literature on Mexican Americans see the oft-cited Octavio I. Romano-V., "The Anthropology and Sociology of the Mexican Americans: The Distortion of Mexican American History," *El Grito* 2 (1968): 13–26; and Miguel Montiel, "The Social Science Myth of the Mexican American Family," *El Grito* 3 (1970): 56–63. For a critique of the methodology employed and the language competency of investigators, see Américo Paredes, "On Ethnographic Work among Minority Groups: A Folklorist's Perspective," *New Scholar* 6 (1977): 1–32. For a discussion of the Harvard study of cultural values in New Mexico in which Talcott Parsons, Clyde Kluckhohn, Munro Edmonson, Florence Kluckhohn, and Clifford Geertz, among others, participated, see Nicolás C. Vaca, "The Comparative Study of Values in Five Cultures Project and the Theory of Value," *Aztlán* 12 (1981): 89–120. For a critique of Mexican American families depicted in research related to the field of education, see Deluvina Hernández, *Mexican American Challenge to a Sacred Cow* (Los Angeles: University of California, Los Angeles, Mexican American Cultural Center, 1970).

19. See Staples and Mirandé, "Racial and Cultural Variations." Nonetheless, the challenge of presenting more accurate descriptions of Mexican American domestic groups does not appear to be limited to insider/outsider differences, because insiders are just as capable of reproducing romanticized, stereotypical versions of the family. In one of the first reviews of principal studies and treatments of the Mexican family by a Mexican American social scientist, it is proposed that these studies of Mexico should be adopted as a "baseline" for understanding "the Mexican family" in the United States. This, however, presents a problem when fundamental rural/urban, class, and regional differences among Mexicans themselves are overlooked. See Fernando Peñalosa, "Mexican Family Roles," *Journal of Marriage and the Family* 30 (1968): 686–89. Unfortunately, it seems that the cumulative effect of past studies by anthropologists, sociologists, psychologists, and educators, among others, has been the construction and reproduction of the "Mexican American family" as a cohesive cultural phenomenon essentially marked by an assortment of negative signifiers.

20. William A. Vega, "Hispanic Families in the 1980s: A Decade of Research," *Journal of Marriage and the Family* 52 (1990): 1015–24.

21. Maxine Baca-Zinn, "Employment and Education of Mexican American Women: The Interplay of Modernity and Ethnicity in Eight Families," *Harvard Educational Review* 50 (1980): 47–62; Lea Ybarra, "When Wives Work: The Impact of the Chicano Family," *Journal of Marriage and the Family* 44 (1982): 169–78; and Zavella, *Women's Work and Chicano Families.*

22. Betty García-Bahne, "La Chicana and the Chicano Family," in *Essays on La Mujer,* eds. Rosaura Sánchez and Rosa Martínez Cruz (Los Angeles: UCLA Chicano Studies Center, 1977), 30–47.

23. Maxine Baca-Zinn, "Political Familism: Toward Sex Role Equality in Chicano Families," *Aztlán* 6 (1975): 13–26.

24. Maxine Baca-Zinn, "Chicanas: Power and Control in the Domestic Sphere," *De Colores*

226 *Adelaida R. Del Castillo*

2 (1976): 19–31; and Lea Ybarra-Soriano, "Conjugal Role Relationships in the Chicano Family" (Ph.D. diss., University of California, Berkeley, 1977).

25. Deluvina Hernández and Cecilia Cota-Robles Suárez, *Low-Income Women Who Head Households: Equity through Education and Employment Programs* (San Antonio: National Chicana Foundation, 1978).

26. For this research, see Marilyn H. Buehler, Andrew J. Weigert, and Darwin L. Thomas, "Correlates of Conjugal Power: A Five-Culture Analysis of Adolescent Perceptions," *Journal of Comparative Family Studies* 5 (1974): 5–16; Baca-Zinn, "Chicanas: Power and Control"; idem, "Political Familism"; idem, "Employment and Education"; Ronald E. Cromwell and René A. Ruiz, "The Myth of Macho Dominance in Decision Making within Mexican and Chicano Families," *Hispanic Journal of Behavioral Sciences* 1 (1979): 355–73; Ronald E. Cromwell, Ramón Corrales, and Peter M. Torsiello, "Normative Patterns of Marital Decision-Making Power and Influences in Mexico and the United States: A Partial Test of Resource and Ideology Theory," *Journal of Comparative Family Studies* 4 (1973): 177–96; Vicky L. Cromwell and Ronald E. Cromwell, "Perceived Dominance in Decision Making and Conflict Resolution among Anglo, Black and Chicano Couples," *Journal of Marriage and the Family* 40 (1978): 749–59; Glen R. Hawkes and Minna Taylor, "Power Structure in Mexican and Mexican American Farm Labor Families," *Journal of Marriage and the Family* 37 (1975): 807–11; Ybarra-Soriano, "Conjugal Role Relationships"; idem, "When Wives Work"; and Zavella, *Women's Work and Chicano Families.*

For commentary and reviews of the literature on Mexican American families, see Michael V. Miller, "Variations in Mexican American Family Life: A Review Synthesis of Empirical Research," *Aztlán* 9 (1978): 209–31; Oscar Ramírez and Carlos H. Arce, "The Contemporary Chicano Family: An Empirically Based Review" in *Explorations in Chicano Psychology,* ed. Augustine Baron, Jr. (New York: Praeger, 1981), 3–28.

27. For research on the historical diversity of Mexican American families see Richard Griswold del Castillo, "A Preliminary Comparison of Chicano, Immigrant and Native Born Family Structure, 1850–1880," *Aztlan* 6 (1975): 87–96; idem, "La Familia Chicano [*sic*]: Social Changes in the Chicano Family of Los Angeles, 1850–1880," *Journal of Ethnic Studies* 3 (1975b); and idem, *La familia: Chicano Families in the Urban Southwest, 1948 to the Present* (Notre Dame: University of Notre Dame, 1984).

28. Griswold del Castillo, "La familia."

29. Segura, "Familism and Employment among Chicanas and Mexican Immigrant Women," in *Mexicanas at Work: In the United States,* ed. Margarita B. Melville (Houston: Mexican American Studies, 1988), 24–32; Torres Raines, "The Mexican American Woman and Work: Intergenerational Perspectives of Comparative Ethnic Groups," in *Mexicanas at Work,* 33–46; Chavira, " 'Tienes que ser valiente': Mexicana Migrants in a Midwestern Farm Labor Camp," in *Mexicanas at Work,* 64–74; Curry Rodríguez, "Labor Migration and Familial Responsibilities: Experiences of Mexican Women," in *Mexicanas at Work,* 47–63; Baca-Zinn, "Employment and Education"; Ybarra, "When Wives Work"; idem, "Separating Myth from Reality: Socio-Economic and Cultural Influences on Chicanas and the World of Work," in *Mexicanas at Work,* 12–23; Zavella, *Women's Work and Chicano Families;* Mora, "The Tolteca Strike: Mexican Women and the Struggle for Union

Representation," in *Mexican Immigrant Workers in the United States,* ed. Antonio Ríos-Bustamante (Los Angeles: UCLA Chicano Studies Research Center, 1981) 111–24; Ruiz, *Cannery Women, Cannery Lives* (Albuquerque: University of New Mexico Press, 1987); Baca-Zinn, "Political Familism"; Hernández, "Lives of Chicana Activists: The Chicano Student Movement (A Case Study)," in *Mexican Women in the United States: Struggling Past and Present,* eds. Magdalena Mora and Adelaida R. Del Castillo (Los Angeles, UCLA Chicano Studies Research Center, 1980), 17–25; Melville, "Mexican Women Adapt to Migration," in *Mexican Immigrant Workers in the U.S.;* Argüelles, "Undocumented Female Labor in the United States Southwest: An Essay on Migration, Consciousness, Oppression and Struggle," in *Between Borders: Essays on Mexicana Chicana History,* ed. Adelaida R. Del Castillo (Encino: Floricanto Press, 1990), 299–312; Baca-Zinn, "Familism among Chicanos: A Theoretical Review," *Humboldt Journal of Social Relations* 10 (1982/3): 224–38; Baca-Zinn, "Chicano Men and Masculinity," *Journal of Ethnic Studies* 10 (1982): 29–44; Segura, "Familism and Employment," 24–30; Sosa Riddell, "Chicanas and El Movimiento," *Aztlán* 5 (1974): 155–65; Ybarra, "When Wives Work"; and Zavella, *Women's Work and Chicano Families.*

30. Argüelles, "Undocumented Female Labor," 299–312; de la Torre, "Hard Choices and Changing Roles among Mexican Migrant Campesinas," in *Building with Our Hands,* 168–80; Chavira-Prado, "Work, Health, and the Family: Gender Structure and Women's Status in an Undocumented Migrant Population," *Human Organization* 51 (1992): 53–64; Pesquera, " 'In the Beginning,' " 181–95; Del Castillo, "Covert Cultural Norms and Sex/Gender Meaning: A Mexico City Case," *Urban Anthropology* 22 (1993): 237–58; Baca-Zinn, "Family, Feminism, and Race in America," *Gender and Society* 4 (1990): 68–82.

31. Beverly Chiñas, *The Isthmus Zapotecs: Women's Roles in Cultural Context* (New York: Holt, Rinehart & Wilson, 1973); May N. Díaz, *Tonalá: Conservatism, Responsibility, and Authority in a Mexican Town* (Berkeley: University of California Press, 1966); Larisa A. Lomnitz, *Networks and Marginality: Life in a Mexican Shantytown* (New York: Academic Press, 1977).

32. Many of these concepts have been based on Mexican psychological and family studies including the work of María E. Bermúdez, *La vida familiar del mexicano* (México, D.F.: Antigua Libería Robredo, 1955); Rogelio Díaz-Guerrero, *Estudios de la psicología del mexicano* (México, D.F.: Editorial F. Trillas, 1967); and Samuel Ramos, *Profile of Man and Culture in Mexico* (Austin: University of Texas Press, 1934).

33. Octavio Paz, *The Labyrinth of Solitude: Life and Thought in Mexico* (New York: Grove Press, 1961), 29–30.

34. Ibid., 77.

35. Oscar Lewis, *Life in a Mexican Village: Tepotzlán Restudied* (Urbana, Ill.: University of Illinois Press, 1951), 319–20.

36. Erich Fromm and Michael Maccoby, *Social Character in a Mexican Village: A Socio-psychoanalytic Study* (New Jersey: Prentice-Hall,Inc., 1978), 153.

37. Bart McDowell, "Mexico City: An Alarming Giant, *National Geographic* 2 (1984): 158.

38. See notes 1 and 30.

39. Fromm and Mccoby, *Social Character,* chapter 7.

40. I thank Norma Iglesias Prieto for bringing this saying to my attention.

41. Fromm and Maccoby, *Social Character,* 109, 151.

42. Ibid., 152, 166.

43. Similarly, Mercedes González de la Rocha argues that male domestic violence (against women) is in part due to their lack of power at the workplace. See González de la Rocha, *Los recursos de la pobreza: Familias de bajos ingresos de Guadalajara* (Jalisco, Guadalajara: El Colegio de Jalisco, 1986), 135.

44. Fromm and Maccoby, *Social Character,* 151, 150.

45. Lola Romanucci-Ross, *Conflict, Violence, and Morality in a Mexican Village* (Chicago: University of Chicago Press, 1973), 58.

46. Louise Lamphere "Strategies, Cooperation, and Conflict Among Women in Domestic Groups," in *Women, Culture and Society,* eds. Michelle Zimbalist Rosaldo and Louise Lamphere (Stanford: Stanford University Press, 1974), 95–112.

47. Margery Wolf, *Women and the Family in Rural Taiwan* (Stanford: Stanford University Press, 1972), 33.

48. Alfredo Mirandé, "A Reinterpretation of Male Dominance in the Chicano Family," *The Family Coordinator* 28 (1979):474–497; and Montiel, "Social Science Myth," 56–63.

49. Marta Cotera, *Diosa y Hembra: History and Heritage of Chicanas in the U.S.* (Austin: Information Systems Development, 1976), *The Chicana Feminist* (Austin: Information Systems Development, 1977); Adelaida R. Del Castillo, "Mexican Women in Organization," in *Mexican Women in the United States;* Alma M. García, "The Development of Chicana Feminist Discourse, 1970–1980," *Gender & Society* 3 (1989): 217; Sonia López, "The Role of the Chicana within the Student Movement," in *Essays on La Mujer,* ed. Rosaura Sánchez and Rosa Martínez Cruz (Los Angeles: UCLA Chicano Studies Center, 1970), 16–29; Anna Nieto Gómez, "Chicanas Identify," *Hijas de Cuauhtémoc* (April 1971): 9, "La Feminista," *Encuentro Femenil* (1974): 34–47, "Sexism in the Movement," *La Gente* 6 (1976): 10; B. Rincón, "La Chicana: Her Role in the Past and Her Search for a New Role in the Future," *Regeneración,* 1 (1971): 15–17; and Mirta Vidal, "New Voice of La Raza: Chicanas Speak Out," *International Socialist Review* 32 (1971): 31–33.

50. Baca-Zinn, "Chicano Men."

51. Lourdes Benería and Martha Roldán, *The Crossroads of Class and Gender: Industrial Homework, Subcontracting, and Household Dynamics in Mexico City* (Chicago and London: The University of Chicago Press, 1987), 148.

52. Lewis, *Tepotzlán,* 319.

53. Baca-Zinn, "Employment and Education," 47–62; Melba J. T. Vásquez and González, "Sex Roles among Chicanos: Stereotypes, Challenges, and Changes," in Baron, *Explorations in Chicano Psychology,* 50–70; Ybarra-Soriano, "Conjugal Role Relationships."

54. Cromwell, Corrales, and Torsiello, "Normative Patterns," 58–59.

55. Baca-Zinn, "Employment and Education," 47–62.

56. Hawkes and Taylor, "Power Structure," 807–11.

57. Frank D. Bean, Russell L. Curtis, Jr., and John P. Marcum, "Familism and Marital Satisfaction among Mexican Americans: The Effects of Family Size, Wife's Labor Force Participation, and Conjugal Power," *Journal of Marriage and the Family* 39 (1977): 759–67.

58. See Jane F. Collier and Sylvia J. Yanagisako, eds. *Gender and Kinship: Essays Toward a Unified Analysis* (Stanford: Stanford University Press, 1987); and Peggy R. Sanday and Ruth G. Goodenough, eds. *Beyond the Second Sex: New Directions in the Anthropology of Gender* (Philadelphia: University of Pennsylvania Press, 1990).

59. Benería and Roldán, *Crossroads of Class and Gender,* 157.

60. Female heads-of-household throughout Latin America and the developing world have long utilized informal consensual unions (free unions) in serial monogamy to secure control of their finances and families. See Susan E. Brown, "Love Unites Them and Hunger Separates Them: Poor Women in the Dominican Republic," in *Toward an Anthropology of Women,* ed. Rayna Rapp Reiter (New York: Monthly View Press, 1975), 322–32; Mari H. Clark, "Women-headed Households and Poverty: Insights from Kenya," in *Women and Poverty,* eds. Barbara C. Gelpi, N.C.M. Hartsock, C. C. Novak, and M. H. Sroeber (Chicago: University of Chicago Press, 1986), 103–19; Nici Nelson, "Female-Centered Families: Changing Patterns of Marriage and Family among Buzaa Brewers of Mathare Valley," *African Urban Studies* 3 (Winter 1978): 85–103.

61. Chiñas, *Isthmus Zapotecs,* 101–08.

62. Díaz, *Tonalá,* 85–90.

63. See Del Castillo, "Covert Cultural Notions."

64. Susan Rogers, "Female Forms of Power and the Myth of Male Dominance: A Model of Female/Male Interaction in Peasant Society," *American Ethnologist* 4 (1975): 727–56.

65. See notes 1 and 30; Fromm and Maccoby, *Social Character;* Rogers, "Myth of Male Dominance."

66. Fromm and Maccoby, *Social Character,* 151.

67. Susan Rogers, "Myth of Male Dominance."

68. The public performance of gender in this context differs from Butler's use of the term in that the individuals in Mexico City actually subscribe to the idea of right and wrong gender roles which they fear they may be violating. Butler's use of performance attests to the cultural fabrication of gender through the public "stylized repetition of acts." Performance in this sense results in a parody of the very notion of an original, authentic, or true sex and gender. See Butler, *Gender Trouble,* 140–41.

69. Contrary to the social science literature of the day, not all studies found that acculturation and urbanization were the impetus behind egalitarian decision making. See Hawkes and Taylor, "Power Structure," 807–11; Baca-Zinn, "Political Familism," "Employment and Education," 47–62; and Ybarra-Soriano, "Conjugal Role Relationships"; idem, "When Wives Work," 169–78.

70. Baca-Zinn, "Employment and Education," 47–62.

71. Cromwell and Ruiz, "The Myth of Macho Dominance," 355–73.

72. Zavella, *Women's Work and Chicano Families,* xiii.

73. Ibid., 169–70.

74. Ibid., 140.

75. Ibid.

76. I address the moral implications of the *fichera*'s profession in "Mexico City Ficheras: The Moral Culture of the 'Mala' Mujer" (paper presented at the invited session of the

Society for Medical Anthropology: Addicts, Prostitutes, Teen Mothers: Going Beyond the Social and Biomedical Labels, American Anthropological Association, Chicago, Ill., 20–24 November 1991).

77. I examine Mexican overt and covert normative behavior and its implications for gendered meaning in "Covert Cultural Norms."

WITH QUILL AND TORCH : A CHICANA PERSPECTIVE ON THE AMERICAN WOMEN'S MOVEMENT AND FEMINIST THEORIES

Beatriz M. Pesquera and Denise A. Segura

"Write with your eyes like painters, with your ears like musicians, with your feet like dancers. You are the truthsayer with quill and torch. Write with your tongues of fire. Don't let the pen banish you from yourself. Don't let the ink coagulate in your pens. Don't let the censor snuff out the spark, nor the gags muffle your voice. Put your shit on the paper."[1]

Quill in hand and fueled by the torch of political dissent, Chicana[2] activists and scholars have charged the American Women's Movement and feminist theories with inadequately addressing racial/ethnic, culture, and class differences among women.[3] The forums for these critiques include personal reflections of Chicana activists as well as scholarly presentations.[4] Few of these critical interpretations have found their way into either mainstream or feminist journals. Thus, Chicana perspectives on feminism are rarely integrated within feminist scholarship.

The omission of Chicanas from feminist discourse is consistent with the historical subordination of Chicanos since the U.S.-Mexico War.[5] However, it is not compatible with feminist theoretical goals that seek, among other things, to inscribe women as subjects by creating discourse that integrates racial/ethnic, culture, and class diversity. In this chapter we explore the attitudes of a select group of Chicana women toward the American Women's Movement and feminist theories. Our analysis of the views of these women reveals the importance of (what we term) the "Chicana triple-oppression lens" that informs their perspective on feminism.

We begin with a brief overview of the major critiques of American feminism from Chicana activists and scholars. Then we explore the perceptions of 101 highly educated Chicanas regarding the American Women's Movement, feminist theories, and the extent to which Women's Studies and women's centers on college campuses address Chicana concerns. We demonstrate that Chicanas' critiques, often eloquent, sometimes harsh, of American feminism flow from a triple-oppression lens grounded in the experiences of being Mexican women from largely poor or working-class backgrounds who work in environments (colleges and universities) that rarely validate their subjective essence.

CHICANA CRITIQUE OF AMERICAN FEMINISM

Chicana feminist writers of the late 1960s and early 1970s viewed American feminism ambivalently. Many Chicanas criticized the movement's predominantly white middle-class leadership as largely unable or unwilling to articulate a nuanced vision of women's empowerment.[6] During this period, few Anglo or Chicana feminists moved to build coalitions between both communities of women.[7] Instead, Chicanas questioned the feminist call to "sisterhood," arguing that unity that responded only to the subordination of women was inadequate because it overlooked the historical racial/ethnic, class, and cultural antagonisms between women.

Chicanas argued that membership in a historically subordinated racial/ethnic group, culture, and class—as well as gender—has culminated in a unique "triple oppression."[8] As Mexicans, Chicanas have been treated as "second-class citizens" since their incorporation into the United States in 1848.[9] Historically, they have encountered racial/ethnic and gender discrimination, which limits their access to education, jobs, and political participation and results in their overrepresentation among the poor and lower working classes. Despite these difficulties, Chicanas have continued to maintain a distinct Chicano/Mexicano culture. This set of circumstances informs a unique Chicana perspective, or worldview, that guides their assessment of the relevancy of social reforms or movements, including American feminism.

Chicana feminists have opposed American feminist writings that equated sexism with racism as ahistorical, inasmuch as gender and race are not analogous systems of oppression.[10] Chicanas expressed skepticism concerning the suggestion that eliminating sexual oppression would end class and racial/ethnic inequality. Chicana activists argued that the American Women's Movement and feminism could not be relevant to Chicanas until racial/ethnic and class concerns were integrated into their political and theoretical formulations. Chicanas doubted, however, that such an integrative approach would emerge in light of the racism and "maternal chauvinism" apparent among Women's Movement activists, as Ana Nieto-Gómez states: "Chicanas, having to deal with racism in the feminist movement and sensing that Anglo women believe they can solve the problems of minority women, have tried to circumvent this maternal chauvinism."[11] Concern about what Nieto-Gómez termed "maternal chauvinism" reverberates throughout the writing of early Chicana feminists. Chicanas angrily decried their omission from feminist agendas, and a review of key feminist writings of the late 1960s and early 1970s affirms the accuracy of this perception.[12] In the rare instances in which Chicanas were included, their experiences tended to be cast in ways that reinforced cultural stereotypes of them as women who did not "want to be liberated."[13] Most often, however, Chicanas have been silent objects within feminist discourse—neither included nor excluded by name. Thus, Chicanas in this period concluded they were not "equal" sisters in the struggle against sexual oppression.

Chicana feminists also criticized what they interpreted as an individualistic upward mobility ethos within the American Women's Movement. They posited an alternative view; their political concerns were rooted in the collective struggle of the Chicano community. Thus, they questioned the validity of trying to become integrated into society when that struggle would leave intact structures of domination/subordination due to race/ethnicity and class, as well as gender. We analyze the meaning of this critique among Chicana feminists today.

THE WOMEN OF MALCS

The 101 women of this study are on the mailing list of Mujeres Activas en Letras y Cambio Social (MALCS), an organization of Chicana/Latina women in higher education. This organization's charter and activities demonstrate familiarity with Chicana concerns, a feminist orientation, and sensitivity to cultural concerns.[14] MALCS was founded in 1983 by Chicana faculty and graduate students as a support and advocacy group, and as a forum for sharing research interests. The founding declaration of MALCS states that "we are the daughters of Chicano working-class families involved in higher education. . . . We are particularly concerned with the conditions women face at work, in and out of the home. We continue our mothers' struggle for social and economic justice."[15] Drawing from a tradition of political struggle, MALCS is dedicated to the documentation, analysis, and interpretation of the Chicana/Latina experience in the United States.

We developed a questionnaire and mailed it to the 178 women on the MALCS mailing list in 1988; 101 were completed and returned for a response rate of 57 percent. The questionnaire asked women to describe their perceptions of the major features of the contemporary American Women's Movement, the major concerns of Chicanas today, and the extent to which the Women's Movement and feminist theory have addressed the needs of Chicana women. They also answered a series of closed-end questions regarding their familiarity with writings on the Women's Movement, their involvement in "feminist" and "women's" activities, and information on their socioeconomic status.

Nearly all the women who answered our questionnaire were associated with institutions of higher learning, either as faculty members (38.6 percent), graduate students (25.7 percent), undergraduates (8.9 percent), or professional staff (8.9 percent). Eleven women indicated they were employed outside of a university setting, and seven declined to provide information on their employment or education. The women's ages ranged from 22 to 65 years, with a median age of 35 years, and a mean age of 38.1 years. This age distribution means that a majority of the women were college age (17–22 years old) during the heyday of the Women's Movement (1967–1976). Moreover, most of the women have activist backgrounds: over three-fourths (78.2 percent) of the informants either belong to, or have previously been involved in, women's organizations, and they overwhelmingly (83.2 percent) self-identified as "Chicana feminist."

We asked the informants to indicate their familiarity with literature on the American Women's Movement. Nearly three-fourths of the women were either very familiar (24.8 percent) or somewhat familiar (48.5 percent) with this literature, while 19.8 percent were slightly familiar and 5.9 percent were not familiar with the literature. Over half of the women also indicated they were either very familiar (23.8 percent) or somewhat familiar (35.6 percent) with feminist theoretical writings; and those who were either slightly familiar or not at all familiar with these writings numbered 24.8 percent and 15.8 percent, respectively.

While neither of these answers can be standardized (e.g., one woman's sense of being "very familiar" with literature on the American Women's

Movement may differ substantially from that of another women), we feel confident that the informants gave fairly accurate self-assessments. We base this evaluation on a content analysis of the different ways women describe the major agendas of the American Women's Movement and the relative ease with which they refer to various types of feminist theories (e.g., socialist feminism). Accordingly, women who indicated they were very familiar with either the American Women's Movement or feminist theoretical writing gave far more detailed and knowledgeable descriptions than did women who indicated they were slightly familiar or not familiar with these writings.

From the responses of this group of highly educated women, we explore the content of the Chicana triple-oppression lens. As academicians (or aspiring scholars), these Chicanas are situated in settings where reforms advocated by the American Women's Movement can benefit them. Their circumstances should enhance their willingness to articulate a positive evaluation of American feminism. The fact that women express views that are more negative than positive suggests a Chicana triple-oppression lens whose strength is probably exacerbated by competition between Chicanas and white feminist scholars in the highly competitive world of the academy.

We must emphasize that this group of Chicanas does not represent all women of Mexican descent in the United States. They are, nevertheless, academicians or highly educated women who inform the public discourse on feminism and women's issues. Moreover, as well-educated Chicanas they constitute one end point of the continuum that forms the Chicana experience. Their perceptions, therefore, offer an excellent source of knowledge on Chicanas and American feminism.

THE WOMEN'S MOVEMENT AND CHICANA CONCERNS

We asked the Chicana informants to describe ways in which the American Women's Movement has addressed or not addressed Chicana concerns. Ninety-five women answered this question; six women did not reply. Over half of the informants indicate that Chicana concerns have been somewhat addressed (53.5 percent) by the American Women's Movement, whereas 38.6 percent feel these needs have not been addressed. Only two women feel that the American Women's Movement has addressed Chicana concerns.

Eighty-two women provided in-depth, written responses in support of their answers. Their responses range from acknowledging the importance of the American Women's Movement to forceful critiques of race-class biases. The latter sentiment prevails both among women who feel that the American Women's Movement has somewhat addressed and those who feel that it has not addressed Chicana concerns. The major difference between these two groups of women is the tenor of the critique; that is, women who feel that the movement has not addressed Chicana concerns articulate more intense antagonism, harsher criticism, and less acknowledgment of benefits gained.

Chicanas tend to portray the American Women's Movement as articulating the issues of relatively privileged, well-educated, middle- and upper-class white women. Informants argue that the social origins of movement activists hindered the development of issues relevant to women outside a narrow social milieu. For example, one respondent noted that "by its very historical origins, the movement has emphasized middle-class to upper-class concerns" (Chicana faculty member, 34 years old). This informant's criticism of the lack of diversity within the movement echoes that of both other women of color and substantial white feminist scholars.[16]

Informants object to what they perceive as a marked tendency within the American Women's Movement to present itself in global terms (i.e., The Women's Movement). Chicanas in MALCS feel that this attitude obscures important racial/ethnic and class differences among women: "The women's movement that stands out in my mind is the 'second wave,' which occurred during the 1960s. This movement was primarily a 'white, middle-class movement' that openly called for the liberation of women. Although the movement seemed to speak in universal liberation terms (for all women), it systematically excluded the concerns of non-white women, as it failed to consider issues of race, class, and cultural oppression" (Chicana faculty member, 40 years old).

Another informant stated that "the movement has failed to adequately address classism and racism and how it impacts on women as a class and in dealing with our areas of common concern [i.e., women and the family]. I think we have been used to present a collective voice on behalf of women but have not been extended the same degree of importance in areas that concern us differently, i.e., class and race issues. In other words, white women also have to overcome their own prejudices as they try to overcome prejudice altogether" (Chicana graduate student, 24 years old). Like other women who feel that the American Women's Movement has somewhat addressed Chicana concerns, this informant recognizes that the movement often articulates issues pertinent to many women (e.g., the family). What she and others object to is the movement's failure to "adequately address" how other forms of inequality, in particular, racial/ethnicity and class, conditions women's lives. She and the other informants take exception to the manner in which the Women's Movement postulates stances on behalf of all women without considering these differences. Ultimately, she challenges white women to confront their own race and class privileges side-by-side with the struggle to eradicate sexism.

In general, the women who feel that the Women's Movement has somewhat addressed and those who feel that it has not addressed Chicana concerns object to an analysis of oppression that grants primacy to gender. They argue that overreliance on a gender critique inhibits the development of a more inclusive perspective sensitive to the ways in which race/ethnicity and class, as well as gender, shape the Chicana experience. As another Chicana observed, "The Anglo-American women's movement addresses the dominant culture's sexist practices but many times failed to address the development of our present economic system and how that brought about the division of labor, the social class differences, and the racist institutions" (Chicana graduate student, 32 years old). This woman acknowledges the need to eradicate sexism, but argues for the incorporation in the discussion of class and race/ethnicity as well.

Many women also voice disapproval of the "liberal-reformist" tendencies they feel predominate within the movement. They argued that the American Women's Movement should be less dedicated to finding ways to integrate women into a male-dominated world and more devoted to developing strategies to end structures of inequality and exploitation produced by American capitalism. These perceptions are captured in the response of one Chicana: "The reluctance of the dominant NOW-type feminism in the United States to face up to the reality of racism and class-based problems facing Chicanas has been the main obstacle to feminist concerns for Chicana issues. At the root of this problem is the narrow definition of feminism that is based on sex differences and not a problem of domination" (Chicana graduate student, 29 years old). This woman, like many of the informants, did not distinguish between the various segments within the American

Women's Movement. While this overgeneralization may have contributed to the harsh tone of the critique, it is important to note that women who made this distinction tended to voice similar criticisms; for example, "The Women's Movement addressed the specific concerns that affect us as a race and/or class only when we demanded it, but only temporarily. There were few changes in white middle-class women's ideology and practice among the women's rights groups and women liberationists" (Chicana graduate student, 30 years old). This woman, like other informants, combines the different branches of the American Women's Movement in her critique to emphasize how the omission of Chicana concerns cuts across political and ideological alignments of feminists within the American Women's Movement.

Despite their criticism of the American Women's Movement, nearly all the informants endorse the key maxim: eradicating female subordination is essential. Many women credit the movement's critique of patriarchy with influencing their own development as Chicana feminists. They acknowledge that Chicanas benefit from the struggle against patriarchy. Despite this view, a majority feel that the gains netted from this particular struggle are inadequate and largely incidental: "All women of all races are helped when a woman any group of women defies stereotypes and promotes a progressive agenda or idea. But Chicana-specific concerns are not usually what 'the larger agenda' of the Women's Movement is about" (Chicana faculty member, 39 years old). In words reminiscent of Chicana feminists in the 1960s and 1970s this woman contends that the American Women's Movement has not prioritized Chicana concerns. According to this view, Chicana concerns are implicit rather the explicit within feminist agendas. Moveover, because white middle-class women tend to define the direction of this struggle, they will likely garner the greatest benefits. "The Women's Movement addresses the problems of women in general (i.e., white women because they're the leaders of the women's movement) and not those of minority women specifically. Though all women should gain from the movement, statistics show that it is white women who have gained" (Chicana graduate student, 47 years old).

Not only is the previous informant critical of the direction taken by the Women's Movement, she also questions its effectiveness to advocate for women outside the social mainstream. She, like most of the women in this study, contends that social policies to redress gender inequality have not significantly improved the life chances of most Chicanas. In general, Chicanas are poorer, less educated, and employed in the lowest-paying jobs vis-à-vis white women, as well as men.[17] Sex discrimination in training and job access is but one barrier Chicanas face. They also experience discrimination based on their race/ethnicity and culture.

A few informants acknowledge that in recent years, the concerns of working-class and racial/ethnic women have been moving from "margin to center," to quote Hooks.[18] Many women feel this change has resulted from the critiques and demands of women of color. As one informant states, "Over the past decade, there appears to be increased concern to address working-women's issues *and* [respondent's emphasis] to incorporate women of color into ongoing organizational efforts. Thus, incorporation in terms of issues and individuals sought out for membership in women's caucuses, organizations, etc., appears to be evolving. Mostly, there appears to be a heightened consciousness (perhaps out of guilt) among white women to address more directly the concerns of women of color" (Chicana faculty member, 37 years old).

While many women indicate that the American Women's Movement had been moving toward a more inclusive agenda, others feel that Chicana feminist efforts have been almost completely ignored. Their view is typified by the sentiment expressed by one respondent, who wrote that "women of color, particularly Chicanas themselves, have struggled as a group since the late 1960s and early 1970s to raise their/our own issues as women from an oppressed nationality group in the United States. Our fight within the predominantly white, middle-class 'women's movement' has been to address the issues of class and race, as *inextricable* [respondent's emphasis] to our gender issues" (Chicana graduate student, 27 years old). This informant articulates the widespread feeling that white feminists need to acknowledge that Chicanas have been actively challenging patriarchy and racial/ethnic and class oppression. The complexity of Chicanas' struggle requires a multidimensional approach. The term "Chicana" embraces political activism, ethnicity, and gender; therefore, Chicanas do not order their oppression hierarchically. Hence, their articulation of a triple-oppression approach that considers race/ethnicity and class, as well as gender.

Many informants assert that the American Women's Movement neglects the cultural heterogeneity of the American landscape. About one-third of the informants who feel that the movement has not addressed Chicana concerns refer to feminism's lack of cultural sensitivity and cultural awareness. "In general the WM [Women's Movement] has been an Anglo movement, not one considering the cultural heterogeneity of women" (Chicana faculty member, 65 years old).

Chicanas' critiques of the American Women's Movement led them to conclude that they should articulate their own issues: "We need to do this—as Chicanas. We can't expect the white women to understand us in a cultural sense—though they may be able to understand us sociologically in a larger sense" (Chicana faculty member, 43 years old). This woman voices a sentiment heard throughout this group—that neither white women nor Chicano men know how to liberate Chicanas. Moreover, there is no compelling reason for them to do so, inasmuch as they derive privileges from the continued subordination of Chicanas.

FEMINIST THEORY AND CHICANA CONCERNS

In this study, more women feel that feminist theories are less relevant to Chicanas than to the American Women's Movement. Forty-eight women (47.5 percent) indicate that feminist theory/scholarship has not incorporated the particular circumstances of Chicanas, while 42 women (41.6 percent) feel it has somewhat incorporated them. Only two women contend that feminist theory has incorporated the particular circumstances of Chicanas. Nine women did not provide information on this issue.

The women who assert that feminist theory has not incorporated and those who assert that it has somewhat incorporated the particular circumstances of Chicanas describe it as grounded in a narrow range of experiences without a global vision. Echoing the voices of early Chicana feminists, the informants also discuss a range of exclusionary practices within feminist scholarship that limits Chicana voices: "Basically, I know of no major feminist theoretical piece which discusses Chicanas. I think there is discussion now in 1988 of women of color, but that is not the same as a discussion of Chicanas" (Chicana graduate student, 30 years old). While this woman acknowledges recent efforts to include women of color, she, like the majority of the informants, asserts that these discussions typically overlook Chicanas. One result of this omission is Chicanas' alienation from American feminism and antagonism toward "white" feminists, who often act as "gatekeepers," limiting access to research and publication outlets necessary to the development of Chicana feminist discourse.

Even more objectionable to Chicana feminists than their exclusion is their inclusion as an "externalized other," whose experiences are appended to theory rather than centered at its heart. As one informant states, "Feminist scholars (excluding Chicanas) rarely talk about Chicanas or care to do any research on us. When we are included in any feminist theory we are used to substantiate a theory on white women. Generally theories are designed to explain the power relations between white males and females and then the experiences of Chicanas are forced into these theoretical frameworks" (Chicana faculty member, 31 years old). This woman, like a majority of the informants, questions the validity of feminist theories that cast Chicanas' experiences into preexisting analytic frameworks. They feel that feminist scholars need to develop an integrative perspective rather than the more obvious additive approach: "Chicanas are seldom represented in feminist theory courses or feminist colloquia unless of course in a marginal sense. As an afterthought many feminist seminars offer a single session which will touch on 'women of color' in general. We have, however, reached a point in history where feminist theorists are a bit self-conscious about failing to consider the particular circumstances of Chicanas, and as a result, the latest publications, etc., have in a limited way begun to solicit Chicana feminist scholarship" (Chicana faculty member, 40 years old). This respondent, like most of the other women surveyed, speaks from personal experiences with Women's Studies courses (e.g., as student, faculty or staff member). Her words display frustration with the misrepresentation of Chicanas and their token inclusion in feminist writings.

Other informants focused attention on recent attempts by women of color to bring the theoretical and political issues to the forefront. One, for example, declared that "unfortunately, it seems that true change in the intellectual debate as well as the political territory comes about only when spearheaded by Chicanas themselves. Chicanas and U.S. Third-World women (i.e., other 'minority' women) have shifted the debate and political agendas through political action, scholarship, cultural/artistic activity, and journalism. . . . There remains, of course, all the work to do which will end only when racism and sexism (and class oppression) are obsolete" (Chicana graduate student, 27 years old). This informant emphasizes that,

242 Beatriz M. Pesquera and Denise A. Segura

by and large, inclusion of women of color in feminist theory has been by women of color themselves. Their goal is a praxis addressing multidimensional forms of Chicana oppression.

Chicanas who discussed the incorporation of Chicana concerns into feminist theories voiced considerable cynicism regarding possible underlying motivations. Their view is captured in the response of one MALCS member, who observed, "I predict that it will become more 'fashionable' to hype the 'Hispanic' presence in the United States and the white feminist academics will give lip service to Chicana issues. Their appropriation of our concerns, however, will only serve their interests and diffuse our own voices" (Chicana graduate student, 36 years old). The respondent notes that research on Chicanas is becoming more popular. She and most of the informants harbor deep misgivings that research on Chicanas will be expropriated by white feminists and to a lesser extent by other non-Chicana scholars who are employed in significantly greater numbers in the academy than are Chicanas, as is noted by several scholars.[19] Study informants fear that non-Chicana scholars will secure recognition more readily for Chicana studies research than the Chicanas who initiated this line of inquiry. This is a particularly sensitive issue for Chicanas who feel they have spent years developing research on their communities.

Consistent with this apprehension, Chicanas in this study and others report that their research is often treated with skepticism in academic departments and denied publication in established research outlets.[20] This experience is not unique to Chicanas, but forms the backdrop for much discussion on the discourse of privilege and power currently underway among many feminist scholars of color.[21] One consequence of this limitation is the establishment of alternative outlets (e.g., Kitchen Table Press, Third Woman Press). To advance Chicana studies Chicana faculty and graduate students have formed groups such as MALCS and collaborative research/writing projects to advance Chicana studies. These groups and activities are one way to empower Chicanas, as well as to provide forums wherein Chicanas struggle to navigate their academic paths.

Study informants' critiques of feminist theories reveal a myriad of ideological and political contradictions. Chicanas are caught in the contradiction of seeking a feminist praxis while experiencing alienation from feminists' theories and feminist theoreticians. They are torn between criticizing feminism's lack of theoretical synthesis while denying the ability of white feminists to capture the essence of Chicana subjectivity. Chicana feminism, then, is struggling to wrestle free of these contradictory locutions to create a discourse that speaks to their multifaceted reality.

Despite their apprehensions and criticisms, most Chicanas view feminist theories as useful building blocks to develop their scholarship. As two informants noted, "I believe feminist theory that addresses the circumstances of women in general and addresses some of the circumstances of Chicanas (e.g., scholarship that deals with sexism, patriarchy, male dominance and control over women, economic and legal oppression of women)" (Chicana faculty member, 26 years old); and, "It is true that a close reading of feminist theory gives us a base from which we can develop our own theories and scholarship reflecting the Chicana/Latina reality" (Chicana graduate student, no age given). Informants value approaches analyzing the social construction/reproduction of gender, but they tend to favor broader analytic frameworks grounded on women of color outside the U.S. context: "More recent feminist scholarship, most specifically Marxist feminist scholarship, on women in Latin America, addresses some of the issues of race and sex/ gender both historically and contemporaneously, and this scholarship is useful for Chicana research" (Chicana graduate student, 46 years old).

While the informants feel that Chicanas should be actively involved in formulating theories of oppression that integrate race/ethnicity, class, and gender, they intimate that this scholarship will develop slowly. As one woman said, "Chicanas who have become participating members of institutions are barely beginning to become part of the written canon which is the only way that the particular circumstances of the Chicana reality can be incorporated into any theory/scholarship" (Chicana faculty member, 44 years old). Informants point out that there are few Chicanas in academic settings where they can develop scholarship. Their observation is supported by the available data: out of more than 57,000 tenured academics in the United States, only 255 are Hispanic women.[22]

Given the paucity of Chicanas in the academic world, many informants express their desire to help make academic institutions more responsive to the needs of Chicanas. It is within this context that informants evaluate the effectiveness of Women's Studies programs and centers to meet the needs of Chicanas.

WOMEN'S STUDIES, WOMEN'S CENTERS, AND CHICANA NEEDS

An important facet of American feminism is the institutionalization of Women's Studies programs and women's centers at colleges and universities. These programs are typically designed to provide support for women, offer courses on women, and support research on women. The extent to which these programs and centers meet Chicana needs is largely unknown. This is important to examine, because it provides another indicator of American feminism's sensitivity to Chicanas.

We asked informants whether or not Women's Studies programs and women's centers existed on their campus and the extent to which they feel they meet the needs of Chicanas. Over three-fourths of the informants (76.2 percent) indicate that there is a Women's Studies program on the campus (10.9 percent of the informants indicated that their campus did not have a Women's Studies program; 12.9 did not reply). More than half of these women (56.4 percent) feel these programs do not meet Chicanas' needs. Only three percent feel Women's Studies programs meet Chicanas' needs while 16.8 percent feel these programs somewhat meet these needs. A little less than one-fourth of the women (23.8 percent) did not answer the question.

Over two-thirds of the women (69.3 percent) said their campus has a women's center (19.8 percent of the informants indicated that their campus did not have a women's center; 10.9 did not reply). Of these women, 47.5 percent feel it does not meet Chicanas' needs. Five percent of the informants said the women's center meets Chicanas' needs, 22.8 percent indicate these needs are somewhat met, and 24.8 percent did not answer the question.

The answers regarding the relevancy of Women's Studies programs and women's centers to Chicanas' needs raise serious considerations for institutionalized feminism. Only a minute proportion of the informants, 5 percent or less, feel that Women's Studies and women's centers meet their needs. If we consider the proportion of women who feel Women's Studies programs and centers somewhat meet Chicanas' needs, women's centers are more favorably evaluated.

Almost one-fourth of the informants did not answer questions on Women's Studies programs or women's centers. This implies that either they have little or no knowledge of these programs/centers, or they are not involved in either. The low number of women who feel Women's Studies programs or women's centers meet or somewhat meet Chicanas' needs corresponds with the high number of women who voice forceful criticisms of their marginality to the American Women's Movement and feminist theories.

CONCLUSION

Women in this study overwhelmingly criticize American feminism for failing to incorporate their concerns adequately within feminist theories, political agendas, and institutionalized programs. They oppose American feminism's tendency to "universalize" the experience of white middle-class women and to either ignore or subsume racial/ethnic, culture, and class differences among women to a general theory of women's common oppression. Many of these women acknowledge the importance of the struggle against patriarchy, but feel this addresses only one dimension of Chicana oppression.

Chicanas contend that the class privilege and racial advantage shared by white middle-class feminists often blind them to Chicana concerns. They advocate "deconstructing" American feminism, to account for ways the tripartite axes of stratification shape women's experiences and demarcate relations of power and privilege in American society.

To reiterate, Chicanas interpret reality thorough a "triple-oppression lens" rooted in their experiences as Chicanas in the United States. By a triple-oppression lens, we mean that Chicanas simultaneously experience reality as members of a historically oppressed group, with a culture distinct from that of the dominant culture. Furthermore, their location in the class structure is mediated by their racial/ethnic status. The social construction of a Chicana perspective, or worldview, is filtered through their racial/ethnic/class status. As a result, Chicanas' interests as women are distinct from and at times contradictory to the interests articulated within American feminism.

A general theory of the common oppression of women proposed by American feminism unravels as we consider class, race/ethnicity, and culture, as well as gender interests. A Chicana perspective is fueled by the combined effects of class, race/ethnicity, and gender on Chicanas' life chances.

Thus, Chicanas question the efficacy of American feminism to address their concerns.

The subordination of Chicana concerns within the American Women's Movement, coupled with informants' views that Women's Studies programs and centers are not meeting Chicanas' needs, presents a formidable challenge to American feminism. The future potential of feminism to forge a progressive praxis depends on the manner in which activist and intellectual currents take into account the intersection of race/ethnicity, culture, and class, as well as gender.

NOTES

Authors' note: We are grateful to Linda Facio and Judith Stacey for their critical comments. We claim equal responsibility for any remaining errors.

1. Gloria Anzaldúa, "Speaking in Tongues: Letter to Third World Women Writers," in *This Bridge Called My Back: Writings by Radical Women of Color,* ed. Cherríe Moraga and Gloria Anzaldúa (Watertown, Mass.: Persephone Press, 1981), 162.

2. In this paper, "Chicana" and "Chicano" refer respectively to a woman and to a man of Mexican descent residing in the United States. "Chicano" is also a broad term that includes both males and females who claim Mexican heritage (e.g., the Chicano community).

3. See, for example, Maxine Baca-Zinn et al., "The Costs of Exclusionary Practices in Women's Studies," *Signs: Journal of Women in Culture and Society* 2 (1986): 290–303.

4. The personal reflections of Chicana activists are typified by the writings of Francisca Flores, "Equality," *Regeneración* 2 (1973): 4–5; and Ana Nieto-Gómez, "La femenista," *Encuentro Femenil* 1 (1973): 34–47. For an example of the critique as reflected in scholarly presentations, see Teresa Córdova et al., eds., *Chicana Voices: Intersection of Class, Race, and Gender* (Austin: National Association of Chicano Studies, 1986).

5. Rodolfo Acuña, *Occupied America: A History of Chicanos,* 2nd ed. (New York: Harper and Row, 1981).

6. Martha Cotera, "Feminism: The Chicana and Anglo Versions, A Historical Analysis," in *Twice A Minority: Mexican American Women,* ed. Margarita Melville (St. Louis: C. V. Mosby, 1980), 217–34.

7. The lack of movement toward coalitions was noted by several activists and scholars. See, for example, Adelaida Del Castillo "La visión chicana," *La Gente* 8 (1974): 3; and Sylvia González, "The White Feminist Movement: The Chicana Perspective," *Social Science Journal* 14 (1977): 67–76.

8. María Linda Apodaca, "A Double-Edged Sword: Hispanas and Liberal Feminisim," *Critica, A Journal of Critical Essays* 1 (1986): 96–114.

9. Acuña, *Occupied America;* U.S. Commission on Civil Rights, *The Excluded Student* (Washington, D.C.: 1972).

10. Apodaca, "Double-Edged Sword."

11. Nieto-Gómez, "La femenista," 46.

12. Cotera, "Feminism"; and Alma García, "The Development of Chicana Feminist Discourse, 1970–1980," *Gender and Society* 3 (1989): 217–38.

13. Enriqueta Longeaux y Vásquez, "The Mexican American Woman," in *Sisterhood is Powerful,* ed. Robin Morgan (New York: Vintage, 1970): 379–84.

14. García, "Feminist Discourse."

15. Adaljisa Sosa Riddell, ed., *Mujeres Activas en Letras y Cambio Social, Noticiera de M.A.L.C.S.* (Davis: University of California Chicano Studies Program, 1983), 3.

16. See, for example, Gloria Hull, Patricia Bell Scott, and Barbara Smith, *All Men Are Black, All Women Are White, but Some of Us Are Brave* (Old Westbury, NY: Feminist Press, 1982); Moraga and Anzaldúa, *This Bridge Called My Back;* Gloria Joseph and Jill Lewis, *Common Differences: Conflicts in Black and White Feminist Perspectives* (New York: Doubleday, 1981); and Jenny Bourne, "Towards an Anti-Racist Feminism," *Race and Class* 25 (1983): 1–22.

17. Julianne Malveaux and Phyllis Wallace, "Minority Women in the Workplace," in *Women and Work: Industrial Relations Research Association Research Volume,* eds. Karen S. Koziara et al. (Washington, D.C.: Bureau of National Affairs, 1987), 265–98.

18. Bell Hooks, *Feminist Theory: From Margin to Center* (Boston: South End Press, 1984).

19. See, for example, Stephen Kulis and Karen A. Miller, "Are Minority Women Sociologists in Double Jeopardy?" *The American Sociologist* 19 (1988): 323–39; and Stephen Kulis et al., "Minorities and Women in the Pacific Sociological Association Region," *Sociological Perspectives* 29 (1986): 147–69.

20. Similar reports are found in Beatriz Pesquera and Adela de la Torre, eds., *Building with Our Hands: New Directions in Chicana Studies* (Berkeley: University of California Press, 1993).

21. Baca-Zinn et al., "Exclusionary Practices," 290–303.

22. Marta Tienda, "The Mexican American Population," in *Non-Metropolitan America in Transition,* eds. Amos H. Hawley and Susan M. Mazie (Chapel Hill: University of North Carolina Press).

CONTRIBUTORS

Leo R. Chávez, associate professor of anthropology at the University of California, Irvine, researches various aspects of the Mexican immigrant experience, including household organization and structure, community formation, and access to medical care. His current focus is on breast and cervical cancer among Latinas in Orange County, California. He recently published *Shadowed Lives: Undocumented Immigrants in American Society* (Harcourt Brace Jovanovich, 1992).

Adela de la Torre, professor of health care administration and chair of Chicano and Latin American studies at California State University, Long Beach, is also a scholar at the Tomás Rivera Center in Claremont. As a health economist specializing in Latino health issues, she has published several articles in the area of Chicana/Latina health, health-care financing, and rural health-care access. Her most recent publication is *Building with Our Hands: New Directions in Chicana Studies,* coedited with Beatriz M. Pesquera.

Adelaida R. Del Castillo, assistant professor in the Department of Mexican American Studies at San Diego State University, received the Phi Eta Sigma Timeos Award for Outstanding Assistant Professor. She was editor of *Between Borders: Essays on Mexicana/Chicana History* (Floricanto Press, 1990) and is currently working on a book on covert norms and the displacement of gender among lower-income groups in Mexico City.

Ignacio M. García, assistant professor of history at Brigham Young University, has also taught at Texas A&M University in Corpus Christi. He is the author of *United We Win: The Rise and Fall of La Raza Unida Party,* which explores the development of a Chicano militant ethos during the 1960s and 1970s.

John A. García, professor of political science at the University of Arizona, has just completed a five-year term as department head. His principal areas of scholarship are Latino political behavior and politics, voting behavior and mobilization, urban politics, and public policy (i.e., immigration, education, and labor force participation). His most recent project was as one of four coprincipal investigators with the Latino National Political Survey. His current research focuses on concepts of identity and political linkages and coalition formation within the Latino community, as well as with the African American community.

María Rosa García-Acevedo has held academic appointments at the Centro de Investigación y Docencia Económica, Universidad IberoAmérica, and the Universidad Autónoma de Ciudad Juárez. She has been a policy analyst for the Ministry of Foreign Relations of Mexico. Her publications include articles and book chapters on U.S.—Latin American diplomatic relations, Mexican immigration to the United States, and U.S. policies toward Mexico. Currently she is completing a comprehensive analysis of the political links between the Mexican government and Chicano organizations.

Susan González Baker, assistant professor in the School of Public Administration and Policy and research scientist in the Mexican American Studies and Research Center at the University of Arizona, specializes in demography and public policy and has published several articles on Mexican migration to the United States and a monograph on U.S. immigration policy. She also conducts research on Mexican-origin women workers in U.S. labor markets and on minority subgroups among the homeless.

Rebecca G. Martínez, doctoral candidate in the Program in Social Relations at the University of California, Irvine, includes among her research interests women and health, anthropology of the body, and relationships of power in the medical setting. She is currently investigating these issues among women in the United States and Venezuela.

Beatriz M. Pesquera, associate professor and director of the Chicana/Chicano Studies Program at the University of California, Davis, has published articles on Chicanas' employment and familial experiences and on Chicana feminism. She is currently completing a book on the intersection of work and family among Chicana workers and, with a coauthor, is preparing a manuscript on Chicana feminism. During 1990–1991, she was a Rockefeller Humanist-in-Residence at the Southwest Institute for Research on Women at the University of Arizona, Tucson. She is coeditor of *Building with Our Hands: New Directions in Chicana Studies*.

Refugio I. Rochín, director of the Julian Samora Research Institute at Michigan State University, has published extensively on various aspects of the experiences of Chicanos and other Latinos in the American economy. His most recent publications are a coauthored study of rural Chicano communities, "Immigration, Colonia Formation, and Latino Poor in Rural California," published by the Tomás Rivera Center, and a study of perceptions of the North American Free Trade Agreement, "Public Perceptions of the North American Free Trade Agreement: Facts and Myth."

Guadalupe San Miguel, Jr., associate professor of history at the University of Houston, central campus, received a B.A. in U.S. history from Columbia University, an M.A. in American history from Stanford University, and a Ph.D. in social education history from Stanford University. His key research interests focus on several areas in education. He has published articles on school segregation, the politics of bilingual-policy development, and what he calls the "quest for educational equality," and a book, *Let All of Them Take Heed: Mexican Americans and the Quest for Educational Equality in Texas* (Austin: University of Texas Press, 1987). His most recent book manuscript on the education of Mexican Americans in the Southwest during the nineteenth century is under review, and he is currently completing another on the politics of identity in school reform activities during the Chicano Movement.

Denise A. Segura, associate professor of sociology at the University of California, Santa Barbara, has received numerous awards, most recently a 1991–1992 Ford Foundation Postdoctoral Fellowship. She has published articles on Chicanas and Mexican immigrant women in the labor market, Chicano education, and Chicana feminism. Currently she is writing a coauthored book on the contemporary and historical dimensions of Chicana feminism.

INDEX

ABOUT THE EDITORS

David R. Maciel, professor of history at the University of New Mexico, has also been a visiting professor at the National Autonomous University of Mexico (UNAM), the University of California, San Diego, the University of Arizona, and the University of Guadalajara. His teaching interests and fields include Chicano history, Mexico, modern Latin America, and the U.S. Southwest.

He completed undergraduate studies in anthropology at San Diego State University and graduate studies in Latin American studies and history at the University of Arizona and the University of California, Santa Barbara. He received two Fulbright teaching and research postdoctoral fellowships to Mexico and additional research fellowships from the Ford Foundation and the National Endowment for the Humanities.

His published research has focused on the Chicano community, Mexican cultural history, and film. He has written *Ignacio Ramírez: Ideólogo del liberalismo social en México; Aztlán: historia del pueblo chicano, El Norte: The U.S.-Mexican Border in Contemporary Cinema,* and *El bandolero, el pocho y la raza: imágenes cinematográficas del chicano,* and other works. In addition, he has published in such journals as *Aztlán, Cuadernos Americanos, Relaciones, Revista de la Universidad, Spectator, Studies in Latin American Popular Culture,* and *Tiempos de Arte.* Currently, he is serving as a coeditor for a multiauthor book on the popular cultural manifestations of Mexican immigration to the United States. In addition, he is in the final stages of completion of a cultural history of Mexican cinema from its origins to the present.

Isidro D. Ortiz is associate professor of Mexican American studies at San Diego State University, where he also serves as chair of the department. His teaching interests and fields include Chicano/Latino politics, California and American politics, and political movements.

He completed undergraduate studies in secondary education with a specialization in history and political science at Texas A & I University and pursued graduate studies in political science at Stanford University. He has received several institutional research grants as well as a grant from the American Political Science Association. He has published articles and book chapters on various aspects of Chicano/Latino politics in the United States and Mexico. He has also served as coeditor of *Chicano Studies: A Multidisciplinary Approach* and editor of *Chicanos and the Social Sciences 1970–1980: A Decade of Development.* His current research focuses on Chicano/Latino elite political strategies and the responses of Chicanos to anti-immigrant racism.